The Vision of His Glory

By
Anne Graham Lotz

The Vision of His Glory

Finding Hope
through the
Revelation of Jesus Christ

By
Anne Graham Lotz

W PUBLISHING GROUP™
www.wpublishinggroup.com

A Division of Thomas Nelson, Inc.
www.ThomasNelson.com

Library of Congress Cataloging-in-Publication Data

Lotz, Anne Graham 1948–
The vision of his glory: finding hope through the revelation of Jesus Christ /
Anne Graham Lotz.
p.   cm.
ISBN 0-8499-4016-8

1. Bible. N.T. Revelation–Criticism, interpretation, etc.
2. Hope–Religious aspects–Christianity. I. Title.

BS2825.2.L688   1996   95-43760
228'.06–dc20   CIP

Printed in the United States of America.

05   RRD   24 23 22 21

Dedicated

to

the hopeless.

Contents

vii

Contents

My Tribute . . .

Each year as I approach the Christmas holidays, I ask the King what He would like for His birthday. He is very creative in His suggestions! They vary widely but have one thing in common: The gift is always sacrificial in nature, something I *would* not do except the King requested it. And it is something I *could* not do except the King enabled me.

One year He seemed to ask for my involvement in carrying out the dying request of an executed murderer. One year I felt His request was for me to add a trip of multiple speaking engagements to my already-completed schedule. One year I thought the gift He desired was for me to tell the Christmas story in my child's public-school classroom.

After having spent five months trying unsuccessfully to secure a professional writer to help me with this book, I was becoming somewhat desperate as the contract deadline drew nearer and nearer yet not one word of the book had been written. As I approached Christmas 1994, the still, small voice of the King seemed to whisper in my heart, "Anne, for My birthday this year, I want you to give Me this book. I want you to write it yourself."

With humility, I want to thank the King for His gift suggestion. And I offer it to Him as my tribute, with love!

My Tribute . . . and Thanks

. . . and Thanks

To my father, whose example of boldly presenting the hope of Jesus Christ to a hopeless world has been and always will be a plumb line and inspiration to millions—including me . . .

To my mother, for pushing me to pick up my pen . . .

To Kip Jordon, for having a vision of this book before I did . . .

To Rolf Zettersten, for his practical help in getting this project started . . .

To my beloved Dan, for the willing sacrifice of home-cooked meals, clean shirts, and my undivided attention until this book was finished . . .

To Sue Ann Jones, for helping me to verbally express the thrill in my heart when I gaze at the vision of His glory . . .

To Word, for enthusiastically embracing this book—and its author . . .

To Helen George and the AnGeL Ministries staff and prayer team, for sharing the responsibilities of ministry so I could add a writing schedule to an already-full speaking schedule . . .

To Dr. Lewis Drummond, for his line-by-line critique, confirming the doctrinal integrity of the manuscript . . .

And to you, for your desire to find hope through a fresh vision of His glory.

For everything that was written in the past was written to teach us, so that through endurance and the encouragement of the Scriptures we might have hope.

Romans 15:4

Introduction

 In Mogadishu, Somalia, on March 21, 1994, a young man was bicycling to work. He was considered the most outstanding Christian in his very small, struggling, isolated Christian community. He had taken seminary courses through correspondence, and he was investing his life in discipling other young believers as he sought to build up the church in Somalia. The church had high hopes for growth and national impact under his enthusiastic, gifted, Spirit-filled leadership.

But early on that March morning, two men drove by him on a motorcycle, and with one blast of a machine gun, blew this young Christian into eternity.

His brutal, senseless murder left behind a young wife and a one-year-old baby who now faced potential devastation. He himself had led his wife to the Lord. When she professed her faith in Christ, her family and tribe disowned her. Upon her husband's death, she was all alone with no means of support. Not only his family but the church and the entire Christian movement in his nation were rocked to its very foundation of faith.

Is there any hope for the future of this young wife and baby? Is there any hope for the future of the church in Somalia? As this Somalian family and church struggle to put the pieces of their lives back together, what about you? Have you faced a devastating tragedy in your life? Has your life taken an unexpected turn? Is there any hope for *your future?*

When life seems too hard to bear . . .

When bad things happen to good people . . .

When evil triumphs over good . . .

When Satan seems to have the upper hand . . .

When all hell breaks loose . . .

When death still stings and the grave seems to have the victory . . .

Is there any hope for the future at all?

The book of Revelation answers with a resounding yes! YES! *YES!*

When stars fall from the sky . . .

When mountains fall into the sea . . .

When demons invade the earth . . .

When the blood of those massacred rises to the height of a horse's bridle . . .

Even when the worst conceivable nightmares become reality . . .

. . . there is one splendid, shining, sure hope for the future—and His Name is Jesus!

The book of Revelation was originally written to give hope to the early church when Christians were being fed to lions, nailed to crosses, burned at the stake, and boiled in tar. It was written *by* a Christian who himself was suffering "because of the word of God and the testimony of Jesus."[1] It was written specifically *to* a generation of Christians yet to come who will experience what Jesus described as "great distress, unequaled from the beginning of the world until now—and never to be equaled again."[2]

Many readers have missed the blessing awaiting them in the book of Revelation because they have been intimidated by its numerical symbolism or overwhelmed by its awesome imagery. They read of mysterious lampstands and sacred seals, worldwide earthquakes and trumpeting angels, monstrous beasts and miracle-working dragons—and quickly turn instead to the soothing poetry of the Psalms or the simple promises of the Beatitudes.

I hope you'll resist that urge and stay with me for a brief journey through what I believe is one of the most thrilling and fascinating books in all of Scripture. Revelation is, above all, a book of hope, and the blessing to be found in its magnificent imagery has been, for me, a continuous, awesome experience of worship as it has led me to a fresh, personal encounter with the Lord Jesus Christ. This book is my humble attempt to share with you how this richness of worship, this wealth of hope, this vision of His glory, is intended for all of us. Indeed, the book of Revelation was written *for you*, confirming God's promise through Jeremiah's prophecy: "'For I know the plans I have for you,' declares the Lord, 'plans to . . . give you hope and a future.'"[3]

If you have never read Revelation, I invite you to experience this most wonderful of adventures. If, sometime in the past, you started to read Revelation but somehow lost your way or became confused or just grew weary of the symbolism, I invite you to try again. I gladly share my journey with you. Take heart, and remember the challenge of Isaiah: "Strengthen the feeble hands, steady the knees that give way; say to those with fearful hearts, 'Be strong, do not fear; your God *will come*, he *will come* with vengeance; with divine retribution he *will come* to save you.'"[4]

Lift up your head!

Open your eyes to the Person of Jesus Christ!

Pilate, the Roman governor who presided over the trial of Jesus, challenged the rioting mob that shouted for His crucifixion with these words: "Behold the man!"[5]

That same challenge has been heard down through the centuries: "Behold the Man." But the vision the mob beheld has changed from that of a bloodied, tortured, mangled prisoner on His way to execution to a vision of the same Man bathed in glory!

The crown of thorns has become a dazzling, bejeweled crown of gold . . .

The seamless robe gambled for by His executioners has become a robe of light, flashing like lightning in its brilliance . . .

The hands that were bound now hold the book by which every person who has ever lived will be judged.

Introduction

The crowds gathered in the courtyard of the judgment hall early that Friday morning jeering, "Crucify Him! Crucify Him!" give way to multitudes of thousands upon ten thousands who fill the universe with shouts of praise to the One Who alone is worthy of all honor and glory and wisdom and thanks and power and strength!

The vision has caused the martyr in the flames of death to smile. It has given strength to the weak,

> faith to the doubting . . .
> courage to the timid . . .
> peace to the fearful . . .
> victory to the defeated . . .
> hope to the hopeless!

Behold the Man! The vision is glorious!

Hope When You Are Depressed . . .

1.   By the Smallness of Your Life

2.   By the Greatness of Your Problems

 . . . *Christ in you,*

the hope of glory.

Colossians 1:27b

1

Hope When You Are Depressed by the Smallness of Your Life

Revelation 1:1–8

 His name is Leoni. He is one of an estimated thirty-five million abandoned children in a South American country who live in the streets, surviving by stealing, begging, and scavenging. Shortly after birth, he was left by his homeless mother on the doorstep of a nunnery, only to be reclaimed months later and taken by his mother to her home, the city streets.

In Leoni's country, parents who cannot support or raise their children for any reason sometimes abandon them, much like unwanted kittens or puppies. It is a matter of record that the abandoned children, who range in age from one to eighteen years, are starved, beaten, raped, and tortured, and sometimes under cover of darkness they are rounded up by the authorities to be shot like rats in a sewer. Always aware of these devastating horrors that constantly surrounded him, Leoni's days were spent begging for food to keep his drunken mother alive. His nights were filled with terror.

Three years after being reclaimed by his mother, Leoni and his mother were arrested by the police and taken to the juvenile courts in the capital city. Because his mother was pregnant with another child she would later abandon, Leoni was assigned to a government orphanage that housed about 550 other young children. Five months later he was transferred to another state orphanage.

What hope for the future does Leoni have? What hope does one small child have in the midst of thirty-five million small children who've been abandoned, attacked, shuffled from place to place? None, if hope is in his country's court system or the government orphanages.

But God has a future for Leoni! A Christian couple, moved by the sovereign grace of God, made his wildest dreams come true when they adopted him into their family. Now, for the first time in his small life, Leoni is loved and secure.

Does your life seem small to you? Perhaps as small as Leoni's actually is? Do you feel abandoned, worthless, lost in the shuffle of life? What hope is there for your future?

If your hope is in this world, there is none. But to those who are depressed by the smallness of their lives God gives hope for the future through the vision of His glory. This vision begins to unfold in the first chapter of the book of Revelation, as we reflect on what God says through prophecy.

Finding Hope by Reflecting on What God Says . . . through Prophecy

The book of Revelation begins by clearly stating its theme. "The revelation of Jesus Christ . . ." The theme of Revelation is not primarily prophecy, or future events, as many suppose; it is Jesus!

Prophecy Was Received from God

The word *revelation* literally means to "unveil." In the book of Revelation, God uses prophecy to "unveil" Jesus, enabling us to see Him in a unique way. And when we see Him clearly, we see a vision of His glory that transcends our smallness.

When Jesus was alive on earth, He was so "veiled" that His own mother, His half brothers and half sisters, even His own disciples did not fully understand Who He was. But we have a clearer view of Him. Through prophecy, God lifts the veil, enabling us to see Jesus in a way that those who walked and lived with Him on earth could not.

Through prophecy, God lifted the veil in the Old Testament so believers could worship Jesus Christ. For example, Adam and Eve could worship Jesus Christ, through prophecy, as the Seed of the woman who, in essence, would take away the sin of mankind and bring man back into a right relationship with the Creator.[1]

Abraham could worship Jesus Christ through prophecy as the One through Whom all the nations of the earth would be blessed.[2] Moses could worship Jesus Christ through prophecy as the Prophet like himself Who would deliver people, not from bondage in Egypt, but from bondage to sin and Satan.[3] Isaiah worshiped Jesus Christ through prophecy as the "Wonderful Counselor, Mighty God, Everlasting Father, Prince of Peace,"[4] and also as the Lamb by Whose wounds we would be healed.[5] Micah worshiped Jesus through prophecy as the Baby who would be born in Bethlehem.[6] Zechariah worshiped Him through prophecy as the King of kings and Lord of lords Who would one day rule the entire world![7]

Although these Old Testament believers and those who listened to them did not fully understand Who Jesus is, through prophecy they were able to "see" Jesus in a way they could not otherwise have seen Him. Because through prophecy, God "unveils" Jesus Christ.

Prophecy Was Recorded by John

God not only unveiled Jesus Christ through prophecy in the past, but through the book of Revelation, He uniquely unveils Jesus as our hope for the future! This "revelation of Jesus Christ" was recorded by the prophet John, but, as Peter explained, "No prophecy of Scripture came about by the prophet's own interpretation. For prophecy never had its origin in the will of man, but men spoke from God as they were carried along by the Holy Spirit."[8]

What God gave and the Holy Spirit inspired, John faithfully recorded: "[God] made it known by sending his angel to his servant John, who testifies to everything he saw—that is, the word of God and the testimony of Jesus Christ" (Rev. 1:1b–2).

Revelation is so thrilling because it is not just a prediction—a weather forecast—of what is to come. It is the prophet John's *eyewitness account* of the future! In this stirring account, he says he personally testifies to everything he saw! For you and me, the book of Revelation describes the future. For the apostle John, it was history! Nearly fifty times, John says "I saw." Almost thirty times he says "I heard." What a personal testimony the apostle John had! If he had the opportunity to share a condensed version of it, perhaps he would express it something like this:

I was a disciple of John the Baptist for some time. One day I was standing beside the River Jordan with John when he pointed out a rather ordinary-looking man, exclaiming "Look! There goes Jesus of Nazareth. He is the Lamb of God Who will take away the sin of the world. He is the Messiah, the Christ, the unique Son of God. There is God, walking the earth in a human body!"

So I left John the Baptist and followed Jesus. I was His disciple for three years. During that time I saw and heard Him in every conceivable circumstance. I saw Him create sight in a man born blind. I saw Him cleanse lepers, walk on water, feed over five thousand people with five loaves and two fish. I saw Him raise Lazarus from the dead, and I heard the Sermon on the Mount. I saw all this with my own eyes!

But I will never forget that Thursday night when Jesus, the other disciples, and I had eaten a meal together in an upper room in Jerusalem. Afterward, He took us to a secluded spot on the Mount of Olives for prayer. But instead of praying, I went to sleep. He awakened me and asked if I would pray with Him. But—oh, how ashamed I am to admit it now—I went back to sleep. Again He awakened me, asking for prayer, and again I went back to sleep. The third time He came, needing me to watch and pray with Him. But since I was still sleeping, He left me undisturbed. When I finally woke up, I saw Roman soldiers placing Him under arrest, taking Him off for trial before the religious leaders.

I followed at a distance, and because I am a relative of the high priest, I was able to slip into the courtyard and watch the proceedings from there. With my own ears I heard Him accused of various false charges. In the end, I heard Him convicted of blasphemy—of claiming to be the unique Son of God.

Then I watched as they took Him to the Roman courts for trial. I saw Him slapped, spat upon, and scourged until the flesh was ripped from His bones and His body glistened with blood. In fact, His appearance was so marred, I could hardly recognize Him as a Man, much less my Master and Friend.

I heard the crowd that had gathered at the judgment hall begin to riot as they shouted in unison, "Crucify Him! Crucify Him!" Then I heard, with my own ears, as seven different times the Roman courts said: "This Man is innocent. This Man is innocent. This Man is innocent." But in the end, I watched as the Roman governor, Pilate, washed his hands of responsibility and concluded: "This Man is innocent, but . . . you can crucify Him!"

I followed at a distance as He was led out of Jerusalem to the place of execution known as Golgotha. There, with my own eyes, I saw Jesus of Nazareth crucified on a Roman cross.

I stood at the foot of the cross and watched for six long, agonizing hours as He hung on it. At one point He even noticed me and asked if I would take care of His mother, who was also standing nearby. At the end of those six horrifying hours, I heard, with my own ears, as He shouted with a loud voice, "It is finished!" And I saw, with my own eyes, as He bowed His head and deliberately refused to take the next breath.

I saw Jesus of Nazareth die on a Roman cross. There was no mistake. He was dead!

And at that point, my life fell apart! I was devastated! Everything I had hoped, all of my dreams for the future, my whole reason for living, had crumbled at that cross! Because I had thought Jesus *was* the Messiah. I had thought He *was* the Redeemer of Israel! I had thought He *was* the unique Son of God—God walking the earth in a Man's body! And He had died on a Roman cross as a common criminal! My whole world was shattered.

I went back to the upper room in Jerusalem with the other disciples. We locked the door and barred the windows, scared that the Romans, now that they had crucified Jesus, would seek out His disciples and put us to death as well.

In my confusion, anger, and grief, the hours ran together. Before I knew it, it was early Sunday morning and someone was pounding on the door.

I was terrified! I thought the Romans *had* come to get us! Then I heard a woman's voice. I opened the door and it was Mary. She was hysterical, saying something about graverobbers and the tomb being empty where Jesus had been buried.

I looked at Peter, and he looked at me. We must have had the same thought because we both ran through that open door, through the early-morning streets of Jerusalem, until we came to the tomb where Jesus had been laid. And sure enough! The stone was rolled away, just as Mary said!

I ran into the tomb, and I will never forget—*never*— what I saw with my own eyes. *NOTHING!* The tomb was empty!

Except for one thing. The grave clothes were still there! And there was something about them . . .

I had witnessed the raising of Lazarus from the dead. When his sister Martha had finished unwrapping him, the grave clothes were a tumbled pile of filthy rags. But Jesus' grave clothes were different. They did not look as though someone had unwound them. The grave clothes were lying there as though the body was still inside! They looked like an empty cocoon, flattened and limp! They looked like the body had just evaporated right through them!

I stood there, looking at those grave clothes and suddenly I *KNEW* that Jesus of Nazareth had risen from the dead! He was alive!

But now I was more confused then ever! I went back to the upper room in Jerusalem with the other disciples. Again, in fear, we locked the door and barred the windows. We talked about what we had seen, and we waited . . .

Sunday afternoon, inside that locked room I suddenly heard, with my own ears, a very familiar voice. The Master's voice. My heart seemed to stop. But He said, "Peace. It is I. Be not afraid."

I turned, and with my own eyes, I saw Jesus of Nazareth standing before me. I saw the wound on His brow where the crown of thorns had been embedded. I saw the wounds in His hands and feet where the nails had been. I saw the wound in His side where the soldiers had thrust in the spear. I *SAW* Jesus of Nazareth risen from the dead!

He was alive!

And for forty days following His resurrection, I walked with Him and talked with Him and listened as He spoke. Then one day, as the other disciples and I were standing with Jesus on the Mount of Olives, near Bethany, I listened to Him with my own ears as He taught us. Then with my own eyes, as He lifted His hands in blessing, I watched as His body slowly lifted up from the ground. I saw His physical body rise up through the air and disappear into the clouds. I *SAW*, with my own eyes, Jesus of Nazareth ascend into heaven!

While I was staring up into the sky where I had seen Him disappear, two men in white suddenly appeared and said, "Why are you standing around, staring off into space? This same Jesus, Who has been taken from you into heaven, will come back in the same way you have seen Him go into heaven."

And now I want to tell you that the same eyes and ears that saw and heard Jesus of Nazareth while He was on earth have seen Him come back!

Let me tell you something of what I have seen!

With my own eyes, I have seen worldwide pestilence, pollution, persecution, and famine so severe that they wiped out a third of the earth's population. I have seen wars fought that were so destructive the blood of those massacred rose to the height of a horse's bridle. I have seen stars falling from the sky and mountains falling into the sea. I have seen a beast rise up out of the sea who rules the world, and a false prophet who does miracles in his name. I have seen demons swarming over the earth, and I have seen angels. I have seen hell, and I have seen heaven. I have seen the sky unfold, and a white horse appear whose Rider is called Faithful and True, followed by the armies of heaven. I have seen Satan bound, and Satan loosed, and Satan thrown into the lake of fire forever and ever. I have seen the old earth pass away and a new heaven and a new earth come down.

And over it all, under it all, around it all, through it all, at the beginning of it all, and at the end of it all, *I have seen Jesus Christ, absolutely supreme as the victorious hope of the ages!*

As thrilling as this narrative is, John's actual personal testimony in the book of Revelation is even more vivid as he describes the glory of Jesus Christ, compelling us to worship Him. God uniquely revealed Jesus to John—and, through prophecy, He has revealed Him to us so that we might read and reflect on the vision of His glory and find hope for the future.

Prophecy Is to Be Read by You

What is your attitude toward prophecy? One attitude is to avoid it because it seems too difficult to understand, too controversial to discuss, too meaningless to be personally relevant. People with this attitude tend to feel more comfortable in the Psalms, the Proverbs, the Gospels, and the Epistles. They leave prophecy to the theological heavyweights such as the seminary professors or preachers or professional Bible scholars.

Others are so fascinated with prophecy they spend hours trying to interpret the symbols, count the numbers, and even make predictions based on their calculations. They tend to forget about personal holiness, obedience, and winning the lost.

Sometimes we lose sight of the fact that prophecy was given to ordinary people like you and me to give us hope for our future: "Blessed is the one who reads the words of this prophecy, and blessed are those who hear it and take to heart what is written in it, because the time is near" (Rev. 1:3). Blessed! Blessed! *BLESSED* are those who do not give just a superficial reading to the book of Revelation, but who continually read, study, apply, and live by it!

And what is this special blessing? It is the blessing of seeing Jesus! It is the vision of His glory that gives hope!

How does reflecting on what God says through prophecy give you hope when you are depressed by the smallness of your life? It begins by helping you get your eyes off yourself.

When was the last time you read prophecy? As you read this book, would you also open up your Bible and read the book of Revelation along with it? Make the time to reflect on what God says through prophecy so you can refocus on Who Jesus Christ really is. Let's begin this refocusing as John did, through praise.

Finding Hope by Refocusing on Who Jesus Is . . . through Praise

God has revealed Himself to us through Jesus Christ, and Jesus is revealed to us through the Bible. Therefore, one of the greatest treasures to be derived from Bible-reading is knowing God through focusing on the attributes of Jesus Christ—attributes that then become a rich source for our praise.

On what is your focus? Is it on other people? On your problems? On your pain and pressures? Often such a focus tends to intensify one's depression. A wonderful antidote for depression is to refocus, through praise, on Who Jesus is.

Praise Him for His Deity

As John proceeds to "unveil" Jesus Christ, he directs our attention to His deity. Jesus Christ is God, an equal member of the Trinity—God as three Persons in One. The concept of the Trinity goes beyond our limited power to comprehend. Every illustration that seeks to explain it seems superficial; however, thinking of water, which retains its basic elements in the form of liquid, steam, or ice, may help. God retains His power, character, personality, and attributes in the Person of the Father and the Son and the Holy Spirit. And although the Trinity is not named as such in the Bible, it is implied again and again.

In the first three verses of the Bible, the Trinity is implied to the careful reader. Genesis 1:1 speaks of God the Creator. Genesis 1:2 speaks of God the Spirit. And Genesis 1:3, coupled with John 1:1–3, speaks of God the Son as the living Word. In Genesis 1:26, God says, "Let us [plural] make man in our [plural] image, in our [plural] likeness. . . ." Then verse 27 says, "So God created man in his [singular] own image, male and female he [singular] created them." The shift in pronouns refers to the fact that God is more than One. He is Three in One.

This same mysterious doctrine, that God is One yet Three in One, is described in Revelation 1:4–5. Verse 4 says, "Grace and peace to you from him who is, and who was, and who is to come. . . ." John is speaking of the God of Genesis 1:1 and Genesis 1:26–27, the God Who so loved us He brought us into existence so we could have a permanent, personal, love relationship with Him. The Bible says when we come to Him through faith in Jesus Christ, we can call Him "*Abba*, Father."[9]

Revelation 1:4 goes on to say ". . . and from the seven spirits before his throne. . . ." Some translations of the Bible say "from the seven-fold spirit." This speaks of the Holy Spirit, referred to by the number seven, which denotes perfection or completeness. The Holy Spirit is perfect and complete in Himself because He is God. He is the same Spirit of God Who hovered over planet earth in Genesis 1, preparing it to receive God's Word and be transformed into a place of beauty that brought God pleasure. He is the same Spirit Who hovered over your heart, preparing you to receive God's living Word so you could be transformed into a person who brings God pleasure. He is the same Spirit Who fully indwells Jesus, Who indwells you and me when we receive Jesus Christ by faith, and Who ever lives before the throne of God. He is the Holy Spirit Paul described in Romans 8:26–27 Who "intercedes for us with groans that words cannot express." Since the same Spirit Who indwells Jesus indwells us and is ever before the throne of God, all He has to do is think and feel, and His prayers are conveyed to the Father. The Bible says we can call Him our "Comforter."[10]

The third member of the Trinity mentioned in Revelation 1:5 is God the Son: "And from Jesus Christ, who is the faithful witness, the firstborn from the dead, and the ruler of the kings of the earth."

Jesus Christ is the "faithful witness" because He witnessed to what God is like, even when that witnessing led to His death on a Roman cross. He is the firstborn of all those who will one day rise from the dead, and He is the Ruler of the kings of the earth, whether or not they acknowledge it at this time.

And Jesus so loves us, that when His Father sent Him to earth to die as a sacrifice for our sin, He came. He confined Himself to a woman's womb for nine months, then submitted to the human birth process. He limited Himself to the body of a two-year-old and then subjected Himself to the changes of adolescence, growing in wisdom and stature and favor with God and man. At the age of thirty-three He willingly died on the cross, being obedient even unto death. He was buried in a borrowed tomb, then on the third day rose up from the dead. He ascended into heaven, where He sits at the right hand of the Father, ever living to make intercession for you and me. He has asked the Father to send down His Holy Spirit to indwell those who receive Him by faith. And one day, He will return to rule the world in peace and righteousness and justice! The Bible says we can call Him Savior, Lord, and King.[11]

To refocus on Who Jesus is, begin by praising Him for His deity. Then praise Him for His humanity. Jesus is not only fully God; He is fully Man.

Praise Him for His Humanity

Jesus is the Savior Who redeemed us. In His humanity, He gave His life to take away our sin, reconcile us to God, and give us eternal life. He "loves us and has freed us from our sins by his blood" (Rev. 1:5b).

Jesus is also the Lord Who rules our lives, giving us eternal purpose and meaning as we live to serve Him. He "has made us to be a kingdom and priests to serve his God and Father—to him be glory and power for ever and ever!" (Rev. 1:6).

And in His humanity, Jesus is the King Who one day will return for us. "Look, he is coming with the clouds, and every eye will see him . . ." (Rev. 1:7b).

I was reminded of Jesus' humanity one day when I was sitting in an airport between flights, feeling very depressed by the smallness of my life. As I watched the hundreds of people rushing through the terminal and did not see anyone I knew; as I watched the television report of world and national news and knew that not one of the important people quoted or pictured even knew I existed; as I thought of my own family members who have achieved so much while in comparison I seemed to be doing so little . . . my thoughts made me feel smaller and smaller. Insignificance, unimportance, and inferiority swept over me.

Have you ever felt like that? Do you feel depressed now by the smallness of your life? It doesn't make any difference if your feelings are reasonable or unreasonable; mine were a mixture of both. There is an antidote for feelings of smallness, of insignificance. Just that week I had begun meditating on the book of Revelation. I picked up my Bible and opened it where I had left off in Revelation 1:3 that morning during my devotions.

As I read those next few verses, an amazing realization came to me. The most important man in our nation—perhaps in the whole world—is the president (personal family and friends excluded!). For how long will he hold this status? Four years? Eight years? Fifty years from now, who will remember his name or his accomplishments, outside the history books?

In comparison, Jesus is the most important Man, not just in our nation, not just on planet earth, but in the entire universe! And He isn't important just for four years or eight years, but forever and ever and ever! Furthermore, the most important Man in the universe thinks I am so important, He gave His own life for me! How can I feel depressed by the smallness of my life when the most important Man in the universe died for me, rules over me now, and will one day return for me? In the eyes of the Lord Jesus Christ, I am important. I am of value. How can I consider myself anything less?

On the day when Jesus returns, everyone will be looking at Jesus. But have you ever considered where He will be looking? He will be looking for you! He has told us, ". . . I will come back and take you to be with me. . . ."[12] His eyes will be searching the crowds of upturned faces, looking for you! While others mourn because His coming brings their judgment, you and I who have been redeemed by His blood will be rejoicing because His coming fulfills all our hopes and dreams!

Praise God for the deity of Jesus Christ! Praise God for the humanity of Jesus Christ! And praise God for the eternity of Jesus Christ!

Praise Him for His Eternity

"I am the Alpha and the Omega . . ." (Rev. 1:8a). This title describes the eternal omniscience of Jesus Christ. The alpha is the first letter and the omega is the last letter in the Greek alphabet. Through the alphabet all of our words, all of our wisdom, and all of our knowledge are expressed. Jesus is the beginning and end of the alphabet, the summation of all wisdom and knowledge.[13]

This means that the eternal Christ has never had a new thought. If Jesus Christ had a new thought, it would reveal He had previously not known something. But since He is omniscient, He knows—and has always known—everything!

What does the omniscience of Christ mean to me personally? It means I have always been on His mind. Think of it: The most important Man in the universe has *always* been thinking of me! Wonder of wonders! I have never been out of His thoughts! Even as He hung on the cross, He was thinking of me by name! Dying for me by name! And when He was raised from the dead on that first Easter Sunday, He was raised with me on His mind!

And not only is He eternally omniscient, He is eternally omnipresent: He is "the Lord God, who is, and who was, and who is to come . . ." (Rev. 1:8b). Jesus Christ always has been, always is, always will be. He is eternally the same yesterday, today, and forever. Although He "made himself nothing, taking the very nature of a servant, being made in human likeness,"[14] He did not undergo some radical personality change when He came to earth. He is the same today as He was at creation, as He was in John's day, as He will be when He reigns on the earth.[15]

What does His eternal omnipresence mean to me personally? It means He is fully present in every age, every generation, every culture, every nation. And if Adam and Eve knew Him as they walked with Him in the cool of the day,[16]

if Enoch walked right into heaven with Him,[17]

if Abraham knew Him as his Friend,[18]

if David knew Him as his Shepherd,[19]

if Mary Magdalene knew Him in His liberating grace,[20]

if Paul knew Him in His transforming power,[21]

why can't I know Him? If He is eternally the same, fully present in every age and every generation, *then I can know Him!* If I do not, the problem is not with Him, but with me!

Twenty years ago, as I was routinely studying my Bible one day, I decided if Abraham could know God, so could I. My life since then has been a pilgrimage of getting to know God through prayer, through the disciplined study of His Word, and through obediently living out what I learn. And because I believe the ultimate human experience is knowing God in a personal, love relationship, I will continue this pursuit until my faith becomes sight and I see Him face to face! Although I do not know Him as well as Abraham did, nor as well as I want to or should, I know Him much better today than I did twenty years ago. And I pray I will know Him better next year than I do today. It is thrilling that God, Who is eternally the same, is knowable to me! And to you!

His omnipresence also brings comfort because I am assured He is fully present with me even as I write this at my desk at home. He is fully present with my children living in different cities and states. He is fully present with my husband at work. He is fully present with my parents wherever they may be. He is fully present with pastors in Bosnia, believers in Rwanda, missionaries in New Guinea, underground "house" church members in China. Being everywhere at once does not deplete or dilute His Person or His power in any way.

Praise God for the eternity of Jesus Christ! He is omniscient, omnipresent, and omnipotent! He is ". . . the Almighty" (Rev. 1:8c). Jesus Christ is all-powerful, fully in charge. No one, nor anything, is mightier than Jesus!

What problem are you facing that is bigger than you are? Praise God for the omnipotence of Jesus Christ! He is the Almighty—mightier than all. Greater, more powerful, than any problem or situation you or I will ever face. In fact, one reason God allows us to have problems and be in situations that seem bigger than we are is so we can discover by experience His "incomparably great power for us who believe."[22]

If our lives are easy, and if all we ever attempt for God is what we know we can handle, how will we ever experience His omnipotence in our lives?

It is when we are in over our heads . . .
>> when we are cornered with no way out . . .
>> when we are up against a brick wall . . .
>> when we are facing the Red Sea in front of us,
>> the desert on either side of us, and the Egyptian
>> army in back of us . . .

That's when we discover His power!

Refocus on Who Jesus Christ really is. Praise Him for His deity! Praise Him for His humanity! Praise Him for His eternity! Just praise Him for Who He is! Isn't He wonderful!

Make time each day to praise Jesus for Who He is. How? By reflecting on what He has said through prophecy. Read the Bible, identifying His attributes so you can live your life in praise of Who He really is. And pray. How do you pray? Sometimes if we feel we are very spiritual, we begin our prayer by thanking God for what He has done for us. Then we begin the long "shopping list" of all the things we want Him to do.

God loves for us to come to Him and ask Him for things. But I wonder what kind of relationship I would have with my husband if I shared only about fifteen minutes a day with him and spent the first minute or two thanking him for what he had done for me and the rest of the time asking him to do something else for me! I doubt we would have a very good relationship! My husband wants me to love him simply for who he is. And Jesus Christ, Who is my heavenly Husband, also wants to be loved for Who He is. Not just for what He has done, or may do, but for Who He is in Himself. Would you make time each day to praise Jesus for Who He is? Read the Bible, gleaning His attributes that you might live your life in praise of Who He is.

How does praise of Christ help you if you are depressed by the smallness of your life? It helps you get your eyes off yourself as it puts your life in proper perspective. You cannot remain depressed when you maintain your focus on the Person of Jesus Christ through praise.

Years ago in a rural, Scottish village, the pastor of a small church was asked to resign. The ruling board of his congregation had evaluated the fruit of his ministry and could find nothing that seemed significant. No baptisms had been held the previous year, no conversions had been recorded, and only one response to a sermon could even be remembered.

That single response had taken place one Sunday when the offering plate had been passed. A small boy had put the plate on the floor then stepped into it. When asked for an explanation, he had replied that since he had no money to give God, he wanted to give himself. He had been reprimanded for disturbing the order of worship, and the entire incident had been all but forgotten.

But the little boy did not forget he had given his life to God. While the church had considered his action disruptive and insignificant, God had accepted and honored it as being very significant.

The small boy who had stepped in the offering plate to give his life to God because he had nothing else to offer grew up and lived out his commitment. He became a great pioneer missionary-statesman used of God to change the course of individual lives, tribes, and nations in southern Africa. His name was Bobby Moffat. He was a man who overcame the smallness of his life by giving Himself totally to God, keeping his focus on Christ.

If you are depressed by the smallness of your life, you can find hope today through the vision of His glory! Reflect on what God has said through prophecy, and refocus on Who Jesus is through praise!

 *"For I know the plans I have for you,"* declares the LORD, *"plans to prosper you and not to harm you, plans to give you hope and a future."*

Jeremiah 29:11

2

Hope When You Are Depressed
by the Greatness of Your Problems

Revelation 1:9–20

 The New York City Marathon is considered the ultimate race, with runners coming from all over the world to compete in it. While much prestige is given to the winner of the race, much respect is also given to those who simply qualify to participate and then actually finish the race. The course covers a distance of twenty-six miles and the record finish is two hours and seventeen minutes.

In 1986, Bob Weiland entered the New York City Marathon along with 50,000 other runners. He and 19,800 of the other runners finished. But while the average runner finished in approximately four *hours*, Bob Weiland finished in four *days*, seventeen hours, and seven minutes. Why? What took him so long to complete the race? Bob Weiland has no legs! He ran the race by sitting on the ground and swinging himself forward step by step with his arms!

Could any runner without legs face a greater problem than a twenty-six-mile marathon? And not only face it but participate and actually finish? But rather than be depressed Bob Weiland overcame the greatness of his problems by keeping his eyes, not on each immediate, painful step, but on the big picture of finishing the race. He focused on his goal.

What problem are you facing that seems greater than you can bear? What situation in your life seems impossible?

Amy Carmichael, the great missionary to India, wrote, "When we are facing the impossible, we can count upon the God of the impossible!"

The apostle John received a fresh vision of the God of the impossible at a time when not only the early church but he himself faced overwhelmingly great problems. When John received this vision that he recorded in the book of Revelation, the Emperor Domitian was on the throne in Rome. Secular history records Domitian as the most cruel of all the Roman emperors. He declared himself to be God, sentencing to death those who refused to worship him.

The early Christians did refuse to worship Domitian; therefore, they were sentenced to die by the thousands. Some were thrown to the lions in the great coliseum; some were burned at the stake. Others were wrapped in the skins of wild animals and fed to the dogs or dipped in tar and lit as torches for the emperor's garden. Still others were crucified, including mothers with their babies draped around their necks.

The early Christians, including John, faced great problems! But rather than focus on each painful step of his walk of faith in the midst of such stress and suffering, the glorious vision enabled John to focus on the goal of Jesus Christ. By sharing the glorious vision, John encouraged those running the race of faith to maintain their focus on Christ as they patiently endured.

Finding Hope . . .
through the Patience of Christ

John was patient in suffering. Early tradition records that he was approximately ninety years old when he wrote the Revelation of Jesus Christ, describing himself and his circumstances this way: "I, John, your brother and companion in the suffering and kingdom and patient endurance that are ours in Jesus, was on the island of Patmos because of the word of God and the testimony of Jesus" (Rev. 1:9).

Patience during Suffering

My parents have not yet celebrated their ninetieth birthdays, but as they have grown older, I have become increasingly aware of the physical toll the aging process takes on the human body. While her mind is razor sharp, my mother has difficulty sleeping, difficulty standing, and sometimes, difficulty speaking. My father's heart to serve God seems to grow stronger with each passing year, but his body is growing noticeably weaker. He has difficulty getting up out of a chair, difficulty in hearing, difficulty in walking. The primary problem for them both is age and the physical limitations it brings. They both suffer, not only from physical pain, but from the frustration of having great ability, ideas, and resources yet being unable to accomplish all they would like because of their deteriorating physical condition.

While no one knows for sure, I would assume the apostle John, at ninety years of age, was suffering in a similar fashion. I expect he knew the pain of arthritis, the weariness of insomnia, the dullness of hearing, the dimness of sight, and the weakness of limb that comes with physical old age.

In what way are you suffering physically? Are you suffering due to the physical limitations of old age? Or perhaps suffering due to some health problem that has nothing to do with old age? One of the problems John faced was in his own physical welfare.

Early tradition also indicates that while he was in exile on Patmos, John was assigned to manual labor. While no one knows what that labor might have been, any hard, manual work for a ninety-year-old would be too much! And I doubt he received any pay for it or any encouragement in it. Undoubtedly he suffered in his work.

Do you? Are you working in a place you don't want to be? Working for insufficient pay, without any encouragement?

Perhaps you are a schoolteacher, pouring your life into your lesson plans and your students. Yet it may be that not one student has ever thanked you, and the parents either are totally uninvolved or involved only when they have a complaint. Maybe the administration nervously seems to scrutinize every move you make, and the pay is totally inadequate to meet your needs. Perhaps you don't want to work, yet you must in order to help support your family.

Or perhaps you are in business, working hard to close a contract. But when it is finally signed, the credit and the commission go to someone else.

Or perhaps you work on a loading dock, where those whose every other word is either profane or obscene, mocking you for not joining in "the conversation."

Or do you faithfully take your place in a factory assembly line, drawing less pay than those who cheat on their time cards?

Like John, are you suffering in your work?

John also suffered because of his witness for Jesus Christ. The problems began shortly after Pentecost, when he and Peter, through the power of the Name of Jesus Christ, healed a man crippled from birth. He was arrested by the authorities and warned not to speak to anyone in Jesus' Name. He responded by saying, "We cannot help speaking about what we have seen and heard."[1]

Although he was released on that occasion, shortly thereafter he, along with the other apostles, was arrested by the religious authorities because of the hundreds of lives that were being changed through the power of Christ. This time he was flogged, then ordered once again, before he was released, not to speak in the Name of Christ. The Bible records that he and the other apostles responded with joy because they had been counted worthy to suffer disgrace for the Name of Jesus![2]

Even as John records the glorious vision, he is a "companion in the suffering and kingdom and patient endurance that are ours in Jesus." And remember, John was the great, old apostle who had seen Jesus with his own eyes, heard Jesus with his own ears, whose hands had actually touched the risen Savior.

Perhaps someone had invited him to speak to their civic club about his extensive travels yet warned him not to speak the Name of Jesus because it might be considered exclusive when there would be people there of different religions. But he didn't hesitate. He told the audience there is only one way, one truth, one life—and His Name is Jesus.[3]

By the Greatness of Your Problems

Or perhaps someone invited the soft-spoken, dignified old "apostle of love" to give the invocation at the opening of the state legislature—without praying in the Name of Jesus because it would be considered offensive. But he offered his prayer in the Name of Jesus anyway because he knew that was a precondition for receiving answers.[4]

Or perhaps he was asked to speak at the chapel of the local university but was told to give an inspirational speech, not a spiritual message, or the faculty would not invite him back. But he went right ahead and told them that Jesus is "the true light that gives light to every man,"[5] and, "Anyone who claims to be in the light but hates his brother is still in the darkness."[6]

I wonder if repeatedly he was warned not to be so bold, not to be so uncompromising, not to be so narrow and exclusive and intolerant of others' views or he would lose his promotion, lose his "job," lose his friends, lose his reputation, lose the support of influential leaders in the community. Yet he continued to give out the Word of God clearly, boldly, without compromise. And it cost him. It cost him his "job," or ministry position, it cost him friendships, it cost him opportunities of service, and it cost him the support of the leaders in the community.

When have you suffered for the sake of the Word of God and the testimony of Jesus? I have been in virtually all of the situations I described above for John. I have been told not to pray in the Name of Jesus, but I did. I have been told just to give an inspirational, nonreligious address, and I gave the gospel. I have been accused of being exclusive, intolerant, unloving, and divisive "because of the Word of God and the testimony of Jesus." I have even been removed from a church, along with the Bible class I was teaching, because I taught the entire counsel of Scripture as the truth that it is. I have suffered in my work but never as severely as John suffered. I have never been exiled on Patmos!

Yet there have been even more times when my witness has not been bold and my word has not been clear, because I was afraid. Surely John knew fear too. Surely he feared the pain of torture, the

23

terror of the lions' den, the agony of the cross. But those fears didn't stop him from proclaiming the gospel.

And what do I fear? A raised eyebrow? Am I afraid I won't be included in the social events of the season? Afraid of criticism and gossip behind my back? How ashamed I am of my fears when I think that the early Christians faced lions and crosses and boiling tar and exile on Patmos!

A pastor I know was invited to give a major address at an institution. The invitation was issued by a group of Christians who had made it clear he was being invited to present the gospel. Several days before he was to speak, the pastor publicly stated he would not "be offensive" to anyone in the audience; he would not name the Name of Jesus in his speech because he wanted everyone who came to feel welcome and included. When I called to challenge him on his stand, he said he was hoping the audience of students and faculty would so enjoy his message they would not only invite him back but would come to his church. Then he added this revealing statement: "I make it a policy to play it safe."

His fear of losing personal popularity as well as losing potential church members prompted him to deny the very gospel for which he stood.

What are you afraid of? If you have not suffered "because of the Word of God and the testimony of Jesus," is it because your fears have kept you silent? Have your fears been the bushel under which you have hidden your light?[7] Let your light shine! John did. Think of the vision of His glory John would have missed had he played it safe!

Instead, John endured with patience not only his suffering but also his solitude.

Patience in Solitude

John was exiled on the Isle of Patmos, an island six miles wide and ten miles long. It was basically a large, barren rock in the middle of the Aegean Sea. And John was stuck on it!

John, who had been an eyewitness to the crucifixion, the resurrection, and the ascension of Jesus.

John, who had been present at Pentecost.

John, who had helped establish the early church, who had been an evangelist to the world, who had pastored churches and discipled believers.

John was in exile on Patmos! Cut off from his friends, cut off from his ministry, cut off from opportunities to serve, cut off from traveling, cut off from those who might pray with him or encourage him or even offer sympathy to him in his condition of suffering and solitude.

What is your Patmos? Is it a hospital bed? Is it a workplace where you are the only Christian? Is it a small house with small children? Is it a rest home for the elderly? Is it a new city or a new job? Being fired from your job or going through a divorce or the death of a spouse can put you on Patmos. In what way have you been cut off, exiled, and placed in solitude? There are all different kinds of Patmos, aren't there? And it requires patience to live in the solitude of Patmos.

Some time ago, my husband and I received a call from a friend—I'll call him Dave—asking if he and his wife could talk with us. We knew Dave had been fired from his job several months earlier. When we met with him and his wife, Dave shared that he was really struggling with the way he was being treated by other Christians. He said not one Christian had called to ask how he was doing. Not one member of his church had offered to pray for him. Not one Christian had asked how he or she might help. Dave said he had finally gone to one of the deacons in his church and asked the deacon to meet with him for prayer. The deacon readily agreed, and they set a time when they would get together. When the time came, the deacon did not show up! He had forgotten!

My husband and I looked at our friend and said, "Dave, you are on Patmos. You are in exile. You have been cut off from friends, from a job, and from support. Perhaps it is because God wants to reveal Himself to you in a new, fresh way."

But Dave's focus was so fixed on what he wanted, what he expected, what he felt he deserved, that he struggled against God's will for his life when it included getting fired from his job without the close support of other believers. He refused to patiently endure the solitude of Patmos. Therefore he could not seem to see the big picture. He did not receive a fresh vision of Christ, and he lost hope.

Patience through Submission

Submission to God's will is essential, not only to receiving God's blessing, but to receiving further revelation from God. The apostle John was submissive to God's will, even when it included exile on Patmos.

John was submissive to his Lord in the way he spent his time, which is implied by the phrase, "On the Lord's Day . . ." (Rev. 1:10a). How about that! Who knew what day it was on Patmos? I doubt the other prisoners knew, or even cared, if it was Sunday, Monday, Tuesday, or any other day of the week. They may have marked their cell walls with a line, then crossed off the lines each week, just to keep track of how much time they were spending in exile. But I doubt anyone was aware when it was the Lord's day. But John knew! And on the Lord's day, John spent time with the Lord!

Sometimes when we are suffering in solitude, we refuse to submit our time to the Lord. Instead of remaining involved in fellowship with other Christians or being involved in Christian activities, we tend to withdraw. We get so depressed with the greatness of our problems that we isolate ourselves from the very people and activities that would help get us through the hard times. For instance, our friend Dave stopped going to church. Have *you* stopped going to church? Or have you stopped attending the Bible study you were a member of? Have you withdrawn from your Christian friends? Have you become so depressed that you are not spending time in prayer?

On the Lord's day, John spent time with the Lord. He was submissive in his time and submissive in his spirit. He wrote, "On the Lord's Day, I was in the Spirit" (Rev. 1:10b).

John was in a sweet spirit; he had a right attitude. If you are suffering in solitude, what is your spirit like? When you are cut off from friends and from fellowship, when you are cut off from your hopes and dreams and plans for the future, do you feel sorry for yourself— Do you ask, "Why me?" Do you complain, "Why doesn't anyone seem to care?" Are you offended with God because He allowed this to happen—even though you have been faithfully serving Him? Our friend Dave's spirit was filled with pity for himself, resentment toward others, and offense with God. Is that how you feel too?

Can you imagine what John—and we—would have missed had he become self-analytical, self-pitying, resentful, bitter, and offended? Instead, his spirit was sweet, and his focus was on Christ.

Jesus said if you desire to truly worship God in a manner He accepts, you *must* worship Him in spirit.[8] This means not only that you and I must be indwelt with the Holy Spirit, not only that we be in an earnest, sincere spirit, but also that we must be in a sweet spirit—a right spirit—if we are going to experience genuine worship of the living God.

John was able to experience genuine worship because he was submissive to the Lord in his time, in his spirit, and also in his will. This submission of his will can be seen in that he was still listening to the voice of God. In the midst of his suffering and solitude, he was still open to instruction and direction and new thoughts. And he said he heard God's voice loudly: ". . . I heard behind me a loud voice like a trumpet" (Rev. 1:10c). Did God's voice seem loud because John had made time to come quietly into God's presence?

For you and me, God speaks, not through dreams and visions, but through His Word. When do you make the time to quietly come into the presence of God, open your Bible, and read with the expectation of hearing His voice speak to you?

This past year I drove from the Gulf Coast of Florida to the Atlantic Coast. My route took me along what is known as "Alligator Alley," an unswerving ribbon of asphalt that crosses the Everglades. Again and again, to break the monotony, I tried to tune in a good radio station, but the dial was almost entirely silent, with only two or three stations available. Because I was unable to pull in anything else, those few stations I received seemed to come through loud and clear. I found myself listening to programs I had not heard before simply because there was nothing else available. Then, as I neared the end of my journey and approached the city of Fort Lauderdale, the radio dial became so jammed with signals it was filled with static. I heard a multitude of languages and music and newscasts and accents. No one station stood out clearly. It was confusing. I would find a program I wanted to listen to, but in a few short miles it had been drowned out by other voices crowding in.

Our lives can be like that radio dial. We can be so jammed with signals coming from every direction that even when we tune in to the voice of God, He can get drowned out by other voices crowding in. If we are to hear Him clearly and loudly, there must be times of quietness built into our daily lives. I wonder if that is one reason He sometimes places us in exile, on Patmos.

It was when John was in exile on Patmos that God spoke to him, and John *listened*. When suffering in solitude, whose voice do you listen to? Voices from without? A professional counselor, therapist, public opinion, medical research, pop psychology, polls of human behavior? Voices from within? Your own thoughts, opinions, complaints, emotions, desires, and prejudices? Has the bombardment of other voices kept you from your daily Bible reading and prayer? There are times when I think God is silent, but in reality, He is speaking; I am just not listening.

The submission of John's will can be seen in that he not only listened to the voice of God, but he opened his eyes to the face of God: "I turned around to see the voice that was speaking to me . . ." (Rev. 1:12a).

In order to "see the voice," John had to be willing to turn around. It can be very difficult for a ninety-year-old man to turn around— literally and figuratively. John had known Jesus and had served Jesus most of his life. For sixty years or more, he had been a preacher, an evangelist, a pastor, a discipler of men, a church planter. He was accustomed to serving the Lord in a particular way. Now, he had to be willing to turn around—to change directions, to shift gears, to see and think and serve in a new way.

Are you willing to turn around? Many Christians are not— especially those who are either older in age or older in spiritual maturity. You don't have to be ninety years old to be set in your ways and lose your flexibility and pliability and softness to the Lord's touch in your life. How open are you to seeing something new, to doing something new, to thinking something new?

Had John been unwilling to turn around, he would have missed the work God had for him to do at the end of his life. God was changing gears in John's ministry. Whereas previously John's ministry had been that of an evangelist and exhorter, now God was calling John to a ministry of worship and writing.

What are you missing because you are unwilling to turn around?

For fifty or more years, my father has conducted evangelistic crusades all over the world. His meetings almost invariably have had the same format, which has included large choirs, testimonies of conversion by various individuals, musical solos, and the preaching of the gospel. In 1994, however, several young men involved in setting up the meetings asked my father to consider a more youth-oriented format, including contemporary musical groups, in order to attract young people. Going against the strong advice of some of his long-time counselors, my father agreed. On June 11 in Cleveland, Ohio, a meeting was held that involved several Christian "rock" and "rap" groups. Sixty-five thousand young people, all under the age of eighteen, showed up, setting a new stadium record for attendance. The music was accompanied by a light show and all sorts of modern theatrics and techniques. The audience was wildly demonstrative, standing to sing, shout, wave, and dance to the music. Then my father stood up to preach the gospel. He was introduced by the leading musical group as a hero of the faith. The entire stadium became quiet and reverent as thousands of young people heard the gospel of Jesus Christ in a personally relevant way for the first time. When the invitation was given, six thousand young people ran forward to receive Christ as Savior! And I thought to myself, "Praise God for a seventy-five-year-old evangelist who, like John, was willing to 'turn around.'"[9]

John turned around to see the voice because he knew that behind the voice, or the Word of God, was the living Person of

God. His desire was not just to hear the Word but to see and know the Person behind the Word.

When you read your Bible, do you read to familiarize yourself with the facts? Do you read to grow in your knowledge of the truth? Do you read it so you can live by and obey it, that you might be blessed? Despite these good intentions, could it be you are stopping short of the ultimate purpose of God's Word, which is to reveal God so you can know Him personally?

Sometimes, when faced with great problems, our tendency is to focus on the *hands* of God—what He has not done for us and what we want Him to do for us—instead of focusing on the *face* of God—simply Who He is. Our depression can deepen through this kind of self-preoccupation. Often, in the midst of great problems, we stop short of the real blessing God has for us, which is a fresh vision of Who He is. When we stop focusing on our problems and on ourselves and focus instead on our almighty and omnipresent God, our problems, as the old hymn promises, "grow strangely dim in the light of His glory and grace."

Patient endurance helps us overcome the depression caused by the greatness of our problems because it gives us the opportunity to grow in our knowledge and personal relationship with the One Who is our hope.

Have you grown so impatient, wanting your problems solved now, that you are missing the vision of His glory God has for you? Stop the pity party, stop the complaining, stop the destructive self-analysis and the impatient struggle with God's will. Get your eyes off yourself, your problems, your circumstances, and look to the face of Christ!

Finding Hope . . .
through Preoccupation with Christ

John refused to let himself become preoccupied with his problems. How do we know that? Because in the entire book of Revelation, he only mentioned his problems one time: here in the ninth verse of the first chapter. It's as though he became so preoccupied with

Christ, he did not have time to think of his own suffering and solitude. If he had been depressed by his problems, he seemed to have forgotten all about them in light of the vision of His glory; instead he became totally preoccupied with Christ.

Jesus Is the Son of Man

John described, "When I turned around to see the voice that was speaking to me, I saw seven golden lampstands. . . . The mystery of . . . the seven golden lampstands is this: . . . . the seven lampstands are the seven churches" (Rev. 1:12b, 20). In John's day, the churches were experiencing great problems of pain, persecution, and pressure. So when John turned around, he saw churches, made up of individual believers, who were experiencing great problems—and "among the lampstands was someone like a son of man" (Rev. 1:13b).

John saw Jesus as the Son of Man—a reminder that Jesus is God, Who Himself, in His humanity, experienced great problems of pain, persecution, and pressure. And now, John was seeing Jesus in the midst of those who also had great problems!

Did you know that Jesus draws near to those who are suffering? When you experience problems, He is close beside you.

Malachi described the Lord as a refiner of gold.[10] When gold is refined, the ore is placed in a large melting pot, then the pot is heated. The refiner watches the pot closely, turning up the heat until the ore is completely melted. When the heat is highest, the refiner is the closest, leaning over to skim off the dross until he can actually see his face reflected in the surface of the melted gold.

Has the "heat" been turned up in your life? Please turn around! Look up! The Refiner is bending close, skimming off the dross until He can see His own reflection in your life! When you suffer, do you think that God is ignoring you? That He doesn't care? That He is unwilling or unable to do anything for you?

Has your suffering been intensified by feelings of loneliness and separation and what you feel is a lack of understanding on the part of God? Turn around and look up!

Jesus Is High Priest

When John, in the midst of his suffering and solitude, turned around and looked up, he saw Jesus "dressed in a robe reaching down to his feet" (Rev. 1:13b). That is a description of the high priest in the Old Testament.[11] Hebrews tells us not only that Jesus is our High Priest, but that "we have not a high priest which cannot be touched with the feeling of our infirmities; but was in all points tempted like as we are, yet without sin."[12]

Jesus understands what it *feels* like to suffer great problems. As a man He suffered physically, mentally, materially, emotionally, and spiritually. And He suffered to an extent we will never experience ourselves. He understands with full, personal comprehension what you are going through, and as your High Priest, "He always lives to intercede" for you before the throne of God.[13] Jesus is praying for you with personal understanding and feeling.

Jesus Is the King of Kings

John said Jesus had "a golden sash around his chest" (Rev. 1:13c). This could be part of the description of the high priest's robe, but it is also a description of a king.

On many special occasions, the world has watched as the royal family of Great Britain has come out on the balcony at Buckingham Palace in London to greet the crowd gathered below. When the queen is in formal dress, she wears an elegant, long gown with a diamond-studded tiara on her head and a golden sash draped from her shoulder, across her chest, then tied at her waist. Before her, her father the king, in dress uniform, would also have worn the golden sash across his chest. The sash symbolizes the monarch's position of dignity and authority.

John saw Jesus, not only as Man and Priest, but as King, in full authority over whatever is taking place, not only everywhere in the universe, but in your life and mine.

Does it seem that your life is out of control? It may be out of *your* control, but it is fully under *His* control. John said he saw Jesus with the golden sash across His chest; He is the King of kings, fully in charge of whatever is going on in your life.

Jesus Is the Everlasting Father

John's gaze went beyond the clothes to the One *wearing* the clothes. He said, "His head and hair were white like wool, as white as snow . . ." (Rev. 1:14a). His white hair reveals His eternal wisdom and purity. Daniel saw Jesus in a similar fashion and described Him as the "Ancient of Days."[14] Isaiah saw Him and said His Name would be called "Wonderful Counselor, Mighty God, Everlasting Father, Prince of Peace."[15]

As the everlasting Father, Jesus is wise. There are no accidents with Him in control.

He makes no mistakes.

He knows exactly what He is doing;

He never has to second-guess Himself.

His hindsight is never better than His foresight.

His wisdom does not improve with age or experience.

Jesus — He does it exactly right the first time.

If you are in God's will, your life is exactly right, regardless of how great your problems are.

Romans 8:28 says, "in all things God works for the good of those who love him, who have been called according to his purpose." In other words, when you are in the purpose, or will, of God, everything that comes into your life can work for your good. You may immediately question how the pregnancy of your unmarried daughter can work for your good, or how God can work even a divorce for your good, or how the loss of your job can be for your good, or how your terminal illness can be for your good. If, by "good," Romans 8:28 meant your comfort, convenience, health, wealth, prosperity, pleasure, or happiness, we would all question it! But your ultimate good is conformity to the image of Jesus Christ.

And when you are in God's will—"called according to his purpose"[16]—everything God allows into your life is used by Him to make you like Christ. And because He is the Everlasting Father, with head and hair as white as wool, Jesus knows just exactly what to allow into your life to achieve that ultimate purpose.

Are you afraid the bad things happening to you are happening because God is punishing you? Or because He just doesn't like you? The white hair speaks not only of His wisdom, but of His purity.

Your heavenly Father is absolutely pure . . .

> in His motives,
>> in His methods,
>>> in His manner.

He is absolutely pure . . .

> in His thoughts,
>> in His words,
>>> in His deeds.

He is absolutely pure . . .

> in His emotions,
>> in His attitude,
>>> in His plans.

It is not in His nature to be mean or vindictive or sadistic or cruel or petty or selfish. He is "Holy, holy, holy . . . the LORD God Almighty,"[17] the everlasting Father.

Jesus Is the Avenger

John's next description of Jesus is astounding: "His eyes were like blazing fire" (Rev. 1:14b). If I saw someone with eyes like blazing fire, I would say the person was angry, wouldn't you? John saw Jesus as the avenger of His people. Jesus was not angry with John but with the cause of the suffering of the believers in the early church, as well as John's own suffering.

The Bible says you and I are the apple of God's eye.[18] The apple of the eye is the pupil. If someone suddenly tried to stick his finger in the pupil of your eye, your instinctive reaction would be to strike out and prevent him from doing so. When someone or something hurts you, it is as though someone has tried to stick a finger in

God's eye! If He does not immediately strike out to prevent the problems, pain, and pressures from coming into your life, He is deliberately repressing His protective reaction because He has something better in mind for you. He is going to use it for your good.

When God called Abraham out of Ur of the Chaldees, He said, "I will bless those who bless you, and whoever curses you I will curse."[19] In other words, God would be so identified with Abraham that He would consider the way others treated Abraham as treatment of Himself.

When you belong to God by faith in Jesus Christ, He so identifies with you that He considers whatever happens to you—and the way others treat you—as happening to Him. This personal identification is why God says, "It is mine to avenge; I will repay."[20]

When John saw Jesus with eyes of blazing fire it was as though God, in Christ, was putting His arms about His loved ones, holding them close to Himself as He looked over their shoulders with eyes that issued a warning to those who would cause them problems: "Watch out! I am angry! You have touched the apple of My eye! I will avenge My own."

Jesus Is the Final Judge

John dropped his astonished gaze from the eyes of Jesus to the feet of Jesus. And what he saw would bring even more discomfort to those who had set themselves against God and against those who belong to Him. He said, "His feet were like bronze glowing in a furnace" (Rev. 1:15a).

These were the same feet that had walked the dusty roads of Palestine . . .

The same feet that had walked on water . . .

The same feet the disciples had neglected to wash because they were too busy arguing about which of them was greatest . . .

The same feet that walked up Calvary . . .

The same feet that were nailed to a Roman cross . . .

The same feet that were bruised by the serpent while crushing the serpent's head . . .

The same feet that walked out of the empty tomb . . .

The same feet that walked with the disciples on the Emmaus Road . . .

The same feet that ascended into heaven . . .

The same feet under which God has placed all things . . .

John saw these *same feet*, looking like bronze, glowing in a furnace. These are the feet of the final Judge of the universe!

When John saw the feet of Jesus looking like bronze, he saw feet that were ready to trample in judgment all that had set itself against God and God's people. Feet that were ready to trample anything and everything that had caused human suffering. Feet that are ready to trample in judgment all that has caused *your* problems and pain and pressures and persecution.

There are three primary sources of problems and suffering: sin, Satan, and self. One day, there will be an accounting when Jesus will judge all three, permanently destroying at their source all problems and suffering for the believer in Christ.

Jesus Is the Living Word

Then John heard the voice behind the pages of Scripture, the voice of the living Word of God.

This was the same voice that had calmed the storm . . .

The same voice that had commanded Lazarus to come forth from the tomb . . .

The same voice that had turned Mary's tears to joy when it called her by name . . .

The same voice that had called into being everything and anything that has ever existed . . .

This is the same voice that even now sustains all things in the universe.[21] John said this voice "was like the sound of rushing waters" (Rev. 1:15b).

Having grown up in the mountains, I have stood many times on the banks of a rushing mountain stream. It is very different than a slow-moving river or even a meandering brook in the valley. The sound of rushing water conveys not only energy, power, and life; if you stand close enough to it, it drowns out all other sounds. Have you ever stood at the base of a waterfall? The sound is so great it fills the air, and you cannot even hear yourself speak.

In this time when so many voices are being raised against Christ and what He has said, we can be assured that one day, they will all be silenced. He will have the last word.

Sometimes when we are depressed, we feel lifeless. It's hard to get out of bed in the morning. We seem to have no energy to do even the most routine functions. If you are depressed by the greatness of your problems, read God's Word! That's where you find help. That's where you find joy. Let the rushing waters of the living Word drown out all other sounds and voices. There is life-giving power in the Word of God!

At the most difficult times in my life—the loss of a baby, the forced removal from a church, the execution of a friend, the robbery of our home—God's Word has sustained me. There have been times when I have only been capable of reading a few verses at a time, yet the supernatural life-giving power of the Word of God has not only helped me maintain my emotional and mental balance, it has given me strength to go on, even if only one day at a time.

There is strength . . .

There is peace . . .

There is hope . . .

There is power . . .

There is *life* in the voice that sounds like rushing water!

Read the Word!

Jesus Is Lord of Lords

"John saw that in his right hand he held seven stars . . ." (Rev. 1:16a). From Revelation 1:20 we know that the stars are the angels of the churches. Angels are messengers of God, celestial beings who live to serve Him day and night. In Revelation 2 and 3, they represent the leaders of the churches who also serve God as messengers, giving out His Word to believers.

I hold in my right hand the instruments I use: my writing pen or my eating fork or my pruning shears. John saw Jesus as Lord, holding His servants in His right hand. The implied promise is this: When you and I face great problems, if we will submit to God's grip in the midst of our pain, pressure, and persecution, He will use us for His glory. And as we serve Him we are secure, knowing that nothing, not even our own mistakes and failures, can snatch us out of His hand.[22] We belong to Him. Praise God! He holds on to us, even when we seem to let go of Him!

Jesus Is the Commander of the Lord's Army

". . . Out of his mouth came a sharp, double-edged sword" (Rev. 1:16b). John saw Jesus as the Captain of the Lord's host, the Commander of the armies of heaven.

And the weapon He used to smite His enemies—

The weapon that ensures victory . . .

The weapon against which nothing or no one can stand . . .

The weapon that "penetrates even to dividing soul and spirit" . . .

. . . is the Sword, which is the Word of God.[23]

When confronting great problems, what weapons are you using? Money? Medication? Manipulation? Meanness? Memory? Where is your sword? If Jesus will use it one day to conquer the world, why do you think it is insufficient for you today?

John saw a double-edged sword coming from the mouth of Christ—double-edged because it offers salvation for the believer but destruction for the unbeliever. It is a sword that divides and separates the rebellious, revealing the deepest secrets of the human heart, even while it gathers and unites the redeemed.

Take up your double-edged sword if you have great problems. It offers conviction and comfort, commands and promises, that will not only see you through your darkest hour but will enable you to be more than a conqueror in Christ.

Jesus Is the Light of the World

The glorious vision of Jesus reached its climax when John saw His face, which appeared ". . . like the sun shining in all its brilliance" (Rev. 1:16c). John had become so preoccupied with Jesus that although his circumstances had not changed, his depression had lifted! In the midst of the darkness, John saw the Light! The Light at the end of the long tunnel—the Light that turned John's night into day—was the face of Jesus!

If we had the opportunity to ask John, "Was it worth it to maintain your testimony? Was it worth it to give out the gospel without compromise? Was it worth it to seek to live for Christ in a hostile world? In the end, when you paid the price of exile on Patmos, was it worth it?" I believe John would answer, "Yes! Yes! Yes! It was worth it! I would go back to Patmos any day, just for the vision of Jesus that God gave me there!"

What vision of Jesus are you missing because you are preoccupied with yourself, your problems, your pain, and your circumstances? In the midst of your depression, turn around. Focus on Christ. Why? Because when you are preoccupied with Christ, there is no time to think of your problems.

John's patience and preoccupation with Christ resulted in his prostration before Christ.

Finding Hope . . .
through Prostration before Christ

John said, "When I saw him, I fell at his feet as though dead" (Rev. 1:17a). John, who had walked and talked with Jesus on earth, who had even leaned his head on His shoulder at the last supper, who was called the beloved disciple—John fell at His feet! When confronted with the vision of Jesus in His awesome glory, holiness, and majesty, as one day we too will see Him, the familiarity he had previously felt with Jesus gave way to one of fear and prostration before Him.

Prostrate in Silence

What does it mean to fall prostrate before Christ as though you were dead? A dead man is silent. I never heard a dead man speak or utter any sound whatsoever. To fall at the feet of Jesus as though dead means there is no more discussion about what you think He should or should not do, no more argument about His will, no more rationalization of your behavior, no more excuses for your sin! Falling prostrate means you are silent before Christ. Dead silent.

Prostrate in Stillness

A dead man is also still. I never saw a dead man move. He doesn't even twitch. To fall at the feet of Jesus as though dead means there is no more wrestling with His will for your life, no more pursuit of goals and plans that are your own, no more walking off in your own direction, no more running ahead of Him or lagging behind Him. Falling prostrate means you are still before Christ. Dead still.

Prostrate in Surrender

John was experiencing what Paul described in Galatians 2:20 when he said, "I have been crucified with Christ and I no longer live, but Christ lives in me. The life I live in the body, I live by faith in the Son of God, who loved me and gave himself for me."

Have you ever so totally surrendered your life to Christ that you have fallen at the feet of Jesus as though dead? This experience is not possible without problems and pressures that first force us to turn around and look up, to turn away from the greatness of our problems and refocus on the awesome power, holiness, glory, and majesty of God. Then we fall at His feet as though dead in total prostration. I doubt John would ever have come to this point in his Christian life had he not been suffering in solitude on Patmos. But it is at this point—for John and for us—that the fullness of life in Christ begins. It is at this point that hope becomes reality and the vision of His glory becomes personal.

Lying there, as a dead man at the feet of Jesus, all John cared about was the hand of God on his life. Once he had glimpsed the glorious vision of the face of Christ, his sole desire was to feel the touch of God and hear the voice of God in his life. "Then he placed his right hand on me and said: 'Do not be afraid. I am the First and the Last. I am the Living One; I was dead, and behold I am alive for ever and ever!'" (Rev. 1:17b–18a). In other words, Jesus is saying, "John, don't be afraid. I was a dead man too. But I've been raised up, and I will raise you up. The life you are now going to live, you will live by faith in Me. I love you and gave My life for you." As John lay prostrate at the feet of Jesus, silent and still, he was surrendered for service.

Prostrate for Service

God picked up John for service. He said, in essence, "John, in the midst of your suffering and solitude, when you are experiencing great problems, I have something for you to do." Then God gave him his assignment: "Write, therefore, what you have seen, what is now and what will take place later" (Rev. 1:19).

Do you long to serve the Lord? People are always coming up to me after a message, or writing me notes after a conference, asking me how to get started in service, how to begin a speaking ministry, how to do something of eternal significance. And I respond, "When have you fallen prostrate at the feet of Jesus? Make yourself available for service. Just say, 'Here I am, Lord, help Yourself to my life. Anything. Everything. I am available without reservation.'" Don't wait until your life is problem-free before you make yourself available. And don't tell God how and when you will serve. Just prostrate yourself before Him in total, unreserved surrender of your heart, mind, soul, and strength.

John, in the midst of his suffering, saw the vision of the glory of Christ, felt the fresh touch of God on his life, and heard God calling him to a new area of service.

How did this help John when he was faced with the greatness of his problems? It helped by giving him a sense of purpose and worth in the midst of his suffering. It gave him confidence that his suffering would not be wasted—it was not in vain. It gave him something to live for. It gave him hope!

Outside Monrovia, Liberia, is a little village named Harbell built on the site of a former Firestone rubber plantation. In the village a small church and school have been established to serve the displaced persons who live there.

The pastor of the church is named Gabriel, and the headmaster of the church-run school is named Emmanuel. The school serves six hundred children and has no books, pencils, paper, or blackboard. When the pastor was asked if he was discouraged, he looked amazed and said, "Brother, we are Christians. We may be helpless, but we are not hopeless!"

Are you a Christian? If you are, how can you be hopeless?

Are you so depressed by the greatness of your problems that you have given up all hope? Instead of giving up, would you patiently endure? Would you focus on Christ until you are so preoccupied with Him alone that you fall prostrate before Him?

And if you never feel the hand of God on your life, if you never hear the voice of God calling you into service, it will be enough to lie at His feet and gaze upon the vision of His glory!

Hope When You Are Deluded . . .

 *Everyone who has this hope in him purifies himself, just as he is pure.*

1 John 3:3

3

Hope When You Are Deluded
by Your Own Importance

Revelation 2:1–7, 12–17; 3:1–6, 14–22

 Several years ago, my father and mother were asked by a major talk show host if they would grant a televised interview from their home in Montreat, North Carolina. My parents agreed. Two weeks before the interview was to take place, my mother did what any self-respecting housewife would do—she began to clean the house furiously. With the help of several friends, Mother polished, waxed, washed, and dusted until the old log cabin we call home looked the best it ever had.

When the day came for the interview, my mother confidently greeted the talk-show host and his technical crew at the front door. While the crew set up the cameras and equipment in the living room, the host reviewed with my parents the questions he would be asking. Finally, the director of the show said all was ready.

The living room was crisscrossed with what looked like miles of cables. Huge television lights had been set up around the room, with cameras placed strategically so views could be taken from every angle. The room had literally been transformed into a television studio.

As the host positioned my parents on the sofa, instructing them about which cameras to look into when they answered his questions, my mother was serenely poised. Looking about the room, she could see it was absolutely spotless. Even the cables, cameras, and equipment didn't mar the polished, waxed, washed, and dusted beauty.

Then the cameras began to roll, and the huge lights were turned on. In absolute horror, my mother looked around at her "spotless" room! The room that had looked perfectly clean under ordinary lighting was revealed under the intense television lighting to have cobwebs in the corners, soot in the fireplace, dust bunnies under the table—even dust in the air!

My mother's living room is like our lives. Under ordinary lighting—as we set our own standards, compare ourselves with others, do what feels good and what we think is right in our own eyes—we can be deluded into thinking we're okay. In fact, we can even think we are better than others, confident God must be pleased with us. Then we go to church or Sunday school or get into a Bible study or perhaps hear a Bible-based message, and the light of God's Word shines into our lives. Under the intensity of His light, we see things we had not seen before—the cobwebs of selfishness, the soot of secret sin, the dust of disobedience. Although the revelation can be horrifying, the "dirt" must be confronted, confessed, cleansed, and corrected if we are to be pleasing to God.

In Revelation 2 and 3, God shines the intense light of His Word into the hearts of seven churches, revealing, in essence, cobwebs, dust, and soot—things that were not pleasing to Him, things the churches were not aware of under the ordinary lighting of their own standards and comparisons. The churches seemed in danger of losing the vision of His glory.

Four of the churches were revealed to be deluded by their own importance. One of them, the church at Ephesus, was deluded by something many would not consider a problem for those seeking to do God's work. But it became a problem for the Ephesian church—and it may be a problem for you. The Ephesian Christians were deluded by the importance of service.

Deluded by the Importance of Service

Ephesus was the most prominent city in the nation we know today as Turkey. And the church in Ephesus was a great church, becoming prominent itself under outstanding Christian leadership. Both the apostle John and the apostle Paul had pastored this church. Paul's young protege, Timothy, very probably was "superintendent" of the district that included this church.

When Revelation was written, not only had the Ephesian believers been under excellent leadership, but they were also in the second generation of faith. Many, having been born to believing parents, had been reared in the church.

I can relate to the believers at Ephesus. I was born to believing parents, raised in the church, and exposed to outstanding Christian Bible teachers and preachers while growing up. And because of this heritage, I understand the tendency to take Who Jesus is for granted, to become "professional" in the expression of my faith, to place my *work* for Christ before my *worship* of Christ.

The Ephesian believers had not only become professional and perfunctory in the expression of their faith, they had become deluded by the importance of service, placing it above their love for Jesus Christ. Have you in some way become deluded by the importance of your service for Christ? Do you think He cares more about what *you do* for Him than what *you are* to Him? When you are deluded by service, the glorious vision reveals hope for you through looking at Jesus.

Finding Hope through Looking at Jesus

The Ephesians were unaware of their delusion until the light of God's Word shone into their hearts, focusing their attention on the Person of Christ: "To the angel of the church in Ephesus write: These are the words of him who holds the seven stars in his right hand and walks among the seven golden lampstands" (Rev. 2:1). We know the stars represent the leaders of the church, and the lampstands represent the church itself. So Jesus seems to be saying: "Look at Me! I hold you in My hand—you belong to Me. You are Mine; you are accountable to Me, and I am present in your midst."

What are you looking at? What is your focus, particularly in your Christian service? Are you looking at yourself, discouraged because you don't measure up in comparison to others? Or are you prideful because, in comparison, you feel you are better than others and doing a more effective job? Do you serve to please your peers or your pastor, forgetting you are accountable to Christ? There is no hope of really seeing yourself as God does unless you first look at Jesus Christ.

It is so easy, in Christian service, to let our eyes focus on ourselves or on others—on someone or something other than Christ. So Jesus said, in effect, "Stop looking at anyone or anything else. Look at Me."

Are you looking?

Finding Hope through Learning from Jesus

Once the attention of the church was focused on Him, Jesus encouraged the believers: "I know your deeds, your hard work and your perseverance. I know that you cannot tolerate wicked men, that you have tested those who claim to be apostles but are not, and have found them false. You have persevered and have endured hardships for my name, and have not grown weary. . . . You hate the practices of the Nicolaitans, which I also hate" (Rev. 2:2–3, 6).

The Christians in the Ephesian church were doing many things right. As a matter of fact, we have the impression they were doing *many things.*

Recently, on a Sunday morning, I had an opportunity to visit what has been described as a megachurch. I was struck by the length of the bulletin. Instead of an order of service, it looked more like a small magazine. Waiting for the service to begin, I browsed through the information given, and I noticed the multitude of activities offered for each day of the week. This is a sampling:

Sunday morning, three worship services were offered, not because of an overflow demand but for the convenience of the worshipers. And the services were of three different types, for three different types of taste: One was for "seekers," one was for believers, and one was for those desiring more ritual and tradition.

Sunday afternoon, a tea was being held for new members, and Sunday night another worship service was to be held, with youth activities scheduled simultaneously in the adjacent fellowship hall.

Monday morning there was an aerobics class called "Jumping for Jesus" where women could exercise to Christian music to work off the weight they had accumulated over the weekend. Monday night a Bible study was offered for men, and the choir gathered to rehearse.

Tuesday morning the women of the church met for a Bible study the pastor's wife taught. Tuesday night a Bible study was offered for women who worked during the day, and the members listened to a tape of the message given by the pastor's wife that morning. There were also planning meetings listed for Tuesday night: the growth planning committee, the youth planning committee, the missions planning committee, and the political action planning committee—to name just a few.

Wednesday morning the Temple Keepers met. Temple Keepers were those who needed accountability from others as they tried to maintain their diets and keep their "temples" in good shape. On Wednesday everyone was invited to a family-night supper where each family was to bring enough food for themselves, then everyone would share what had been brought. After supper, the families were divided into age groups for Bible study and discussion.

Thursday morning, each Sunday school had a representative that visited the rest homes and prisons in the area. They led hymn singing, Bible reading, and even played games when time permitted. Thursday night was the deacons' meeting. It was also the night that evangelistic teams went out, canvassing the neighborhood with surveys, seeking opportunities to witness.

Friday morning preparations were made for the soup kitchen, which opened to the indigent for lunch. The clothing closet was also sorted out on Friday mornings and made available after lunch to those who had come for a bowl of soup. Friday night was prayer meeting. Although apparently very few people, if any, showed up to pray, the meeting was always held on Friday night. A class for candidates for baptism was also conducted.

Saturday morning was the men's breakfast. Much was said about the elaborate menu of eggs, grits, ham, sausage, bacon, toast, pancakes, waffles, coffee, and three kinds of juice. Following the breakfast, the worship committee met to plan the services for Sunday. Saturday night the youth were having a pizza party, followed by a movie and an all-night lock-in. A special outreach for couples was being held Saturday night as well. A candlelight dinner was described, and a special speaker who was being flown in for the occasion would give a motivational talk, followed by a musical concert.

Sunday morning the week began again, with three worship services. The church was busy, busy, busy.

How busy are you in Christian service? Are you involved in some type of Christian activity every day of the week? How often are you in church? More than three or four times each week?

Would Jesus say to you, as He did to the Christians at Ephesus: "I know. I *know* your deeds, your hard work, your perseverance." Did you think Jesus *didn't know* all that you are doing for Him? Did you think He *doesn't see* your work behind the scenes, in the kitchen, in the maintenance room, in the nursery, in the parking lot, or in the home—where no one thanks you or encourages you because no one even notices what you do? While others get the attention, the acclaim, the awards, and the affirmation, Jesus says, "I've noticed. *I KNOW*. Thank you for all you are seeking to do in My Name." Would you accept His encouragement?

Having affirmed the Ephesian believers in their service this way, Jesus then convicted them of something they were doing that was *not* pleasing to Him, something the light of His Word revealed. He said, "Yet I hold this against you: You have forsaken your first love" (Rev. 2:4).

When I first fell in love with my husband, I was preoccupied with thoughts of him. I was almost obsessed about spending time with him. My love was affectionate, emotional, passionate, fervent. His every wish was my command. When we were first married, I starched his shirts and ironed his underwear! And none of it was a burden because I was in love!

Have you ever been "in love" with Jesus like that—perhaps when you first met Him and received Him into your life as your Lord and Savior? Do you remember being preoccupied with thoughts of Him? Do you remember when your quiet devotional times were never long enough? Do you remember when the thought of Him provoked an emotional, passionate, fervent response in your heart? Do you remember how you plunged into service, thrilled to think you could do something for this One you loved, this Savior Who had done so much for you?

Have things changed? Somewhere along the line, without your conscious awareness, did your work for Jesus overtake your worship of Jesus? Have you become so busy you no longer have time for extended prayer and Bible reading? When you do find time to pray, are you primarily focusing on requests concerning your service, not on Jesus and your relationship to Him? When you read your Bible, is it to prepare for a Sunday school or Bible study lesson, not just to listen to His voice speaking to you personally?

If this describes you, Jesus says, ". . . you have fallen" (Rev. 2:5a).

You have fallen in your usefulness to God.

You have fallen from God's pleasure in your life.

You have fallen in your testimony before others.

You have fallen in the effectiveness of your witness.

You have fallen away from a love relationship with Jesus.

For twelve years, I taught a weekly Bible class of five hundred women in our city. I never missed a class. During that time, through the disciplined study of His Word, God gave me a wonderful love for Jesus. At the end of the twelve years, I knew with absolute certainty God was calling me to leave the class and go into an itinerant, Bible-teaching ministry. At the time, I was also responsible for the leadership training of sixty-three women. On the last day I was with the sixty-three women, I shared Revelation 2:1–7, warning them about putting the mechanics of the class above their ministry, of putting their work for Christ before their worship of Christ. Because I myself was deeply in love with Jesus at that time, I warned them of this, even as in my own heart I prayed, "Lord, don't let me fall into that pit. Don't let me lose my first love for You."

I left the class and went out into the world. Literally. Three months later I found myself in Fiji, helping to lead a conference of five hundred pastors who had come in from the surrounding islands. Five months later I was in Brazil, leading another conference for approximately fifteen hundred pastors and evangelists from all over the country and squeezing into my schedule a youth conference of more than two thousand young people. In between Fiji and Brazil, I was teaching in seminars and conferences every week in the United States. Although I was aware that I had to drag myself into my quiet time, where my heart no longer seemed to be uplifted in worship and I didn't feel any real joy, I thought I was just tired. I thought I must be suffering from prolonged jet lag, the consequences of time and food changes.

Then one morning, in my devotions, I read Revelation 2:1–7. And Jesus seemed to speak to me: "Anne, I *know* your deeds. I know all about Fiji and the extra sessions that were dumped on you. I know you took them because of your commitment to Me. I know all about Brazil and the women's sessions you booked into your free time because of your heart's desire to get others into My Word. I *know* your hard work and your perseverance. I *know* you have endured hardships for My Name and have not grown weary. Thank you, Anne, for all you are doing to serve Me. Yet I hold this against you: You are losing your love for Me."

When I came to that verse the first time, I kept on reading. I couldn't be hearing Him speak those words to me! I had vowed not to lose my first love for Him! I went around the world telling others how to love Him! Surely He wasn't speaking to me! But He was! He kept drawing my attention back to those verses until I listened to what He had to say.

I would have denied it and vehemently argued—except it was *Jesus* Who was speaking to me! I knew when He speaks, it's the truth. Finally, the light of His Word penetrated my delusion. Deep in my heart, I acknowledged I wasn't just tired; I *was* losing my love for Him! I cannot tell you how devastatingly painful that revelation was to me. I yearned to love Him, and I thought I did; but He did not agree.

One characteristic of Christ that I value and seek to emulate in my dealings with others is that He never convicts without also correcting. He not only points out what is not pleasing to Him in our lives, but He tells us exactly what we need to do about it.

With tears streaming down my cheeks, I asked, "Lord, what would You have me do?" In verse 5 I found His reply. "Remember the height from which you have fallen!" (Rev. 2:5a). He was saying, "Anne, remember what it was like to love Me with all your heart, mind, soul, and strength." I remembered. That love was the "height" in my relationship with Christ. And when I lost it, it was a long way down.

Then He said, "Repent" (Rev. 2:5b). *Repentance* means to stop. Stop going in one direction, turn around, and go in the opposite direction. Because a "first love" is an emotional, affectionate, passionate love, and because emotions really can't be controlled or dictated, I responded, "Lord, how? I want to repent of losing my first love for You. I want to stop not loving You emotionally and affectionately and passionately. But how, Lord? I am willing to repent, but I don't know how."

Again, from verse 5, He seemed to speak to me. "Do the things you did at first." And I said, "What things? Things I did when I was first born again? Things I did when I first began to serve You?" As I waited and listened, He seemed to point out two "first things" I needed to do.

I needed to return to Calvary, where the burden of my sin and guilt had been so great that I had confessed it and plunged beneath His blood to receive cleansing. I needed to return to Calvary and take a good, long look at what it had cost Him to take away my sin and bring me into a right, loving relationship with Himself. I needed a fresh vision of His "first love" for me. On my knees, in prayer, as I returned to the cross, it was as though my heart was broken by the One "who holds the seven stars in his right hand and walks among the seven golden lampstands," the One Who was smashed and poured out for me there.

And then He seemed to say I was to return to the things I did when I first was "in love" with Him. As I searched my life to see what I had been doing then that I wasn't doing when convicted of losing my love for Him, I found something. Although I had been having times of daily Bible reading and prayer, although I enjoyed fellowship with other believers and was serving the Lord, I was not spending time in concentrated Bible study on my own. I had been traveling around, giving out messages that had been previously prepared, and I had studied nothing new and fresh for months!

I got my Bible, picked up my pencil and a legal pad, and began that very day to do an in-depth study of His Word. Within a week of my repentance and obedience, my joy and passionate love for Him returned. As it so happened, the study I began was on the book of Revelation. The fruit of my repentance is the messages that came from that study and, ultimately, this book.

If you have unconsciously lost your first love while staying busy in service, remember the height from which you have fallen. Repent. Return to the things you did at first. The first things of the cross. And do again the things you may have been doing when you were in love with Jesus that you are not doing now. Daily prayer? Daily Bible reading? Fellowship with other believers? Witnessing? Church involvement? Bible study? It can be different for each of us. Or it may be there is something that was not in your life when you were in love with Jesus. Maybe something has crept into your life and taken away your love. A sin? A habit? A relationship? An attitude? Would you ask Jesus to shine the light of His Word into your heart and pinpoint what has cost you your love for Him? Then repent.

To give added incentive for obedience, Jesus warned the Ephesian believers (and me), "If you do not repent, I will come to you and remove your lampstand from its place" (Rev. 2:5c). A lampstand is, very simply, a stand on which you place a lamp so the light of the lamp can not only be more visible but have a broader range. I felt Jesus was warning me that if I did not regain my first love for Him, He would take away my opportunities for service—my opportunities to let my light so shine that others would see my good works and glorify my Father in heaven.[1]

There was a time in my life when I was scared to death that God would call me into service—whether it would be to Africa or just across the street. Then there was a time in my life when I was scared to death God would *not* call me into service, and I wanted to serve Him with all my heart. So I heeded His warning.

There is a principle in this letter to the Ephesian Christians that I don't want to ever forget. The principle is this: Our *love* for Christ is more important to Him than all of our *service* to Him. Strict obedience and service alone are not enough. Love for Jesus *must* come first. Jesus said the first and greatest commandment is to "love the Lord your God with all your heart and with all your soul and with all your mind."[2] Our *worship* of Christ must always come before our *work* for Christ.

Finding Hope through Listening to Jesus

The vision of His glory gives you hope when you are deluded by the importance of your service by promising you an experience of abundant life: "He who has an ear, let him hear what the Spirit says to the churches. To him who overcomes, I will give the right to eat from the tree of life, which is in the paradise of God" (Rev. 2:7). When you put your love for Him first, Jesus promises a deeply satisfying awareness of His love, peace, joy, and presence in your life.[3]

Are you listening? Apparently the Ephesian Christians were not. Perhaps they were just too busy and continued to be deluded by the importance of their service. The result? Except for the biblical record, their testimony in Asia has been completely erased.[4]

Only the light of God's Word is intense enough to reveal the delusions under which we so often operate. God's Word revealed the Ephesian believers were deluded by the importance of service. In the same way, God's Word revealed the believers at Pergamum were deluded by the importance of society.

Deluded by the Importance of Society

Pergamum was a very religious city in Asia. It was the seat of emperor worship and had a temple to Zeus that was one of the seven wonders of the ancient world. It also had a temple to a "healing god" who was worshiped in the form of a serpent.[5]

In addition, Pergamum was known as an intellectual center. It contained a medical university that housed a library with over two hundred thousand volumes.[6]

The Christians in Pergamum, rather than separating themselves from the falsely religious and intellectual society around them, accommodated themselves to it.

The city in which I live is similar to Pergamum in that it is very religious. There is a church on almost every corner. And people still *go* to church. It is also a very intellectual city. There are more Ph.D.'s in our area, per capita, than in any other area in the United States. We are surrounded by major universities, smaller colleges, and research institutions established to take advantage of the educational facilities. In such a setting it is a constant battle not to be so deluded by the importance of society around us that we accommodate the truth and our testimony to it. This delusion once again is exposed by the light of God's Word.

Finding Hope through Looking at Jesus

The believers at Pergamum glimpsed the vision of His glory when Jesus revealed Himself to them through His Word. He said, "These are the words of him who has the sharp, double-edged sword" (Rev. 2:12). As we have considered previously, the sharp, double-edged sword is God's Word. Jesus seemed to say to those who were seeking to be progressive and sophisticated, accommodating the truth to the world around them and being deluded by the importance of society, "Look at Me! I am the Truth! The Bible is My Word! The words I speak to you are truth! You cannot progress beyond the truth!"

The Bible is absolutely true in everything it says. It is the "double-edged sword" that is true on both sides of every issue:

It is absolutely true in what it says about heaven *and* hell.

It is absolutely true in what it says about salvation *and* judgment.

It is absolutely true in what it says about God *and* the devil.

It is absolutely true in what it says about you *and* me.

It is absolutely true in what it says about history *and* science *and* theology *and* sociology.

It is the truth! And you cannot accommodate truth to the world around you or it ceases to be truth!

Jesus began His letter to the Christians who were deluded by the importance of society in Pergamum by telling them to get their eyes on Him. What are your eyes focused on? Are you looking to higher education, science, or technology as the source of final truth? Or are you holding to your faith in God's Word in the face of society's influence? Perhaps you are married to someone who is very religious but lacks a personal relationship with God through faith in Jesus Christ. Or perhaps you have a best friend who is academically brilliant, rejecting simple, childlike faith as being naive, intellectual suicide. If you are watching (and emulating) someone or something else, if you're afraid to "rock the boat" by speaking the truth, you may be like the Christians at Pergamum, deluded by the importance of "getting along" in the surrounding society. Would you instead keep your focus on Jesus?

Despite their failures, Jesus applauded the Christians at Pergamum for their loyalty and faithfulness to Him in the midst of a sophisticated society. He went so far as to mention by name one of the believers who had been faithful even to death.

Do you call yourself a loyal Christian? Because of your identification with Christ, have you been criticized by friends, neighbors, and coworkers? Instead of compromising your testimony, have you maintained it? Then perhaps you need to learn the hope of His encouragement.

Finding Hope through Learning from Jesus

As Jesus continued to speak to the believers at Pergamum, it was with warmth, showing His appreciation and His encouragement for their loyalty: "I *know* where you live—where Satan has his throne. Yet you remain true to my name" (Rev. 2:13a, italics are mine). He said, in effect, "I *know* how difficult it is to live where Satan's throne is—where Satan rules as the prince and the power of the air. I *know* what it is like to live in the world! Thank you for your loyalty and faithfulness to Me where you live."

But then He told them, "Nevertheless, I have a few things against you: You have people there who hold to the teaching of Balaam. . . . Likewise, you also have those who hold to the teaching of the Nicolaitans" (Rev. 2:14a, 15). No one is sure what the Balaamites and Nicolaitans taught specifically, but generally speaking, they so distorted, diluted, and denied the truth of God's Word they caused people to stumble and doubt it. They so accommodated the truth to the godless, immoral society around them they stripped it of its life-changing power.

I once attended a Bible study led by a seminary professor who made much of his several Ph.D. degrees as well as the New Testament version he preached from, which was in Greek. He began the study by relating all the academic arguments as to why the book we were about to study should not have been allowed into the Canon of Scripture. Then he proceeded to say there was strong disagreement as to who had actually authored the book, in spite of the fact the author had identified himself in the text. He concluded by saying it really didn't make any difference, because only someone who could read Greek was qualified to understand the real meaning of the words.

The whole impression he gave was that there was no reason to read this book since it shouldn't have been in the Canon of Scripture anyway and we couldn't believe what was written since no one knew if the author was legitimate or not. And, he implied, even if we did read and study it, we couldn't understand it unless we knew Greek!

As the professor lectured, his Bible slipped from the podium and fell to the floor at his feet. I saw him glance down, and I knew he was aware of what had happened. But the professor never skipped a beat. He continued his message without his Bible, then closed in prayer and walked to the door to speak to those who had come.

The professor was a modern-day Balaamite and Nicolaitan. He was a false teacher who professed to give out God's Word while destroying people's faith in it. While the Bible lay crumpled and ignored at his feet, the words that came from his mouth were his own ideas and opinions.

The real tragedy is the impact a man like this professor can have on a church congregation. He was personable, kind, and beloved by the church body he was addressing. That church body had identified with Christ, maintaining a witness in the community for Him. They had invited this professor to teach their Bible conference, welcoming him into their midst. And I watched in sorrow as he helped lead the entire church away from God's Word until the congregation died spiritually. It remains a big, beautiful, *dead* church to this day.

Jesus told the believers in Pergamum, "I have a few things against you: You have people there who hold to the teaching of Balaam . . . and Nicolaitan." His warning at this point was not to the false teachers and professors but to those within the church who tolerated and associated with them.

Recently I participated in an international conference held in one of the most beautiful countries in the world. As I talked with those who had planned it prior to the opening session, I discovered that many in the Christian community throughout the country were being impacted by "Balaamites and Nicolaitans." Believers from every denomination were being persuaded that while it was good to place their faith in God's Word, they needed to go beyond that and experience emotional, supernatural signs and wonders.

God graciously gave me the opportunity to share with the several thousand people gathered at the conference what our Lord said to the church at Pergamum. He said, in essence, "If you have gone beyond My Word, you have gone too far!"

Have you gone beyond God's Word? What have you been told needs to be added to it to make your Christian experience more complete? More meaningful? More fruitful? "Watch out that no one deceives you."[7]

Who is your pastor? Your professor? Your Sunday school teacher? Your Bible teacher? Whose books do you read, and whose tapes do you listen to? Whose sermons do you hear, and whose videos do you watch? In your desire to know God more fully and to serve God more effectively, are you being persuaded to go beyond His Word by adding an experience or an emotion or signs and wonders? In your desire to be intellectually progressive and religiously sophisticated are you tolerating a false teacher in your midst? Are you tolerating someone who says God's Word is true in faith and doctrine but not in science and history? Are you tolerating someone who says the Bible *contains* the Word of God but is not *entirely* His Word? Are you tolerating someone who says God is infallible but the authors of the

Bible, when they wrote it, were not, and therefore the Bible has errors? Are you tolerating someone who is causing you to doubt and deny and distort and dilute the truth of God's Word?

"Repent therefore!" (Rev. 2:16a). Jesus told the Christians at Pergamum to stop it—stop going beyond God's Word. Stop allowing others to sow seeds of doubt in your mind! Remember how Satan began his deception of Eve in the Garden of Eden with, "Yea, hath God said. . . .?[8] That's what distorters of the truth are saying today. Are you trying to be so open-minded you are entertaining Satan's lies and giving your attention to this deception?

Jesus told the church if it did not repent He would, "come to you and fight against them with the sword of my mouth" (Rev. 2:16b). You and I do not stand in judgment over God's Word; God's Word stands in judgment over you and me!

An illustration of this occurs later in Revelation 19, where a dramatic scene is described in which the armies of the world gather to make war against each other. At the height of the battle, when the human race is on the verge of annihilation, the heavens open and a Man Whose Name is the Word of God appears, riding a white horse. He is followed by the armies of heaven. Those who had gathered for war on earth see Him. They recognize Him as the King of kings and Lord of lords because His Name is clearly written on His thigh. And they unite together to make war against Him! They gather their soldiers, turn around their battleships, aim their missiles, arm their bombs! And all He does is speak a Word! He just flicks the sharp, double-edged sword that comes from His mouth, and they *all drop dead!* The meaning is clear: We do not stand in judgment over God's Word! God's Word stands in judgment over you and me!

Would you choose, right now, to place your faith in God's Word as the truth? You may not understand everything in it, but would you accept it as the inspired, authoritative, inerrant Word that it is? Would you just take it on faith because of Whose Word it is? God is a Gentleman. He does not lie. You can take Him at His Word.

Finding Hope through Listening to Jesus

Following His warning, Jesus said, "He who has an ear, let him hear what the Spirit says to the churches. To him who overcomes, I will give some of the hidden manna" (Rev. 2:17a). Manna was bread from heaven that God gave His children to eat when they were wandering in the wilderness.[9] When the Israelites built the tabernacle, the Ark of the Covenant, which symbolized the presence of God in the midst of His people, was positioned within the Most Holy Place. Moses then was instructed by God to hide some of the manna in the Ark.[10] Years later, Jesus said *He* was the living Bread that had come down from heaven.[11] He was the Manna God had given His children to eat. When the disciples said they didn't understand what it meant to "eat" of Him, the living Bread, He said He was speaking of His Word.[12] In other words, it is through His Word that we are led into a rich, satisfying, personal experience of the reality of Christ.

Hidden manna is bread that is not easily or quickly received. It is not obvious. Jesus promises hidden manna to those who not only overcome doubt, denial, distortion, and dilution of His Word but who also repent of tolerating those who do. He is promising a personal, intimate relationship with Himself through insights into His Word—insights that are sweet, tasty truths and deep, satisfying understanding reserved for those who approach God's Word by faith.

God's Word is a wonderful book of history, poetry, and prophecy. Even if you are only a casual reader you will be blessed by the most superficial reading. The Bible is the most outstanding piece of literature in the world. But its depths and treasures, the hidden manna, are only given to those who overcome their lack of faith in its truth.

Jesus continued, saying, "I will also give him a white stone with a new name written on it, known only to him who receives it" (Rev. 2:17b). No one is certain what this white stone represents, but in the Old Testament, when the high priest went into the most holy place, he wore a breastplate that was embedded with twelve stones. Each stone was engraved with one of the names of the tribes of

Israel. The last of these stones was a white stone, or jasper, like a diamond.[13] Perhaps this is a promise that if we place our faith in His Word, we can be assured He will carry us by name on His heart into the presence of His Father. If we are loyal to His Word, He will be loyal to us!

It may be that the white stone also illustrates another precious truth brought to light thorough a tradition stemming from the ancient legal profession. When a person was placed on trial in a court of law, his or her case was heard by a panel of judges. At the conclusion of the trial, each judge on the panel would render his decision by dropping a stone into a jar. A black stone denoted a verdict of guilt, a white stone a verdict of innocence.

At the final judgment, our guilt or innocence will be determined, not by a panel of judges but by one Judge, Who is Jesus Christ Himself. Perhaps this promise of a white stone to those of us who place our faith in His Word is the reassurance that at the final judgment, He will render on our behalf a verdict of innocence!

The light of God's Word penetrated into the lives of those in Pergamum who were deluded by the importance of society's intellectual and religious sophistication. But the Christians at Pergamum, like the professor I observed, seemed to have allowed the Bible to slide into crumpled, discarded oblivion. They refused to open their eyes to what God's light revealed. They refused to listen to what God's Spirit was saying. The result? Like the church at Ephesus, the church at Pergamum has vanished from the map![14]

The third church that seemed to operate in delusion was the church at Sardis. Apparently the Christians in Sardis were more concerned with their reputation than they were with their relationship with Christ. They were deluded by the importance of status.

Deluded by the Importance of Status

Sardis was one of the richest, most powerful and famous cities in the world. The planting of a Christian church in its midst had great potential for the entire area.[15] In time, however, the city seemed to impact the Christians more than they impacted the city. The wealth, power, and fame of the city began to permeate the fellowship of believers until they became smug and self-satisfied, impressed with the outward trappings of their success.

Finding Hope through Looking at Jesus

The vision of His glory reveals Jesus as One Who holds the balance scales, weighing the church against the perfect standards of His Holy Spirit. He proclaimed, "To the angel of the church of Sardis write: These are the words of him who holds the seven spirits of God and the seven stars" (Rev. 3:1a).

Have you ever heard someone say, "Well, when I get to heaven, God is going to weigh my good deeds against my bad deeds. And since my good deeds outweigh my bad deeds, He is going to let me in"? That person was right in one respect—God *will* weigh his or her deeds. But He doesn't weigh a person's good deeds against bad deeds. He weighs *all* his or her deeds against the Holy Spirit. And if that person has ever done one wrong thing, had one sinful thought, disobeyed God even once—in other words, if he or she is not per-fect—that person will be outweighed by the Holy Spirit and thus be condemned.[16] Since no one is perfect, that is a hopeless thought. But the vision of His glory reveals it is not as hopeless as it seems!

God will judge you and me either according to our own works or according to the work of Christ. If we are judged according to our own works, we are automatically condemned since it is impossible to do enough good works or to do them all so perfectly that they measure up to the holy, righteous standards of God. If we are judged by the work of Christ, we are saved because He is perfect.

Jesus was saying to the believers at Sardis, "Look at Me! I have weighed you in the balances and found you wanting!" The same conviction applies to us today. In our wealthy, materialistic society we need to stop our preoccupation with the trappings of success, and we need to stop determining people's value by the clothes they wear, or the cars they drive, or the houses they live in, or the jobs they hold, or the education they possess. We need to get our eyes on Jesus, Who measures us not according to how many status symbols we have acquired but according to His Holy Spirit.

As the light of His Word penetrated the lives of the believers at Sardis, nothing was revealed that they could be encouraged about. The only right thing about the church at Sardis was that they knew some people who were right! What an indictment! Like Lot in the Old Testament, who was blessed because of his association with Abraham,[17] I wonder how many people today, *within the church*, are indirectly blessed by God, perhaps even spared His immediate judgment, because of their association with those who are truly righteous before Him. Indirect, secondhand blessing is better than none, but it is much less than God desires for us. And in the end, it will not save us.

Finding Hope through Learning from Jesus

Jesus said the Christians in Sardis were the walking, talking dead! He told them, "I know your deeds; you have a reputation of being alive, but you are dead" (Rev. 3:1b). The Sardis Christians made a great show of being spiritual. They were legalistic, fundamental, pharisaical, but it was all to impress other people. They were Bible-toters and Bible-quoters. They pretended to be more spiritual than they were, putting on a religious show. And they had lots of people fooled! They knew all the right phrases and clichés, but they were hypocrites. They cared more about what others thought than about what God thought.

Despite this devastating indictment, Jesus wanted the Christians in Sardis to know it wasn't too late to change. He commanded Sardis to, "Wake up! Strengthen what remains and is about to die, for I have not found your deeds complete in the sight of my God. Remember, therefore, what you have received and heard; obey it and repent" (Rev. 3:2–3a). What the Christians at Sardis had received and heard was the gospel. They had even given the gospel to others. But they had not obeyed it themselves.

Have you, like these long-ago Christians, been lulled to sleep by the materialism, fame, and fortune that seem to be sweeping through the American church today?

Have you become enamored by church buildings that are much more than just facilities—they are multimillion-dollar showplaces?

Have you fallen under the spell of Christian speakers and musicians who command four- and five-figure honoraria before they will "minister"?

Have you become engrossed in books by Christian celebrities that are read with more eagerness than the Bible?

Have programs and business techniques taken the place of your dependence upon God through daily prayer?

Have you chosen entertainment over the gospel?

Have you sought out psychological counseling instead of repenting of your sin?

Are you part of a church that sends out social workers instead of missionaries?

Wake up! Do you have a reputation for being alive, but in fact you are dead? Wake up! Stop fooling yourself! Repent! Be real! Learn from Jesus' words to the believers at Sardis. Because their entire motivation was to impress others, Jesus told them, "I have not found your deeds complete in the sight of my God."

Around the time I was born, my father's evangelistic ministry became worldwide in scope. He was on television, on the radio, in the newspaper, and featured in magazines as well as preaching to huge audiences. As a result, our family was always under scrutiny. I lived my life in conscious awareness of the opinions of other people. I tried to please everybody. But as I began to live out my teenage years, my desire to please others conflicted with a desperate desire to express who I was as an individual. I began modeling, bleached my hair, and wore what was considered heavy makeup. On one occasion, I was cornered into publicly disagreeing with my father on a political candidate. The uproar was deafening, not from within my own home, where my parents and siblings loved and accepted me, but from without, where some Christians sought to press me into their preconceived mold of what the daughter of a well-known evangelist should be like.

The situation boiled into a crisis the summer of my seventeenth year. I was confused, angry, and rebellious within. A friend took me aside and pinpointed what my problem was. He told me I was a phony, caring more about my image and what people thought than about what God thought. He told me I was looking at God through a prism—that my relationship with God was colored and distorted by what everyone else thought and said and did. In trying to please everyone, I was pleasing no one. He said I needed to look at God directly.

Right then and there, I decided I would live my life to please God alone. I knew if I lived to please God, my parents and those I cared most about would be pleased. I just refused to worry about others I couldn't seem to please anyway.

The decision to repent of my hypocrisy and be real was a very freeing decision. From that day forward I have lived my life, day in and day out, publicly and privately, as I am, a sinner saved by grace who is seeking to grow into Christian maturity to the glory of God. My life is open for all to see, which tends to be frightening. Yet if someone observes me as being angry today, perhaps that same person will observe me less angry tomorrow and actually see my patience next week. Perhaps, if others observe the faults, failures, shortcomings, and sin in my life, they will also observe the spiritual growth as I gain victory in these areas and am changed from glory to glory by the Spirit of God.[18]

Finding Hope through Listening to Jesus

There is no greater cure for hypocrisy than to live in the light of the second coming of Christ. Jesus is not fooled by our phoniness! He warned the Christians at Sardis (and us), "But if you do not wake up, I will come like a thief, and you will not know at what time I will come to you" (Rev. 3:3b). Any day we may find ourselves standing face to face before Him, stripped of all pretense, exposed for who and what we really are before the entire universe.

So why not claim His promise given to those who overcome hypocrisy in their Christian lives and choose to be real from the inside out? The promise is this: "He who overcomes will . . . be dressed in white. I will never blot out his name from the book of life, but will acknowledge his name before my Father and his angels" (Rev. 3:5). To be dressed in white is to be dressed in the righteousness of Christ,[19] as well as in works that are pleasing to God.[20] When we live our lives for Christ—when we live as an "overcomer"—we no longer have to pretend to be spiritual and righteous and good. In Christ, we *are!*

Not only are the service and works of an overcomer acceptable, but the overcomer is personally acknowledged and accepted by God. One reason I had lived a life of hypocrisy and phoniness was because I desperately wanted to be accepted by others. I wanted to be well-thought-of and well-spoken-of by others—by society. The vision of His glory gives hope to those deluded by the importance of society by revealing our citizenship is not of this world. Instead we are accepted in heaven! Why should we pretend? There is no need when we have His hope!

Have you been deluded by the importance of status symbols of wealth and power and success and spiritual maturity within the church? "He who has an ear, let him hear what the Spirit says to the churches." The church at Sardis did not have ears to hear, and despite all of its status, wealth, and reputation, it lies in ruins today.[21]

Deluded by the Importance of Self

The last church to be considered in this chapter is the church at Laodicea. Laodicea was the banking capital of the surrounding region as well as a manufacturing city noted for the quality of its black wool. A medical school in the city produced a salve for the eye that was much in demand.[22] Yet the church at Laodicea couldn't seem to "see" what the light of God's Word was revealing in the lives of those who called themselves Christians. The church was deluded by its self-importance.

Finding Hope through Looking at Jesus

The vision of His glory underscored the credibility of Christ to those at Laodicea. He revealed Himself as "the faithful and true witness" (Rev. 3:14b). He was saying, "Look at Me! I have the final word. I am a faithful witness to the truth. What I am about to say is absolutely accurate." The Laodiceans must have had a hard time believing what He then disclosed about them.

Finding Hope through Learning about Jesus

As He searched the Laodicean church with the light of His Word, Jesus found *nothing* to praise them for! They were doing *everything* wrong! And they were proud because *they* thought they were doing everything *right!* Can you imagine an entire church of so-called believers, and not one of them was doing anything right? Not one of them was pleasing to God. Yet apparently the vast majority of members thought the church was wonderful when in reality the entire church was a sham!

It wasn't that they were uninvolved or apathetic. On the contrary, Jesus said, "I know your deeds" (Rev. 3:15a). The Laodiceans were busy in Christian service, but none of it was acceptable to God. Wouldn't it be a terrible thing to pour out your life in service to the Lord, only to find out in the end none of it was acceptable or pleasing to Him? How could this be?

Jesus exposed the one sin that had permeated everything about the Laodiceans: "You are neither cold nor hot. I wish you were either one or the other! So, because you are lukewarm—neither hot nor cold—I am about to spit you out of my mouth" (Rev. 3:15b–16).

I love hot, black coffee, and even when working at the computer on this book, I usually have a cup beside me. But I will get so engrossed in what I am doing that time will pass more quickly than I realize. Again and again, while concentrating on my work, I will absent-mindedly pick up the cup of coffee that has been sitting on my desk for many minutes only to find it is lukewarm. I am glad I am working in private, because my instinctive reaction is to immediately spit the coffee back into the cup!

What an eternal shame it would be if my life caused the Lord to react in the same disgusted way! Yet indifference to Christ was, and still is, disgusting to the Lord! It was as though the Laodiceans had glimpsed the vision of the glory of Jesus—

The Lord of glory . . .

By Your Own Importance

The Rose of Sharon . . .
> The bright Morning Star . . .
>> The Chiefest among ten thousand . . .
>>> The Lamb upon the throne with nail prints
>>> in His hands and feet—[23]

And they simply shrugged!
> They didn't care!
> The Laodiceans didn't take Christ seriously.
> They didn't take the Bible seriously.
> They didn't take the cross seriously.
> They didn't take sin seriously.
> They didn't take the lost world seriously.

Being a Christian was like a holy hobby to them!

What about you? Do you put your tennis and golf, your home and business, your career and children, your exercise and eating, your pleasures and plans before Christ?

Like the Laodiceans, do "You say, 'I am rich; I have acquired wealth and do not need a thing'" (Rev. 3:17a)? Maybe *you* think you have eternal life and are therefore rich. Perhaps you think treasures are waiting for you in heaven and therefore you have acquired wealth. Could it be you're thinking, "I have the blessings of God— good health, loving family, adequate income. I don't need to repent of sin—or anything else"? Listen to what Jesus said: "But you do not realize that you are wretched [still in your sin], pitiful [unacceptable to God], poor [without eternal life], blind [ignorant of your condition] and naked [devoid of righteousness in God's sight]" (Rev. 3:17b). The Laodiceans were so deluded by their own importance they had never even been born again!

In my first year of teaching the Bible class, I asked various women to help me lead and disciple the class members. One of the women I asked, whom I will call Betty, was a lovely lady about forty years of age. She was known for her leadership in a large mainline church. She agreed to help. Each week, we prayed, read, and discussed the Scriptures together in preparation for our involvement with the larger group of women. Betty accepted the responsibility of discipling fifteen other women, and she met regularly with them for Bible study, prayer, and fellowship. Everything seemed to be going smoothly. More women were coming to the class than we could handle, lives were being changed through the power of God's Word, and we were bonding with the other women who were involved in leadership.

One day, after about two months, Betty came with tears in her eyes, and told me, in essence, that all her life she had been deluded by self-importance. In anguish, she told me she had been born and raised in the church, she had been baptized, she took Communion regularly, she knew how to pray and quote Scripture, and she had carefully cultivated a reputation as a Christian lady, but she had never been born again! She thought she was spiritually rich, had acquired wealth, and did not need a thing. But through the Bible study, God had shined the light of His Word into her life. He revealed to her that in His sight she was wretched, pitiful, poor, blind, and naked. Betty immediately repented of her sin and received Christ by faith as her personal Savior and Lord.

You may be thinking the Laodiceans were hopeless because Jesus was already disgusted with them. But that's not true. With a voice that must have pulsated with emotion, He said, "Those whom I love I rebuke and discipline" (Rev. 3:19a). Jesus *loved* the Laodiceans! And He still loves today those who are proud. He loves those who are deluded by self-importance into thinking they are right with Him when they have never even been born again. He loves you, and He loves me, and He tells us, "So be earnest, and repent" (Rev. 3:19b). Crucify your self; repent of your pride and self-esteem. Jesus said, "Apart from me you can do nothing."[24] Did you think you could do something, independent of Jesus? That's pride! Paul said, "I know that nothing good lives in me."[25] Did you think there was at least one small, good thing in you? That's pride! All of our righteousness is as filthy rags in God's sight.[26]

Finding Hope through Listening to Jesus

How shocking this next statement must have been to this proud church. Jesus announced, "Here I am! I stand at the door and knock. If anyone hears my voice and opens the door, I will come in and eat

70

with him, and he with me" (Rev. 3:20). It's hard to believe: Jesus was on the *outside* of this church, knocking to be let in! How could any church let such a thing occur? How could such a church even exist? How? It could happen because the Laodiceans had become proud of themselves, deluded by their own self-importance.

God hates pride![27] Pride makes us indifferent to Jesus. And if we are deluded by pride into focusing on our own self-importance now, we will be repudiated later by Christ before His Father.

Would you examine yourself in the light of God's Word? Does Jesus live within you because at a specific point in time you confessed your sin, repented, placed your faith in the blood of Jesus to cleanse you from your sin, and invited Him into your life? Don't let pride keep you from the cross. Invite Jesus into your life as your Savior and Lord. He said if you invite Him to come in, He *will* come in and eat with you, and you will know it! You will have an increasing confidence and assurance that you are right with God, that your sins are forgiven, and that you have eternal life.

When you overcome your pride, humbly inviting Jesus to come into your life by faith, you receive a wonderful promise: "I will give [you] the right to sit with me on my throne, just as I overcame and sat down with my Father on his throne" (Rev. 3:21b). One day, those of us who acknowledge that we were deluded by self-importance and then repented will *truly* be important. We will be invited to sit on the throne at the center of the universe to rule and reign with Christ. But the way up is down.

Are you listening? "He who has an ear, let him hear what the Spirit says to the churches" (Rev. 3:22). The Laodiceans were not listening. Their church lies deserted and ruined today.[28]

How does the vision of His glory offer hope when you are deluded by the importance of your service, your society, your status, and yourself? It offers hope because it focuses your attention on Jesus Christ.

In the light of Who He is and what He says, we see ourselves as He sees us while there is still time to repent and correct the things that are not pleasing to Him. We have the sure hope that "we all, with open face beholding as in a glass the glory of the Lord, are changed into the same image from glory to glory, [even] as by the Spirit of the Lord."[29] We have the hope that one day, by His grace and power, we will be like Him![30]

 *I pray also that the eyes of your heart may be enlightened in order that you may know the hope to which he has called you.*

Ephesians 1:18a

4

Hope When You Are Deluded
by Your Own Insignificance

Revelation 2:8–11, 18–29, 3:7–13

 Beth Evans is a friend who was recently talking to a nurse in the intensive care unit of a hospital. The nurse stated her support for abortion based on her professional experience in the ICU, not only in that hopsital but previously in another city. Her reasoning was that the majority of premature babies who enter the ICU are in that condition because of poor prenatal care due to the mother's negligence. The nurse went on to point out that most mothers of the premature infants she cared for were either on drugs, had AIDS, were alcoholics, or had been abused in some way.

Since the birth and care of these babies put enormous pressure on the hospitals, which absorb most of the cost for the low-income mothers, and since the babies would be sent home to situations where they would not be well cared for, why should they be born? The nurse believed it would actually solve problems, save expense, and stop the cycle of poverty and abuse if these small, unloved, unwanted, insignificant babies were eliminated.

So Beth told the nurse her own story. Ten years ago, she and her husband received the joyous news that they were expecting their first child. After a few weeks of pregnancy, Beth felt there was something unusual about her condition. She went into the doctor's office for an ultrasound and was then informed she and her husband were not just expecting their first child but their first *four* children! She was carrying quadruplets!

The doctor then advised Beth, "Have a D and C and try again." Because the human womb was not meant to carry four babies, the doctor said to go through with the pregnancy would exact great cost to Beth physically, and in any case, the babies would in all probability be abnormal due to prematurity. When Beth and her husband informed the doctor they had decided to carry the babies as long as they could without interrupting the pregnancy, the doctor explained their option to "selectively reduce" the number of infants in the womb. When they asked what he meant, he explained he could abort some of the babies, reducing the number to three or two or even just one. When Beth and her husband decided to allow God to determine which ones would live or die, the doctor counseled: "Then don't name them your favorite names because of the high probability they will not all survive. Don't think you will walk out of this hospital with healthy babies. You will not."

After weeks of forced bed rest, Beth's babies were born. Each one of the babies, two girls and two boys, weighed in at approximately three pounds each. The first time Beth saw them in the ICU, they had been paralyzed by a drug given to keep them from fighting the respirator. They had needles and tubes attached to their heels, wrists, and belly buttons. Each wore a black mask to help with the jaundice. Each little body appeared lifelessly still, incredibly small, somewhat subhuman, totally insignificant. But they were her children to whom she had given life and to whom she now committed herself for the rest of her life as their mother.

As Beth related her story to the ICU nurse defending abortion, she pointed out her four healthy, energetic nine-year-olds and softly observed, "I can't imagine which one of my babies I could have done without."

What do you feel is so insignificant you want to "do without" it—to discard it? A relationship? A child? A marriage? An opportunity for service? Your future? Your own life?

By Your Own Insignificance

The vision of His glory gives hope to those who are deluded by their own insignificance because it reveals, in Christ, there is no such thing as an insignificant person or an insignificant place or an insignificant position!

Hope When You Are Deluded by the Insignificance of Your Testimony

Three of the seven churches Jesus addressed in Revelation 2 and 3 seemed to be deluded by their own insignificance. The first of these was Smyrna, a beautiful port city on the coast of what is now Turkey. Its one claim to international fame was that it was the birthplace of the Greek epic poet Homer.[1] But the church in Smyrna was also noted all over the Christian world of its day for its suffering.

We have considered previously the persecution of Christians that was inflicted by the Roman emperor Domitian. When he declared himself to be God, demanding to be worshiped, the Christians refused. He therefore commanded that they be burned at the stake, crucified on crosses, and thrown to the lions.

All the suffering experienced by the first-century believers was summed up in the experience of the believers at Smyrna. Their testimony of the gospel of Jesus Christ seemed to them to be totally insignificant in the face of the insane madness they faced daily as they sought to live for Christ in the Roman world of their day.

How effective do you feel your testimony of the gospel has been? Instead of receiving a positive response to it from your family, friends, and coworkers, have you received continuous rejection, criticism, and persecution? Are you on the verge of being deluded into thinking your testimony is insignificant, especially when compared to the reaction it provokes? Then, once again, you need to look at Jesus.

Finding Hope through Looking at Jesus

Jesus revealed Himself to the believers at Smyrna as One Who identified with their suffering. With hope ringing in His voice, He said,

"To the angel of the church in Smyrna write: These are the words of him who is the First and the Last, who died and came to life again" (Rev. 2:8). Jesus said, in essence: "I died. I know what it's like to suffer. I was persecuted even unto death! But I came to life again! I was not defeated by the suffering. I know what it's like to be hated by the world, but take heart! I have overcome the world."[2]

There is no satisfying answer to the problem of human pain and suffering. But one thing we know for sure that gives comfort in the midst of our suffering is that God, in the flesh, understands. He knows what it *feels* like to suffer in a way we never will.

Is your suffering physical? Do you have migraine headaches? Think of the crown of thorns embedded on His brow! Do you suffer with arthritis? Think of Jesus, hanging on the cross, with all His bones out of joint. Do you have heart disease? Think of the feeling of suffocation He experienced as the weight of His body, hanging by nails in His hands, prevented Him from taking a deep breath. Do you have cancer? Think of the raging fever that wracked His tortured body as He hung under a tropical sun. God, in the flesh, understands physical suffering![3]

Is your suffering emotional? Think of our Lord's rejection by those He loved when "He came to that which was his own, but his own did not receive him."[4] He was not only rejected in life, He was even rejected in death. One reason Jesus was crucified outside Jerusalem was because He was considered unworthy to remain within its walls.[5]

When we think of the crucifixion of Christ, we imagine it taking place, as the beloved old hymn depicts it, "on a hill far away." But according to history, if He was executed in the customary way, He was crucified beside the main road going into Jerusalem—not "far away"! And He would have hung only one to eighteen inches off the ground. In other words, He was stripped of His clothes then smashed onto the cross at eye level on the main road going into the city!

Jesus gave His life as the Lamb of God sacrificed for the sin of the world. And people on their way to market or to conduct business in the city passed Him by without even noticing Him! Yet He was giving His life for them! Some did notice; they stopped to read the sign over His head that stated, *This is Jesus, the King of the Jews*[6] and then mocked Him! Those who should have known Who He was hurled insults: "If God really loved You, He would never have let You get into a situation like this."

When have you poured out your life for someone who didn't notice? Or noticed but didn't really care? Has someone taunted you with the circumstances of your life as proof God doesn't love you? If so, remember that God understands emotional suffering!

Is your suffering spiritual? Do you struggle with the guilt and shame and memory of some sin—either yours or the sin of someone against you?

The Bible says Jesus, Who knew no sin of His own, became sin for you and me when He hung on the cross.[7] He felt the guilt of it. The shame of it. He was haunted with the memories of it. And not just your sin, but all the sin of every person of every generation of every age of every nation in all the world since the beginning of time to the end of time! He felt the weight of it!

I have never smoked a cigarette. Therefore, I am very sensitive to the smell of cigarette smoke. When I check into a hotel room or ride in a car, I can immediately detect if someone before me has smoked there. As sensitive as I am to smoke, can you imagine how sensitive Jesus is to sin!

Jesus had never sinned. And having never sinned, think of the awesome sensitivity He would have to even the smallest sin! Yet not just one small sin, not just your sin or my sin, but the sin of the whole world was laid on Him.[8]

No wonder He cried out, "My God, my God, why have you forsaken me?"[9] Your sin and mine had become a barrier, separating Him from His Father for the first time in all eternity.

Have you ever felt separated from God? Forsaken by God? He understands. In fact, He has known spiritual suffering Himself to a degree you and I will never fully comprehend!

Finding Hope through Learning from Jesus

In whatever way you may be suffering at the present time, Jesus understands—personally! He comforted, "I know your afflictions and your poverty—yet you are rich! I know the slander of those who say they are . . . [religious] and are not. . . . Be faithful [to maintain your faith in Me] even to the point of death" (Rev. 2:9–10).

Professor Marshall Hill was my interpreter when I spoke several years ago in a church that was established in a country hostile to Christ. Before we delivered the message, he told me something of his story.

He said he was serving on the staff of a church when he was turned into the authorities by another staff member for preaching the gospel. He was imprisoned for twenty-five years, much of it in solitary confinement. During his imprisonment, the manuscript of the New Testament commentary that had been his life's work was seized and destroyed. When he was finally released from prison, the authorities declared him a "nonperson," which meant in the eyes of the authorities he no longer existed. This designation made it impossible for him to find a job. He was effectively stripped of everything and lived in poverty. His testimony, as well as his life, had never seemed so insignificant!

Then the same church where Professor Hill had previously served and been betrayed reluctantly invited him to come back on staff because he was the only one the church could find who knew Greek, Hebrew, Latin, and English as well as his native language. Professor Hill agreed, and when I had the privilege of meeting him fifteen years later he was still serving in that church with the same staff member who had turned him in to the authorities forty years earlier!

I looked at Professor Hill and knew I was seeing someone who had been afflicted, who was poor, who had been slandered by the religious community—yet he was rich! The smile on his face went from ear to ear! His eyes sparkled with the joy of the Lord! He told me of the peace in his heart, of his renewed sense of purpose in ministry, of the fresh vision he had for reaching his people for Christ! He was committed to being faithful to Christ, even unto death![10]

Jesus knew the suffering of the Smyrna church would delude the believers there into feeling their testimony was insignificant.

But their testimony wasn't insignificant. He said: "I know your afflictions."

Did you think Jesus didn't know what you were going through? Or that He knew but didn't care? Or that He cared but was just helpless to do anything about it? Nothing could be further from the truth. He knows *exactly* what you are going through. He knows every pinpoint of pain and every little flicker of feeling you endure. And He cares. If He has not intervened to deliver you, it is because He has something better for you.

The testimony of the Smyrna Christians was actually so significant that God has recorded it in His Word to be preserved and exalted for all eternity! He does not point out one single thing that needs correcting in their lives. Instead, He pours out His commendation and comfort and encouragement.

Still . . . without tarnishing their beautiful witness in any way, there seems to be a tendency on their part to do something wrong. It may be your tendency also if you are deluded into thinking your testimony is insignificant.

Jesus said: "Do not be afraid of what you are about to suffer" (Rev. 2:10). Obviously the believers were afraid, which is why He told them not to be. But I wonder if they were so afraid of further suffering they were on the verge of compromising their testimony.

Wang Ming Dao was a Chinese pastor who had been led to Christ by another Chinese. At the time of the Communist takeover, he was pastoring the largest church in what was then Peking. He was tolerated for a couple of years then thrown into prison by the Communists because of his testimony and ministry. While in prison, under torture, afraid of even more severe suffering, Wang Ming Dao recanted his faith and was therefore released by the authorities. In the days and weeks that followed, Wang Ming Dao was seen wandering through the streets of the city, weeping and mumbling, "I am Judas! I have betrayed my Lord!"

Unable to bear his shame any longer, he went to the authorities, confessed his faith in Christ, and asked to be placed back into prison. The authorities complied with his request, and he was imprisoned for twenty-seven more years! When released once again, at the end of his life, Wang Ming Dao was considered by the Chinese church as a hero of the faith he had once recanted.

Although this may be an extreme example, there is a "Wang Ming Dao" in each of us. Fear of further criticism, of escalating hostility, of permanent rejection, of increased persecution, or of continued suffering can cause us to back down, to compromise or silence our testimony. We may not recant our faith, but we hide our light under a bushel.

Are you afraid? Jesus said, "Do not be afraid" (Rev. 2:10). Take God's peace, maintain your testimony, and leave the consequences to Him. Be like Queen Esther of Persia, who, when challenged to take a stand against Haman's plotted holocaust of the Jews, said: "I will go to the king, even though it is against the law. *And if I perish, I perish.*"[11] Queen Esther took her stand, did what she believed was right, and left the consequences to God. In the end, she was received by the king and did not perish. The Jews to this day celebrate the Feast of Purim to commemorate her courage and the deliverance of God's people that resulted. There are times we too must take a stand and let the chips fall where they may.

Shadrach, Meshach, and Abednego took such a stand when they were commanded, along with all the provincial officials of Babylon, to bow down and worship King Nebuchadnezzar's golden image. When they refused the first time, they were given a second chance and warned, "If you are ready to fall down and worship the image I made, very good. But if you do not worship it, you will be thrown immediately into a blazing furnace. Then what god will be able to rescue you from my hand?"[12]

The three Hebrew men gave a classic response: "O Nebuchadnezzar, we do not need to defend ourselves before you in this matter. If we are thrown into the blazing furnace, the God we serve is able to save us from it, and he will rescue us from your hand, O king. But even *if he does not*, we want you to know, O king, that we will not serve your gods or worship the image of gold you have set up."[13] The three Hebrew men maintained their faith in God, willing to suffer whatever consequences resulted. And they were thrown into the blazing furnace! God did not deliver them from the fire of suffering and persecution, but He was present with them in the midst of it.

When King Nebuchadnezzar looked into the furnace, he saw four men instead of three! And the fourth man, he said, looked like the Son of God! The Lord God was, indeed, in the furnace with His children!

These heroes of the faith would surely agree with Paul, who said, "For God did not give us a spirit of timidity, but a spirit of power, of love and of self-discipline. So do not be ashamed to testify about our Lord."[14]

In a similar way, Jesus encouraged the believers in Smyrna when He said: "You will suffer persecution for ten days" (Rev. 2:10b). I am not sure what the ten days literally represent, but the principle is that suffering is temporary. It only lasts ten days; there is an end or limit to it.

If you are so deluded by the insignificance of your testimony that fear of the suffering it provokes is causing you to flinch, to be silent, to compromise, to back down, maybe the Lord would say to you, "Deliverance is on its way! An end is in sight! There is a limit to the criticism, ostracism, persecution, and rejection. *It will end!*" If not today, then tomorrow. If not tomorrow, next week. If not next week, next month. If not next month, next year. If it lasts your entire lifetime, it is still temporary compared with eternity!

If we could mark out our lives on a time line that included all eternity, the line itself would be miles and miles long, with our lives lived on earth just a dot on the line. And the suffering we experience during our lives on earth would be such a small mark it would be undetectable. Why would we consider trading deliverance from that speck of suffering for something that impacts the rest of the entire line? Are you in danger of sacrificing your heavenly reward for earthly relief? Focus on the big picture! Remember the compassionate challenge Jesus gave those suffering in Smyrna: "Be faithful, even to the point of death, and I will give you the crown of life"

(Rev. 2:10c). Your testimony is significant because your eternal reward is at stake!

Finding Hope through Listening to Jesus

Are you suffering? Are you so deluded and distorted by your pain that you have lost all hope . . .

Of ever feeling good?

Of ever having peace?

Of ever knowing comfort?

Of ever experiencing joy?

Of ever being loved and completely understood?

Then Jesus has a promise for you if you will focus, not on your pain but on Him, maintaining your faith and testimony at all costs: "He who has an ear, let him hear what the Spirit says to the churches. He who overcomes will not be hurt at all by the second death" (Rev. 2:11).

The second death is hell—a place of outer darkness, gnashing of teeth, eternal suffering, and pain. The hope given to us by the vision of His glory when we overcome our fear of suffering for Christ is that one day we will be permanently, eternally, totally, personally delivered from all pain, suffering, rejection, criticism, and persecution. The Lord Jesus Himself will wipe away our tears, and we will live in His presence forever!

Take up your cross daily and follow Christ, but don't forget: The power and the glory of the resurrection follow the cross, and the crown follows the resurrection!

According to church history, the first bishop of the church was Polycarp, ordained into the ministry by the apostle John and greatly beloved by the believers. He was arrested by the Roman authorities because of his clear testimony then was told he would be set free if he would curse Christ. His reply rings down through the centuries: "Eighty and six years have I served Christ and He has done me nothing but good; how then could I curse Him, my Lord and Savior?" Polycarp was burned alive at the stake.[15] Although Polycarp suffered unto death, he maintained his testimony in Christ—even to this day.

He has therefore been permanently released from all suffering and will receive the crown of life.

Are you listening to what the Spirit is saying? The Christians at Smyrna were! The city has survived the centuries, and a Christian church still exists there today![16]

While the believers at Smyrna seemed to be in danger of delusion, thinking their testimony was insignificant, the Christians at Thyatira were deluded by the seeming insignificance of their moral purity.

Hope When You Are Deluded by the Insignificance of Your Purity

Thyatira was the home of Lydia, the businesswoman converted by the apostle Paul who helped him plant the church in Philippi.[17] The town itself was so obscure and the church so small, scholars wonder why it was singled out for attention by our Lord. But His attention to Thyatira is a solemn warning to those who may think their lives are so small, so obscure, so insignificant, they can get by with sin.

Finding Hope through Looking at Jesus

The image John describes is an unsettling one as he records the voice of Christ thundering, "These are the words of the Son of God, whose eyes are like blazing fire and whose feet are like burnished bronze" (Rev. 2:18b). This is the same way John described Jesus in Revelation 1 as He angrily looked at the cause of John's suffering. This time, Jesus was angrily looking at the church at Thyatira! I pray I never see Jesus looking at me with eyes of blazing fire—angry—and feet of burnished bronze—coming in judgment! What caused Him to look at the Christians in the Thyatira church this way?

Jesus revealed, "I know your deeds, your love and faith, your service and perseverance, and that you are now doing more than you did at first" (Rev. 2:19). That's amazing! They seemed to be doing everything right! They showed love for the Lord Jesus along with their deeds—the thing the Ephesian church had lacked. They had faith, which the Laodicean church had lacked. They had service and faith and perseverance, which the Smyrna church had seemed in danger of losing. So what was missing? What could be so wrong with a church that seemed so right? The answer comes in the next verse: "Nevertheless, I have this against you: You tolerate that woman Jezebel, who calls herself a prophetess" (Rev. 2:20a).

Jezebel was a leader in the church. I expect she was gifted, articulate, attractive, with a very charismatic personality. Apparently she had convinced the majority of Christians in the church that if they were going to win their friends to Christ, they had to be like their friends. They had to go where their friends went, dress like their friends dressed, talk like their friends talked, entertain like their friends entertained, listen to the music, eat the food, and drink the drinks their friends did. I expect she argued that if you separate from the world instead of compromising and becoming like the world, you will offend the world; then how will you get those unbelievers to listen to your presentation of the gospel?

Jezebel must have denied that it is when, through the life of the believer, Jesus is lifted up in all of His uniqueness, including His holiness and purity, that others are drawn to Him and are saved.[18]

Whatever her tactics were, Jezebel led the entire church into sin! Jesus admonished the believers in Thyatira, "By her teaching she misleads my servants into sexual immorality and the eating of food sacrificed to idols" (Rev. 2:20b). Specifically, she led the Christians into a lifestyle of immorality. And the believers were so deluded by what they thought was the insignificance of their purity they followed her leadership! The church at Thyatira had become so much like the surrounding world that the casual observer would be hard-pressed to tell the difference! What was missing in the church that would provoke the wrath of the Son of God? *Holiness and purity!*

Surely there has never been a time when there has been more immorality *within* the church than there is today. When performance is exalted above character, even within the church, we need to read our Lord's letter to Thyatira very carefully. Jesus said He had given Jezebel "time to repent of her immorality, but she is unwilling" (Rev. 2:21).

And so He allowed Jezebel, who had sown the wind, to reap the whirlwind. She suffered the consequences of judgment for her sin, but even more tragically, her lifestyle affected her children, and they also reaped the consequences.

If you and I do not repent of the sin in our lives, it will be passed on to our children and magnified in their lives. I have a friend who, at the same time he professed to be a Christian leader, was repeatedly unfaithful to his wife. Not only did the husband's sexual immorality result in the destruction of the marriage, but the real tragedy now is to see his sin reproduced in his children as they too have adopted immoral lifestyles. And the consequences of disease and unwanted pregnancies that have resulted have been devastating.

The Lord's warning to the believers at Thyatira was that if they did not remove the sin in their midst, He would! And He did!

In the past few years, the front pages of our newspapers have reported in lurid detail the immorality of some Christian leaders. Tales of marital infidelity, financial dishonesty, and the manipulative tactics of preachers of the gospel have given the tabloids and television talk shows a brisk business.

The network news carried an interview with one such preacher and his wife as they tearfully described as an attack of Satan the legal investigation into their ministry and their subsequent indictment by the grand jury. That preacher was later convicted in a court of law for crimes against the state, and he was imprisoned. His wife then left him to marry his best friend, and his family has disintegrated.

I wonder . . . was it an attack by Satan, or was it the Son of God, with eyes of blazing fire and feet like burnished bronze, Who refused to tolerate such behavior by His people? Especially by the leaders of His people!

As one shameful story about immoral Christian leaders after another hits the press, it is as though once again Jesus has gone into the temple to drive out the moneychangers.

The incredible aspect to many of these stories is that even after a leader's sin and shame are exposed, a large enough following is retained to continue television and radio programs.

Who is instructing you in spiritual matters in your church or through tapes, books, videos, and television programs? How much do you know about that person's character? Does his "walk" match his "talk"?

Watch out! Our Lord's anger and His letter were not addressed to Jezebel; they were directed to those who not only tolerated her but who listened to, supported, and followed her!

In what way have you allowed immorality to creep into your life? Five or ten years ago, if we had turned the television dial and heard and seen what we do today, we would have been shocked, protesting our outrage to those responsible, boycotting the sponsors of such programs. Today, we have become so anesthetized by the bombardment of sin from every side, such scenes and language don't even faze us. Jesus told the Christians at Thyatira (and us today), ". . . repent of [Jezebel's] ways" (Rev. 2:22b). We need to repent of such complacency that allows seeds of immorality and impurity to be sown into our hearts and minds.

Several years ago, in a police "sting" operation, the head of a statewide church organization was picked up for soliciting a male prostitute. Having known this church leader myself for years, the news of his shameful behavior and subsequent arrest was a shock! I wondered, how had such a perversion begun? With one thought? With a second look? How deluded we can be to think such thoughts and looks are insignificant when Jesus said they can be the hooks that drag our entire lives down to destruction![19]

What sin in thought, word, or deed are you committing because you see another "Christian" committing it and he or she seems to get by with it?

Jesus told the Christians at Thyatira to stop using Jezebel's example and position of leadership as an excuse for sin.

While teaching my Bible class, I felt led to rebuke a lovely Christian lady for blatant sin in her life. She looked at me with a surprised, hurt expression on her face, then defended her behavior by saying, "But my pastor does it!" My response to her was, in that case, her pastor was wrong!

Be careful! There are whole denominations today that sanction sin! What others say or do around us is not an acceptable excuse for sin. God will call you and me into account for the sin in our lives, not someone else's. God is not mocked. He demands holiness and purity in His people! What are you substituting for holiness? Positive thinking? Modern morality? There is no substitute from God's perspective.

It is interesting that toward the end of His letter to the church at Thyatira, Jesus addresses the remnant of believers: "Now I say to the rest of you in Thyatira, to you who do not hold to her teaching" (Rev. 2:24). Those who seek to live godly, holy, pure lives will always be a remnant, even within the church!

As a minority, Jesus instructs these believers to "hold on to what you have until I come" (Rev. 2:25). What did they have? They had the Word of God, they had eternal life, they had their commitment to purity, they had the praise of the Son of God, they had hope— they had the vision of His glory!

Finding Hope through Listening to Jesus

The hope offered to those who make the commitment to holiness and purity, is "authority over the nations" (Rev. 2:26b). While this promise seems to involve our future service for Christ following His return to earth, it also has present application. "Authority over the nations" implies that the remnant will have power in their service.

Genuine spiritual power to change lives—not the power enjoyed by megachurches or television ministries or celebrity status or money or educational programs but *real power* to change lives—is directly related to moral purity and personal holiness.

Are you listening? "He who has an ear, let him hear what the Spirit says to the churches" (Rev. 2:29). The Christians at Thyatira were not listening. Nothing remains of that church today.[20]

Hope When You Are Deluded by the Insignificance of Your Own Ability

The last church to be considered is the small, humble church at

Philadelphia. This church, although surrounded by a pagan society, faithfully lived for Jesus Christ. Our Lord had no rebuke or correction for this church, only praise. Yet the believers were so humble, they tended to be deluded by the insignificance of their own ability.

Finding Hope through Looking at Jesus

The vision of His glory given to the Philadelphian church revealed Jesus to be the One "who holds the key of David. What he opens no one can shut, and what he shuts no one can open" (Rev. 3:7b).

Several years ago, I was presented with the key to the city in which I had been holding meetings. It was a gracious gesture on the part of the mayor, letting me know I was accepted and welcomed in that city.

Jerusalem is known as the City of David,[21] and heaven is referred to as the New Jerusalem.[22] The "key of David" represents acceptance in and free access to heaven. And Jesus holds the key! He is the One Who determines who can come into heaven and who must stay out. He Himself, not Peter, as jokes would have us believe, is the One Who opens the door to those who have received Him by faith, and He is the One Who shuts the door to those who have rejected Him.

What makes you think He will open the door of heaven for you? When were you presented with a symbolic "key to the city"? The only place the key is bestowed is at Calvary.

But in this instance, there is perhaps another meaning to the key of David. It could also represent the key to doors of opportunity for service on earth.

Who did you think held the key to the doors of opportunity for you? Your spouse? Your boss? The chairman of the board? Your pastor? One of your parents? A professor or educational institution? A publisher? The loan officer at the bank? To whom or what are you looking for opportunity? Jesus is the One Who holds the key! Would you look to Him?

Finding Hope through Learning from Jesus

Jesus had nothing but words of praise for the Philadelphian church. It must have been deeply encouraging to hear Him say, "I know your deeds. See, I have placed before you an open door that no one can shut. I know that you have little strength, yet you have kept my word and have not denied my name" (Rev. 3:8.) Can you imagine coming under the intense scrutiny of Christ and receiving nothing but praise because your entire life, inside and out, backward and forward, up and deep down, is pleasing to Him! What a testimony this beautiful body of believers had.

This passage is very precious to me because it was from these verses that God called me into service approximately twenty years ago. I had sought to establish a Bible class in our city but had been refused the opportunity to lead it by those who held authority in my life. Shortly thereafter, my husband and I took his parents and our three small children to Cape Cod for a brief vacation. As we drove along the interstate, my husband and his father were carrying on a conversation, two of the kids were screaming, I was trying to help the third one find something to eat, and my mother-in-law was reading this passage out loud, to no one in particular!

In the midst of all that confusion, the words she was reading penetrated my consciousness, and I asked her to pass me the Bible. As I read the words for myself, God seemed to clearly speak to me. *Personally.*

It was as though He were saying, "I know your deeds, Anne. I know you haven't done much for Me in the way of service. I know you have never taught a Sunday school class or led a Bible study on your own. I am fully aware of your deeds (or lack of them). I know that you have a little strength. In fact, that's all a young mother with three small children has! But you have kept My Word. You have maintained your Bible reading and your daily devotions. And you have not denied My Name. You have been loyal, even to the point of foolishness at times—like when you confronted the divinity school professor for his contradiction of My Word in front of a packed chapel. See, I have placed before you an open door that no one can shut. I am going to open the door for you to establish and teach a Bible class in your city."

And He did! One by one, the barriers came down. The last barrier to fall was the one in my own heart and mind. It was the barrier of delusion as to the insignificance of my ability. I felt I couldn't do it.

Although the Philadelphia believers did everything right, their tendency was to be deluded, thinking their ability was insignificant. When Jesus told them that He knew they had a little strength, He revealed they may have felt inadequate. That's the way I felt—and still feel.

Would you say you only have . . .

A little strength?

A little time?

A little money?

A little education?

A little knowledge?

Has the "littleness" caused you to feel inadequate? Has your feeling of inadequacy become your excuse for not taking the opportunities God gives you?

When Jesus opened the door of opportunity for me to establish a Bible class in my city, and as one by one the barriers that had hindered it came down, I was at last faced with the reality of getting into the pulpit and teaching. I knew the open door He had set before me included the implied command to walk through it. But I used my feelings of inadequacy and inferiority as an excuse for disobedience.

Jesus seemed to say, "Anne, I have opened a door for you—walk through it."

I said, "I can't."

And He said, "I know without Me you can do nothing, but through Me you can do all things."

I said, "Lord, I am inadequate."

He said, "I agree. But My grace is sufficient."

I said, "Lord, I am weak."

He said, "I've told you I know you have only a little strength, but My strength is made perfect in weakness."

One by one, He took my reasons for not serving Him—and agreed with them! I loved Him for His honesty with me. He didn't say, "Anne, you can do this! You just have to try harder! You have more strength than you realize! Your background has equipped you more than you know." Instead, He acknowledged what I *knew* to be the truth, which was that I could not, in myself, do what He was commanding. But He left no room for argument as to what He would do through me if I simply made myself available to Him in obedience and dependence.

His command was clear: "Anne, walk through the open door I have placed before you, 'hold on to what you have, so that no one will take your crown'" (Rev. 3:11).

And I respectfully answered, "Lord, I know what I don't have. I don't have time, or strength, or education, or money, or ability. What do I have that I am to hold on to?"

And He said, "Anne, you have Me! And you have My Word! Walk through the open door, holding on to what you have."

And because I call Him "Lord," at that point I had no option. I said: "Yes, Sir!" and started teaching the class. My fear was more like stark terror! Fear of public failure, fear of critical comparisons, fear of upturned faces, and fear of total inadequacy caused me to literally throw up before every lecture I gave for the first two months! But as fearful as I was to teach, I was even more fearful to disobey the One I called Lord!

That was twenty years ago! The interesting thing is that as I have continued to walk through the open doors He places before me, I have not grown in self-confidence. I have less confidence today in myself than when I began teaching because I now know by experience that all my reasons for not serving were very accurate. I *am* totally inadequate. The difference is that my confidence *in Christ* has increased. I now know, also by experience, that my Redeemer is faithful and true in every situation. I know, by experience, He will never command me to do anything He is unable or unwilling to do in me and through me.

I will never forget my first trip to India. I flew in from Hong Kong, arriving in Madras around midnight. Catching a few hours of rest, I left at five the next morning to take another plane to the southern coast. After a night of "rest" in a hotel where the ever-present idols seemed to watch my every move (and where I watched every move of the rats and snakes in the "garden" outside my window), I left to cross the southern tip of India in a car. For ten hours we bumped along roads that at times looked more like ruts, stopping only twice: once to dedicate a church tucked away in the jungle and once to have tea at Donavur Fellowship, Amy Carmichael's home for unwanted girls and boys.

At 6:00 that evening we arrived at our destination, the home of the bishop of Tinneveli, where I was to stay. As I was being shown to my room, I was told very graciously that the car would return for me in one hour. When I asked why, I was told I was addressing all the bishops of the area, after which I would speak at an evangelistic meeting in a soccer stadium! I can assure you, during the hour before the car returned, I stayed on my knees, telling the Lord, "I can't do this!"

As I stood on the platform that night with a dozen distinguished bishops in their long, white robes—barefooted because they had removed their shoes in reverence to the God they served—I looked out into a sea of thousands of Indian faces turned in my direction. The lights around the platform had attracted clouds of bugs, all of which seemed to cling to my long, blue dress. And inwardly I was telling the Lord, "I can't do this."

I was introduced to the crowd that had gathered, then found myself stepping into the pulpit with an Indian gentleman to my left who was to serve as my interpreter. Even as I was still protesting silently, "Lord, I really can't do this," I opened my mouth—and did it! An hour and a half later, when I gave the invitation, hundreds of Indians responded to give their hearts to Christ! And I felt I had been branded for life with the Lord's response: "Anne, you can't. But I can!"

What an adventure it has been! From the weekly Bible class in my city, He opened other doors to pulpits in Fiji, in India, in South Africa, in China, in Brazil, in Eastern Europe, in Australia, in Russia, in Spain, in Argentina, in Japan, in Northern Ireland, in the Philippines, in Honduras, in Mexico. As the doors continue to open,

He continues to be enough. I walk through the open doors, still terrified, still holding tightly to what I have, yet growing in my confidence in Him and in His Word. Praise His Name! I know, without a doubt, to God alone be the glory for the things *He* has done!

What doors has He opened for you? If you are deluded into thinking your insignificant ability is an excuse for refusing to walk through them, it is not. Weakness, inadequacy, inferiority, inability can create a deep dependency upon God alone. And God will use those who are totally dependent upon Him. He holds the key!

What is our motivation to serve Him when He gives us the opportunity? Besides the fact that He is our Lord and we therefore have no option, He told the Philadelphian church, "I am coming soon" (Rev. 3:11). Time to serve Him on earth is short. We are to work while it is day because the night is coming when no man can work.[23]

Finding Hope through Listening to Jesus

The vision of His glory gives hope to those who overcome the delusion that their ability is insignificant. Jesus promised, "Him who overcomes I will make a pillar in the temple of my God. . . . I will write on him the name of my God" (Rev. 3:12). The pillar represents strength, the temple of God is His presence, and His Name written on us is His identification with us.

Several years ago I gave a television interview in South Africa. The interviewer, who had come to the meeting the previous evening, said, "Anne, you have such confidence and speak with such authority in the pulpit. How do you do it?" I smiled, then briefly shared my testimony of fear and inadequacy coupled with my growing confidence in Christ. But to myself, I thought how God was confirming through the interviewer His promise to me that I would be a "strong pillar in the temple of my God."

It was a promise that my obedient, dependent service would be so rooted in His presence and His person that others would see only the strength and identification with God and never know how inadequate I truly am!

Are you listening to what Jesus promises? "He who has an ear, let him hear what the Spirit says to the churches" (Rev. 3:13). The Philadelphian church had an ear to hear and a will to heed. The city and the Christian church there have survived the centuries.[24]

Do you have an ear to hear what the Spirit is saying to the churches? The church at Smyrna, deluded by the insignificance of the believers' testimony, discovered it had eternal value. The believers at Thyatira succumbed to the delusion that their purity was insignificant, and thus they provoked the wrath and judgment of the Son of God. The Christians at Philadelphia were deluded by thinking their abilities were insignificant, yet they discovered Christ was all they really needed.

When you overcome the delusion of your own insignificance, the vision of His glory gives you hope by revealing your significance *in Christ.*

"He who has an ear, let him hear what the Spirit says. . . ."

Hope When You Are Discouraged . . .

But now, Lord, what do I look for?
My hope is in you.

Psalm 39:7

5
Hope When You Are Discouraged by the Majority of the Ungodly

Revelation 4

 Elijah thundered into history when the Northern Kingdom of Israel was the furthest from God it had ever been. Six kings had ruled, each one more wicked than the one before, until the stage was set for the seventh king, who did more evil in God's sight than all the others combined. Under his leadership, not only the world but the people who called themselves by God's Name disintegrated morally and spiritually.

Elijah preached with such power that heaven opened and fire came down! He single-handedly turned the entire Northern Kingdom back to God, temporarily ending the spiritual and moral drought. Then he prayed with such power that the heavens opened again and rain came down, ending the three years of physical drought that had plagued the land.[1]

Elijah had poured out his life in *obedience* to God, and he had poured out his life in *service* to God! He had preached, he had prayed, and he had put an end to the "ministries" of 850 false prophets as he sought to free his people from their influence. He had literally done everything he knew to do, repeatedly risking his life and reputation in order to bring deep, permanent change to his nation. At least he thought he had!

Just when Elijah thought he had the victory, the king's evil queen, Jezebel,[2] issued a death threat against him. A feeling of helplessness and hopelessness must have swept over him. Who was he, one man, against the wealthy, organized, deeply entrenched, powerful forces of evil? And so Elijah ran and ran and ran. When he finally stopped running, he was so discouraged by the majority of the ungodly, he was suicidal.[3]

Only someone who has been involved in service, only someone whose heart is broken for a lost world and is desperate to bring it into a right relationship with God, only someone who has poured out his or her life in surrendered obedience and service to that end can fully understand the depths of Elijah's discouragement. There just seems to be too much evil and too many ungodly people. Making broad, sweeping, lasting change for the good can seem so hopeless.

My father was recently interviewed on television by Diane Sawyer. She asked if, after having preached for fifty years to over 120 million people face to face on every continent of the globe, after having presented the gospel through television, radio, and the printed word, he was pleased with his "success." My father's answer startled her because he replied: "I don't think of myself as successful at all. I feel like a failure." Pressing him to explain himself, she inquired, "Did you think you could change the world?" He responded softly, "I thought maybe, after a lifetime of preaching. . . . But the world is worse today than when I began my ministry."

Do you have that same deep sense of failure? In spite of your obedience, your dependence, and your service to God, do things seem to be worse, leaving you overwhelmed and hopelessly discouraged by the majority of the ungodly?

King David advised, "Do not fret because of evil men."[4]

The one who is indwelt by the Holy Spirit of God . . .

The one who is obeying the Word of God . . .

The one who is living in the will of God . . .

The one who is walking in the way of God is a majority!

A majority of one—because of whose we are!

100

Lift up your head! Open your eyes to the vision of His glory—a glorious vision of hope God has given in His revelation of Who Jesus is! He is the Lord!

Finding Hope in Expecting the Lord to Enter to Claim His People

In Revelation 4:1, John said, "After this, I looked. . . ." By saying "after this" John refers to the preceding chapters and God's involvement with the churches. From this point on in the book of Revelation, there is no further mention of the church on earth. Some Bible scholars believe as John is caught up into heaven, he *may* represent the entire church that one day will be caught up to be with the Lord. Although the "catching up of believers" cannot be based with any certainty on Revelation 4:1, we do know with certainty that it will take place.[5] I have included it here for your own information, encouragement, and blessing.

The apostle Paul described this historical event clearly in 1 Thessalonians 4:13–18: "Brothers, we do not want you to be ignorant about those who fall asleep, or to grieve like the rest of men, who have no hope. We believe that Jesus died and rose again and so we believe that God will bring with Jesus those who have fallen asleep in him. According to the Lord's own word, we tell you that we who are still alive, who are left till the coming of the Lord, will certainly not precede those who have fallen asleep. For the Lord himself will come down from heaven, with a loud command, with the voice of the archangel and with the trumpet call of God, and the dead in Christ will rise first. After that, we who are still alive and are left will be caught up together with them in the clouds to meet the Lord in the air. And so we will be with the Lord forever. Therefore encourage each other with these words."

Bible scholars refer to this event as the "Rapture of the church." Paul told the Thessalonian believers, who were only three weeks old in their faith, that he did not want them "to be ignorant about those who fall asleep"—those who placed their faith in Jesus Christ as their Savior and Lord and later died.

Have you recently buried a friend or loved one who had been born again by faith in Christ? Paul says that while we grieve, it is not "like the rest of men, who have no hope."[6]

The same week my third child was born, my grandmother died. No one in all the world outside of my own parents meant more to me than my grandmother.

When I was small, she and my grandfather lived right across the street from where I lived with my family. Whenever I got sick or just wanted someone to read to me or sew for me or fix me something special to eat, I went across to my grandmother's house. She taught me, read to me, played with me, fed me, and nursed me. When she died, I felt as if a part of myself had died. To this day, in unguarded moments, I still weep with that yearning, homesick feeling just to hear her voice or to see her smile or to feel her hug.

Paul says it is all right to grieve, even twenty years after her death. But I am not to grieve as one who has no hope, because we believe that the same Jesus Who died on the cross to offer us forgiveness of sin, and the same Jesus Who was raised from the dead to give us eternal life is the same Jesus Who one day will come again! And when He comes, "God will bring with Jesus those who have fallen asleep in him." When He comes, He will bring my grandmother with Him!

Paul must have thought you and I would think this was unbelievable, because his next statement emphasized this is "the Lord's own word," not Paul's wishful thinking or active imagination!

Paul said that those believers who are alive on earth when Jesus returns will not hinder those believers who have already died. "For the Lord himself will come down from heaven, with a loud command, with the voice of the archangel and with the trumpet call of God, and the dead in Christ [that includes my grandmother!] will rise first."

When my grandmother died, everything she really was—her mind, her emotions, her will, her personality—all of her that resided inside the "tent" of her body, went to be with Jesus.[7] What was left—my grandmother's body—was buried in a little church cemetery in Swannanoa, North Carolina. Any moment the trumpet may sound, and her body will be raised up from the ground, with chemical and physical changes to make it like His glorious body.[8] She will then be clothed by this new body so that when I see her (if I am alive on earth at the time of the Rapture of the church), she will be residing in her new "tent," coming with Jesus for me!

"After that, we who are still alive and are left will be caught up together with them [Jesus and my grandmother!] in the clouds to meet the Lord in the air. Therefore, encourage each other with these words." Those who are discouraged by the majority of the ungodly can be encouraged by remembering the Lord is coming back to claim His own!

Paul said, in a voice that seemed to almost whisper with intense excitement and anticipation, "Listen, I tell you a mystery: We will not all sleep [physically die], but we will all be changed—in a flash, in the twinkling of an eye, at the last trumpet. For the trumpet will sound, the dead [my grandmother!] will be raised imperishable, and we [believers who are alive on earth] will be changed."[9]

What will it be like on that day when the trumpet call sounds from heaven? Quicker than you or I can blink, believers will feel their feet lifting up off the ground; they will be aware of certain chemical and physical changes taking place in their bodies, preparing them to live in eternity. And they will look up—into the face of Jesus! They will be swept into the clouds of His glory![10] And if they can drag their eyes away from His beautiful face, they will see He is surrounded by their loved ones who had trusted Him by faith and who will have been raised from the dead!

If you are deeply discouraged by the majority of the ungodly, would you take this promise as personal encouragement? Jesus Christ is coming again to earth! Approximately one out of every twenty verses in the New Testament refers to His return to earth. Jesus Himself said: "If I go and prepare a place for you, *I will come back* and take you to be with me."[11] Immediately following the ascension of Jesus, while the disciples were gazing up into the sky where they had just seen Him disappear, two men dressed in white suddenly stood beside them and said: "This same Jesus, who has been taken from you into heaven, *will come back* in the same way you have seen him go into heaven."[12]

Just as His first coming to earth covered thirty-three years and many different events, so His second coming will cover at least seven years and many different events. And because all biblical prophecy has been fulfilled that is necessary for these events to take place, they may begin to unfold at any moment! Certainly not to be dogmatic, since no one can know for sure, but based on God's Word, I believe the first of the events that are considered the second coming of Jesus Christ will be the Rapture of the church. Bible scholars may disagree with the timing or chronology of the Rapture in the events of the second coming, but no true believer can disagree that at some point in time, still future to us, it *will* take place. This is, as Paul told the Thessalonians, "according to the Lord's own word!"

Jesus Christ is coming! He is coming! On any day, at any moment, "in the twinkling of an eye,"[13] "at an hour when you do not expect Him,"[14] "He who is coming will come and will not delay."[15] The Bible says so!

Praise God! He has given us a glorious vision of hope for the future, and it is Jesus! He will physically, visibly enter time and space to claim you and me for Himself!

On that day, when we are caught up in the clouds to be forever with our Lord, we will see Him, not as a helpless Baby in a manger, not as the Good Shepherd leading His own sheep, not as the suffering Savior dying on a cross—we will see Him absolutely supreme as King of kings and Lord of lords!

Finding Hope in Knowing the Lord
Is Enthroned at the Center of the Universe

John was caught up into heaven, where he saw a throne with Someone sitting on it. He relates, in awe, "After this I looked, and there before me was a door standing open in heaven. And the voice I had first heard speaking to me like a trumpet said, 'Come up here, and I will show you what must take place after this.' At once I was in the Spirit, and there before me was a throne in heaven with someone sitting on it" (Rev. 4:1–2).

Enthroned in Sovereignty

We know God the Father sits on the throne at the center of the universe.[16] And we know also that God the Son sits at the right hand of the Father on the throne at the center of the universe. Isaiah saw Him there.[17] Ezekiel saw Him there.[18] Jesus Himself said He was seated there.[19] The apostle John clearly identifies Him as being there.[20]

The throne is mentioned twelve times in this fourth chapter of Revelation. The repetition strongly implies the Lord Jesus Christ's position as that of a King invested with full authority and majesty and sovereignty. He is *seated* on the throne in absolute control of everything that is taking place in the universe.

What has caused you to doubt that Jesus is seated on the throne with power and authority?

Was it when the doctor gave you an unexpected diagnosis of a terminal illness that you cried out, "Jesus, are You on the throne?"

Was it when your unmarried teenage daughter came home and told you she was pregnant?

Was it when your company fired you from your job just before you were due to retire, denying you your pension?

Was it when your house burned to the ground?

When your loved one was crippled in a car accident?

When your son was sent to prison?

When your spouse left you for another person?

Did you cry out, "Jesus, where are You? Are You in control? Are You on the throne?"

John saw Jesus at the center of the universe in full, absolute authority. Even when He seems silent and inactive, even when bad things happen to His children as they did in John's day, even when the wicked prosper and the ungodly are in the majority, *the Lord is still on the throne!*

Rulers in this world rise and fall, earthly thrones are occupied, shaken, then vacated, but Jesus is always securely seated on the throne at the center of the universe, in absolute sovereignty! John saw Him there! And what a sight it was!

Enthroned in Beauty

In the Old Testament, when the high priest went into the Most Holy Place once a year to sprinkle the blood of the lamb on the mercy seat to make atonement for sin, he wore a breastplate that covered his heart and chest. As we discussed in chapter 4, the breastplate was encrusted with twelve stones, each one carved with one of the names of the tribes of Israel. Wearing this breastplate signified that when the high priest went into God's presence, he carried the names of God's children on his heart. The first of those stones was a carnelian. And the last was a jasper.[21]

When John described the One Who sat on the throne, he said He "had the appearance of jasper and carnelian" (Rev. 4:3a). A jasper was a clear stone, much like a diamond. A carnelian, or sardus stone, had more the color of a ruby. John was saying Jesus and the Father were clothed in the light as it would look if reflected from a jasper and carnelian. It is as though John was describing God saying, even by the colors He wore, "I love you. I love you. I love you. I carry you by name on My heart forever." When seated on the throne at the center of the universe, preparing to judge the world, Jesus gives you and me evidence we are on His heart!

John must have had a difficult time dragging his eyes away from the beauty of Jesus Christ. But in obedience to what he had been commanded to do, he proceeded to describe the court of heaven that encircled the throne.

Finding Hope by Seeing the Lord Encircled by the Court of Heaven

If you have lived in the United States during the past few years, I expect you have either seen or heard of the popular television program entitled "The Lifestyles of the Rich and Famous." On the program, the host, Robin Leach, described lifestyles that were the epitome of comfort, ease, and luxury as he conducted televised tours of homes that looked like small palaces, vacation spots that looked like paradise, and possessions that would rival King Solomon's! Because the general public seems to have an insatiable curiosity to see into everything that surrounds a celebrity, the program became one of the most popular on television.

Similarly, Buckingham Palace, the official residence of the queen of England, was opened for public viewing last year. The lines of people and the reservation lists of those wanting to see it were so long it was virtually impossible for the average tourist to get in. Everyone wanted to glimpse the types of things with which the queen surrounded herself. The most popular room on the tour was the throne room, where the queen receives visiting dignitaries and conducts her official business.

The apostle John was given a guided "tour" of the court of heaven. He saw into the very place where the Lord of lords and King of kings sits on His throne, conducting the official business of the universe! And through his eyes, we are invited to "look" also.

As we follow John on this guided tour, keep in mind that the description of what he saw should fit the life of anyone who has enthroned the Lord in full authority at the center of his or her life. As we move through John's description, would you examine your life? If you claim to be under the Lordship of Jesus Christ, how closely does it match the description John gave of the court that encircles the Lord's throne in heaven?

Security

John said, "A rainbow, resembling an emerald, encircled the throne" (Rev. 4:3). Do you remember the first time a rainbow appeared? It was after the flood, when God gave it as a sign of His covenant with Noah. You remember Noah. Talk about someone who could have been discouraged by the majority of the ungodly! He was the only righteous, godly man living on earth in his day! God came to him and told him to build an ark. And although Noah, to our knowledge, had never seen a boat or even a large body of water, he obeyed God. For 120 years, day in and day out, he worked on the ark until one day it was finished, and God invited him, along with all the animals, to come inside.[22]

The Bible says Noah was a preacher of righteousness.[23] After entering the ark, I imagine he stood in the doorway and preached to all the people who had gathered to watch the crazy old man! I can just hear him urging them, "Repent, judgment is coming! Repent, judgment is coming! Get right with God!" How the people must have laughed!

Seven days went by, and nothing happened. I expect the sky was still blue, the sun was still shining, and everything went on as it had since the creation of the world. Finally, God shut the door of the ark.

Have you ever wondered what Noah heard next?[24] However it could be explained scientifically, the Bible says water crashed on the ark from above and erupted from below. The sound must have been deafening as the ark was jarred and jolted by the force of the water. Through the sound of the deluge, I wonder if he heard the screams of the people and animals on the outside of the ark.

After forty days and nights of steady rain, Noah heard absolutely nothing. What a deafening silence that must have been! Except for the presence of God on the ark and the peace of God in his heart, Noah's mind might have snapped, causing him to exit reality due to the trauma he had experienced. Instead, Noah experienced physical, emotional, mental, and spiritual security on the ark.

After 371 days, God opened the door of the ark and told Noah, his family, and all the animals to come out. Noah did, and built an altar, sacrificing a good portion of the animals in thanksgiving to God for his salvation from judgment.

But what would Noah think, and how would he feel the next time he saw a storm approaching? When he heard thunder and saw lightning and felt the rain, would he be terrified and think, *Oh, no! After being saved, am I going to come under God's judgment after all?*

God, Who understood Noah's fear and insecurity, gave him a

sign of His covenant. "I have set my rainbow in the clouds, and it will be the sign of the covenant between me and the earth."[25] In other words, every time Noah saw the rainbow, he was to remember that God remembered His commitment to the human race.

My husband told my daughter that for her sixteenth birthday he would take her for a weekend in New York City. She clung with great anticipation to his promise. She posted little notes all over his office with the date and continually reminded him of their upcoming trip together. She had no trouble remembering his promise! But her remembering would mean little if her father did not remember, since he was the one who was responsible for the trip. She needed to remember that *he remembered* his promise to her.

God said, in essence, "Noah, when you see the rainbow, you remember that *I remember* I am committed to you." The rainbow symbolized Noah's assurance of salvation. It was the sign of his security.

When the storms of life come, when you fall and fail, are you terrified that you may lose your salvation from God's judgment? That you are not eternally secure? God knew you and I would feel that way. And so He gave us a sign. It is the sign of the new covenant.[26] The sign is not our good works or our faithfulness or our righteousness! It is the sign of the cross! You and I do not look at who we are or who we are not. We do not look at what we have done or what we have not done. When we "see" the cross, we remember *God remembers* He is eternally committed to you and me based on nothing more or less than our acceptance of the finished work of His Son.

When you live under the Lordship of Jesus Christ, you have the deep assurance you are absolutely secure and safe from judgment. You will *never* come under His wrath for your sin!

Sincerity

As John's wandering gaze traveled from the central throne past the emerald rainbow, it took in a magnificent circle. "Surrounding the throne were twenty-four other thrones, and seated on them were twenty-four elders. They were dressed in white and had crowns of gold on their heads" (Rev. 4:4). The white robes symbolized the righteousness of these elders before God, qualifying them to reign with Him. The crowns signified they had been given honor and authority. And the fact that they were seated on thrones indicated they were prepared to judge.

There is some debate as to whether these elders were angels or representatives of redeemed men and women. The more obvious fact is that they were kings who served the King of kings!

In the Old Testament, the only ones allowed to serve God in the temple were those who had descended from Aaron[27] and were of the tribe of Levi.[28] After several generations, there were so many descendants who qualified to be priests there were too many to serve in the temple at any one time. So the descendants of Levi and Aaron were divided into twelve orders, with two priests from each order serving in the temple on a rotating basis. Therefore, at any given time, there were twenty-four priests serving God within the temple.

These twenty-four elders were in the court of heaven to serve the Lord Who is the King of kings. The highest positions of honor and authority in the universe are positions of service to Jesus Christ! The entire picture is one of dignified seriousness, instant availability, and deep, genuine sincerity in service. There was no confusion, no casualness, no resistance, and no procrastination in the Lord's court.

How seriously do you take your service to the King? Do you throw together the Sunday school lesson you are going to teach Sunday morning on Saturday night after watching the ball game? Do you show up for your responsibility at church ten minutes late? Why do we seem to serve our secular employers with greater seriousness and commitment than we do the King? We would never throw together an important presentation or show up late for work in the business world. Why do we do such things in our Christian service? Is it because our employer is visible and the Lord is not? Is it because we are confident the Lord understands? He understands all right. He understands we don't take our service to Him seriously!

I have a dear friend who has a husband and four small children and who has felt led to teach a Bible class. I have watched as she has turned down invitations from friends for lunch or ball games or other activities so she would have time to study. I have watched as she has fasted one day a week for her class. I have watched as she has prayerfully agonized over a passage of Scripture until it opened up for her. I have watched her when I knew her children were sick, company was expected, and her husband was away. And each week, I have seen her go to her Bible class thoroughly prepared, always looking neat and well-dressed. I have seen her serious commitment not just one day but day after day, week after week. And I know I am watching someone who has enthroned Jesus Christ as Lord. Because when Jesus Christ is enthroned as Lord, He is served seriously and with dignity.

The way John saw the elders were seated also gives the impression they were poised to be instantly available for service. If He should call on you, how readily available are you to serve?

I have another friend who is not a gifted teacher, but she takes her service to the Lord seriously by making herself and her home instantly available to Him at any moment, day or night. Along with her regular weekly commitments to a Bible study and prayer ministry, she has kept babies for working mothers, played the piano for a church that had no pianist, housed missionaries traveling on furlough, counseled those desperate for a listening ear, taken meals to the sick—all at a moment's notice. She considers herself "on call." She serves the Lord seriously and instantly. Why? The answer is obvious to all who know her. She has enthroned the Lord in her life.

My mother stayed at home to raise five children while my father traveled all over the globe preaching the gospel. She considered her parenting and housework an equal call into service with my father's evangelism ministry. In fact, over the kitchen sink she has a board on which are painted these words: "Divine service will be conducted here three times daily." My mother knows what it means to enthrone the Lord in every area of her life, understanding that the task may be great or small, public or private, but if called to it, it is still service to the Lord Who is King.

111

Activity

Suddenly, as John's gaze was taking in the circle of enthroned "kings," things started to happen! John exclaimed, "From the throne came flashes of lightning, rumblings and peals of thunder" (Rev. 4:5a). The atmosphere was electric, highly charged with activity and energy! It would seem to be an uncomfortable place for any apathetic, complacent spectator who never likes to be outside his or her comfort zone.

In American football, the opposing teams line up on the field. One is in a defensive position; the other is in an offensive position. The offensive team is led by the quarterback, who is given the ball then seeks to either pass it or hand it off to a teammate who will try to advance it against the defensive team. When the quarterback is given the ball, he is surrounded by teammates who form a pocket of protection around him until he can get the ball off.

One of the most exciting plays in football is when the opposing, defensive team breaks through that pocket of protection and flushes the quarterback out into the open. The quarterback then scrambles to improvise, sometimes getting crushed under the opposing team for a loss of yardage, sometimes making spectacular passes under tremendous pressure, and sometimes carrying the ball himself in a desperate attempt to gain yardage.

The highly charged atmosphere of the Lord's court would seem to effectively "flush" all those present out of any pocket or comfort zone they may have grown accustomed to.

Like you and me, the disciples of Jesus preferred to stay in their comfort zone. One evening they were in a boat, crossing the Sea of Galilee, when a storm arose. As they strained at the oars with the wind against them, they saw through the mist the figure of Christ coming toward them, walking on the water!

When the disciples became aware it was indeed Jesus, eleven of them stayed comfortably where they were, but Peter shouted out, "*Lord*, if it's you, tell me to come to you on the water."[29] When Jesus invited him, "Come," Peter climbed out of the boat, risking life and reputation. Because Jesus was Peter's Lord, Peter was not content to remain where he was!

When you observe those who call themselves Christians being apathetic, complacent, uninvolved, and stagnant in service, you can be assured Jesus Christ is not enthroned in their lives as Lord! It is impossible to know Him, to love Him, to surrender to Him as Lord—and do *nothing!* His very presence flushes us out of our comfort zone, demanding and provoking activity!

Purity

In stark contrast to the electric excitement of the lightning and thunder, John's gaze now rests on the burning intensity of God's holiness: "Before the throne, seven lamps were blazing. These are the seven spirits of God [or the seven-fold Spirit of God]" (Rev. 4:5b). The seven-fold Spirit of God is the Holy Spirit. Where God is, is holy. The seven lamps were blazing, speaking of the intense, purifying effect of the holiness of God's Spirit.

What sin are you toying with? What *habit* of sin are you tolerating in your life? What *attitude* of sin—bitterness, selfishness, pride, resentment, anger, jealousy, unforgivenness—are you nurturing, instead of crucifying?[30]

When, by faith, you invited Jesus Christ to come into your life as your Savior and Lord, He came in, in the Person of the Holy Spirit. And the Holy Spirit *is holy*, totally separate from sin. One of the first things the Holy Spirit does when He comes into you is to give you the *desire* to be holy. Increasingly, as you yield your life to Him, He gives you the *power* to be holy. The intense, purifying fire of the Holy Spirit burns away anything and everything that is not pleasing to God.

On the Sunday before His crucifixion, Jesus triumphantly entered Jerusalem, praised by the people as their Messiah and King. As soon as He had been acknowledged as King, He went to the heart of Jerusalem, which was the temple, and cleansed it.[31] All this occurred because the heart of the people who called Him their King was to be holy. As happened in Jerusalem, when we acknowledge Jesus as King of our lives, the Holy Spirit begins to work in our hearts to separate us from sin and all that is displeasing to God.

Authority

As John's view moved around the throne room, he saw "before the throne there was what looked like a sea of glass, clear as crystal" (Rev. 4:6a). The sea described in this phrase would act like a gigantic mirror, reflecting the throne throughout the universe. Not even the smallest place or person will be exempt from the presence and authority of the Lord. Everything and everyone will be visible under God's omniscient gaze. What will He see reflected in you? As He gazes into the mirror will He see Himself reflected in your life? Is Jesus your Lord? How clearly do others see Him reflected in the mirror of your life?

The story is told of a little boy who went to church and listened carefully to the pastor's sermon. When church was over, the little boy was puzzled. As he left with his parents, he saw the pastor across the parking lot. He ran over, calling, "Pastor, may I ask you a question about your sermon this morning?"

When the pastor readily assented, the little boy said, "You said Jesus is a Man."

The pastor confirmed: "That's right."

Then the little boy said, "But I am just a little boy."

The pastor looked amused but kept a serious expression on his face as he replied, "That's right."

Then the little boy said earnestly, "But you said if I asked Him to, Jesus would come live inside of me."

Again, the pastor nodded affirmatively. "That's right," he said.

"But, Pastor," the little boy said in exasperation as though he was pointing something out to a child, "if Jesus comes to live inside of me, He will be sticking out all over!"

To which the pastor firmly responded, "That's right!"

When Jesus Christ is enthroned as Lord, His power, Person, and presence should be "sticking out all over" you and me.

Has the mirror of your life become tarnished or even cracked by sin so that the reflection of Christ in your life is murky, at best?

What do you need to do to polish the mirror? The mirror is polished as we submit to the authority of Christ—confessing our sin, repenting of our sin, yielding our lives totally to His control, and embracing His will even when it includes suffering, sadness, sacrifice, and self-denial.

Piety

As John's gaze moves outward, he describes something we might expect to see in a Steven Spielberg movie: "In the center, around the throne, were four living creatures, and they were covered with eyes, in front and in back. The first living creature was like a lion, the second was like an ox, the third had a face like a man, the fourth was like a flying eagle. Each of the four living creatures had six wings and was covered with eyes all around, even under his wings. Day and night they never stop saying: "'Holy, holy, holy is the Lord God Almighty, who was, and is, and is to come'" (Rev. 4:6b–8).

Although these four living creatures at first seem almost like mutant monsters, under careful scrutiny, they appear to be just the opposite: John's description of these beings gives the impression of absolute piety and devotion to the Lord as they never cease to worship Him.

I assume these creatures are the cherubim and seraphim of the Old Testament. The first time one of them appeared, it was at the door to the Garden of Eden. After Adam and Eve had sinned, they were separated from God and banished from His presence. God stationed at the entrance to the garden the cherubim with a flaming sword that turned every which way. They were to guard the way to the tree of life, preventing Adam and Eve from eating its fruit and thus living forever in their sin.[32]

Isaiah, when he had his vision of the Lord seated on the throne, described these creatures as shaking the doorposts of the temple with the sound of their praise.[33] When Isaiah, in the light of the Lord's holiness, was convicted of sin and confessed it, one of these creatures flew to the altar, took a live coal, and placed it on Isaiah's lips that he might be cleansed and ready to speak God's Word.[34]

Ezekiel described these creatures as preceding his vision of the glory of the Lord, which he received while in exile beside the Kebar River in Babylon.[35]

The four living creatures are described as being covered with eyes, enabling them to see everywhere at once. They were very alert in their service to the Lord. They each had six wings, enabling them to move quickly, faster than the speed of light, in their service.

In John's description, these creatures are the highest of God's created intelligences. They are closer to the physical presence of God than any other created being and are always associated with His presence, which they guard. They are next to God Himself in power and authority.

It is this last aspect of their service that seemed to present a temptation to the one named Lucifer, who was described as the Morning Star. He wasn't satisfied with being next to God in power and authority; he wanted to be God.[36] His pride caused him to be thrown out of heaven, along with the angels who participated in his rebellion, and he now resides on earth where he is described as the prince and power of the air, better known as Satan, or the devil.[37]

The appearance of the four living creatures seems even more bizarre when we envision John's describing them (as Ezekiel did), with each having a different "face": "One had the face of a lion, the second like an ox, the third had a face like a man, the fourth was like a flying eagle."

It is fascinating to note that the Lord Jesus Christ seems to be described this way in the four Gospels. The Gospel of Matthew describes the Lord as a lion, the King. The Gospel of Mark describes the Lord as an ox, or humble Servant. Luke's Gospel describes Jesus in His humanity as the Son of Man. And John's Gospel describes Jesus in His deity as the Son of God, the flying eagle!

This description has a very special application for you and me. We have already considered the service of these four living creatures: They have been actively serving God since the Garden of Eden and, I would assume, even before. All through the Old Testament we can glimpse their work. Yet this passage from

Revelation says, "Day and night they never stop" worshiping the Lord.

How can they do all that work yet never stop worshiping the Lord? Is this a contradiction? No! These four living creatures never ceased to worship the Lord, and from their worship flowed their work! Unlike the church at Ephesus described in Revelation 2:1–7, these creatures kept their priorities in order. And as they worshiped the Lord continually, with their work coming from and motivated by their worship, they began to look like the One they worshiped!

Paul said, "For those God foreknew he also predestined to be conformed to the likeness of his Son."[38] And he went on to say this conformity takes place as we behold His glory.[39]

Have you ever met someone who so lived his or her life in worship of Christ, serving Him in the love and light and joy of His presence, that you felt you could see Jesus reflected in the person's outward appearance? I have.

I remember meeting an older woman whom I looked at twice, not knowing who she was but being struck with her countenance. The sparkle in her eyes, the humility of her demeanor, the sweetness of her expression, the smile on her lips seemed to radiate Christ. Upon inquiry, I discovered she had been a medical missionary to Africa for years. While on the mission field she had been brutally beaten and raped by guerrilla soldiers. But the intense, undeserved suffering in her life had pressed her close to the Lord, not driven a barrier between Him and herself. She lived her life in genuine worship, placing her faith in Him and learning to thank Him for trusting her with suffering even when she didn't understand the answers to "Why?" The result was an outward appearance in which even a casual observer could see a reflection of the character of Christ! The piety and devotion of her life was evidence she had enthroned Jesus Christ as Lord.

If you and I want to reflect the very character of Christ in our own characters in such a way that it even affects our outward appearance, we must learn the lesson from the four living creatures. Day and night they never ceased to worship the Lord, and from their worship of Him came their work for Him. They were absolutely devoted to Him in their service.

Finding Hope in Hearing the Lord Enveloped in a Crescendo of Praise

John has described what he saw when the door of heaven opened, and he has almost completed his guided tour of the Lord's court. As he concludes, he describes not what he saw, but what he heard!

Praising the Lord in *Continuous* Worship

"Day and night they never stop saying: 'Holy, holy, holy is the Lord God Almighty, who was, and is, and is to come'" (Rev. 4:8b). Worship of Jesus Christ is continuous in heaven. It never ceases.

> After the profanity,
> > the blasphemy,
> > > the obscenities,
> > > > the hypocrisies,
> > > > > the superficialities,
> > > > > > the insincerity of voices on earth . . .
> . . . it will be the pinnacle of glory to hear the Name of Jesus exalted,
> > magnified,
> > > honored,
> > > > praised,
> > > > > glorified,
> > > > > > and worshiped—
> > > > > > > without interruption and
> > > > > > > without end!

Praising the Lord in *Contagious* Worship

As the four living creatures praised the Lord continuously, their praise was contagious. John said, "Whenever the living creatures give glory, honor and thanks to him who sits on the throne . . . the twenty-four elders fall down . . . and worship him" (Rev. 4:9–10). As the vision of His glory continues to unfold, following the praise of the four living creatures and the twenty-four elders, millions of angels pick up the chorus. When the angels praised the Lord, "every creature in heaven and on earth and under the earth and on the sea, and all that is in them" sang praises to the Lord. Praise is contagious!

Who is praising the Lord because you and I are praising Him? Surely the atmosphere in our homes and churches and schools and businesses and society in general would be totally different if everyone who professes to belong to Christ would live in continuous praise of Christ!

Praising the Lord in *Costly* Worship

When Isaiah heard the four living creatures praising God in the temple, the door posts and thresholds shook.[40] When Christ is praised, things begin to happen, especially in the temple of our lives and in the temple we think of as His church. In fact, we are told that God inhabits the praise of His people.[41] But such powerful praise is costly.

The twenty-four elders, or kings, who were seated around the King of kings left their thrones, fell down before the Lord, and laid their crowns before the throne saying: "You are worthy, our Lord and God, to receive glory and honor and power" (Rev. 4:10b–11a). Their crowns represented not only their positions of service, but the praise, achievements, glory, honor, and rewards they had received in service.

All through Scripture, we are urged "to get a crown that will last forever";[42] to finish our race that we might receive the crown stored up for all those who "love His appearing";[43] to persevere in order to receive the crown;[44] "receive the crown . . . that will never fade away";[45] to "hold on to what you have, so that no one will take your crown."[46]

No one knows exactly what "the crown" will be, but whatever it is, it must be vitally important and of extraordinary value in eternity. Perhaps it is linked to the warning Paul gave us concerning the Judgment Seat of Christ.[47]

No one who has placed faith in Jesus Christ as Savior and Lord, having received His forgiveness and eternal life, will ever be judged for sin. Jesus took God's judgment for our sin at the cross and said, "It is finished." Praise God! His death alone is sufficient to make atonement for my sin!

However, all true believers in Christ will stand before the Judgment Seat of Christ to give an account for their lives lived from the time they received Him as Savior until they see Him face to face. Paul gives insight concerning that time still to come.

At the Judgment Seat of Christ, your life and mine will pass through the fire of God's holiness. If you or I have lived our lives in obedience to God's Word, surrendered to God's will and walking in God's way, our lives will come through as gold, silver, and costly stones. It may be, then, that the gold, silver, and costly stones make up the crown we receive in eternity.

On the other hand, if we have lived our lives in disobedience to God's Word (we just didn't have time to read it), in resistance to God's will (because it was different than what we wanted), and walking in our own way (we got caught up in what everyone else was doing and did what seemed right in our own eyes), then our lives will be like wood, hay, and stubble. Paul said we will still be saved but as though by fire. Instead of having an abundant entrance into heaven,[48] we will just squeak through the door with nothing to show for our lives lived on earth.

On the day when you see your Lord face to face; when you see the scar on His brow where the thorns had been as He wore your crown; when you see the nail prints in His hands and feet, placed there by your sin; and when for the first time you fully comprehend what it cost Him to welcome you into His heavenly home, don't you think you will want to give Him something in return for all He has given you? On that day, will you have a crown, received as a reward for your life lived for Him on earth, that you can lay at His nail-pierced feet? Or will you have the ashes of a wasted life to press into His nail-scarred palm?

Jesus Christ is absolutely supreme as the Lord of the universe! Would you make Him supreme as the Lord in your life, so on Judgment Day you can lovingly lay your crown at His feet?

Genuine praise is costly! It costs us our lives laid down in worship and our lives laid down in work for the Lord Who is King! Such praise is the overflow of a life lived in the light of the vision of His glory! If you are discouraged by the majority of the ungodly, would you fix your eyes on the Lord Who is enthroned at the center of the universe, encircled by a court in heaven, enveloped in a crescendo of praise, and Who may, at any moment, enter time and space to claim you as His own?

 *But as for me,*
I will always have hope.

Psalm 71:14

6

Hope When You Are Discouraged by the Minority of the Godly

Revelation 5

Have you ever wanted to ask Abraham, "Was it worth it to leave Ur of the Chaldees, wander around Canaan, live in a tent, and in the end have nothing more to show for it than basically one son, the cave of Machpelah, and the still unfulfilled promises of God?"[1]

Have you ever wanted to ask Moses, "Was it worth it to give up the pleasures and treasures of Egypt to lead a million or more former slaves through the wilderness for forty years and never even get into the promised land yourself?"[2]

Have you ever wanted to ask Jeremiah, "Was it worth it to preach over sixty years and never have even one positive response to your message?"[3]

Have you ever wanted to ask Daniel, "Was it worth it to pray three times a day and wind up in the lions' den?"[4]

Have you ever wanted to ask Isaiah, "Was it worth it to volunteer for service to God, saying 'Here am I, send me,' when, as a result of that service, you were sawed in two?"[5]

Have you ever wanted to ask John the Baptist, "Was it worth it to speak the truth to Herod's face and lose your head?"[6]

Have you ever wanted to ask Mary, "Was it worth it to say 'Be it unto me according to Your will,' when that submission resulted in a Son Who was crucified on a Roman cross?"[7]

Have you ever wanted to ask Peter, "Was it worth it to open the door for the gospel to be preached to the Gentiles, only to be crucified upside down?"[8]

Have you ever wanted to ask John, "Was it worth it to preach the gospel and plant churches all over the known world, and in the end, wind up in exile on Patmos?"[9]

Have you ever asked yourself, "Is it worth it to live a life of faith in God when no one else is? Is it worth it to me?"

Is it worth it to get up on Sunday morning, go to Sunday school and church, when you were out late Saturday night?

Is it worth it every morning to get up thirty minutes earlier than your schedule requires in order to pray and read your Bible when you really want to sleep to the last minute?

Is it worth it to share the gospel with your friend and, as a result, lose the friendship?

Is it worth it to fill out your income tax statement honestly, and pay more taxes?

Is it worth it to tell the truth, when lying would get you a promotion or a salary increase?

Is it worth it to get involved with the homeless, the hopeless, the helpless in Jesus' Name and for His sake, and risk hostility and rejection?

Is it worth it to deny yourself, take up your cross daily, and follow Christ, when no one else in your church seems to take his or her faith that seriously?

Is it worth it to live your life in obedience to God's Word, surrendered to God's will, walking in God's way, when the entire world seems to be going in the opposite direction?

Is it worth it to live a godly life and become a member of the minority? Is it worth it?

My personal answer to all of the above is a resounding, unhesitating "yes YES! *YES!* It's worth it!" Living a godly Christian life is worth whatever it costs—a thousand times over! Why? *Because He is worth it!*

The vision of His glory in Revelation 5 describes the "worth-it-ness," or the worthiness, of Jesus Christ and gives thrilling hope to those who are discouraged by the minority of the godly. Our hope is in Who Jesus is!

Finding Hope in the Unequaled Position of Jesus Christ

Following his "guided tour" of the Lord's court, John continued to gaze through the open door of heaven. He ". . . saw in the right hand of him who sat on the throne a scroll with writing on both sides and sealed with seven seals" (Rev. 5:1). Although no one can be certain, it seems reasonable to assume from the context that the scroll represents the deed to planet earth, and it was in the grip of God the Father. Whoever possessed the scroll had the authority, in God's eyes, to proceed to rule the world as well as the ability to fulfill God's purpose for the human race.

"And I saw a mighty angel proclaiming in a loud voice, 'Who is worthy to break the seals and open the scroll?'" (Rev. 5:2). In other words, "Who has the right, in God's eyes, to rule the world? Who is able to fulfill God's purpose for the human race! Who is worthy?"

We can think of many people who have been willing. Alexander the Great would have been willing. The Roman emperor Nero would have been willing. King George III of England would have been willing. Hitler would have been willing. The Ayatollah Khomeini would have been willing. Saddam Hussein would be willing. I expect the presidents of Russia and of the United States would be willing!

But that wasn't the question! The question was, "Who is *worthy?*" Who is worthy to rule the world and complete God's purpose for the human race?

The answer is a stunning revelation of the failure of the human race: "But no one in heaven or on earth or under the earth could open the scroll or even look inside it" (Rev. 5:3). The entire universe—every planet, every galaxy, every generation, every race— was carefully searched for one person who was worthy in God's eyes. But no one was found.

Not Enoch, who had walked so closely with God that one day he walked right into heaven.[10]

Not Abraham, whom God called His friend.[11]

Not Sarah, who by faith conceived and bore a child when she was ninety years of age.[12]

Not Moses, the meekest man in all the earth.[13]

Not Samson, the strongest man in all the world.[14]

Not David, the man after God's own heart.[15]

Not Solomon, the wisest man in all the world.[16]

Not Elijah, who didn't see death but instead was caught up to heaven in a chariot of fire.[17]

Not Jeremiah, who was compared to Jesus by those who knew Jesus.[18]

Not Isaiah, the greatest of the Old Testament prophets.[19]

Not John the Baptist, whom Jesus said was as great as any man ever born.[20]

Not Mary, the mother of Jesus.[21]

Not Peter, who led three thousand people in one day to respond to the gospel he presented and who opened the door for the gospel to be preached to the Gentiles.[22]

Not Paul, the greatest evangelist of all time who was the human author for most of the New Testament.

Not even John, who was recording this vision!

Not one of the millions of sons of Adam and daughters of Eve was found to be worthy to open the scroll or even look inside!

John was distraught. He wrote, "I wept and wept because no one was found who was worthy to open the scroll or look inside" (Rev. 5:4). The old apostle stood there and sobbed in utter despair and hopelessness! The godly were not just a minority; it seemed the truly godly were nonexistent!

Did this mean that the "curse" of God on the human race and planet earth would never be lifted?[23]

. . . that paradise was lost forever?

. . . that the cross was impotent to save mankind from God's wrath?

. . . that there was no atonement for man's sin?

. . . that in the end, evil would win out over good, hate would win out over love, and death would win out over life?

. . . that Satan would have the ultimate victory?

. . . that Jesus Christ, and the minority who placed their faith in Him, would go down in eternal defeat?

Who can blame John for weeping! Surely horror gripped his soul and hopelessness gripped his heart and helplessness gripped his mind! He must have sobbed and sobbed with shame for the failure of the entire human race to be what God had originally intended it to be!

If you have ever felt like a failure, you have *generations of company!* Surely John was also sobbing with shame for his own failure to be what God had originally intended *him* to be!

As the old apostle stood there with tears streaming down his lined, weather-beaten face and running into his long, gray beard, one of the elders[24] got up from his throne and went over to where John was standing.

As he wiped the tears from John's face, he said gently, "Do not weep!" (Rev. 5:5a). And then, in a voice that must have pulsated with the passionate anticipation of victory, he announced, "See, the Lion of the tribe of Judah, the Root of David, has triumphed. He is able to open the scroll and its seven seals" (Rev. 5:5b). In other words, "John, there is *one* Man Who is able! There is *one* Man in all of the universe Who is worthy in God's eyes to rule the world and fulfill God's purpose for the human race! *Only One!* One Man Who is unequaled in His position!"

And certainly if this Man is unequaled in His position as Lord of the universe, if He is well-qualified and worthy to rule the world— *and He is!*—then He is able also to rule your life and mine. Why is it we settle for an unworthy lord? We allow ourselves to be ruled by our emotions or the opinions of others or our business or our appetites or our comfort and convenience or our career or our bank account or the goals we have set and the plans we have made for the future. Every day we hear stories of those who, when it's too late, make the tragic discovery that the lord they served was unable to rule rightly. Their lives end in broken dreams and broken hearts and broken hopes.

John said the entire universe was searched for someone who was worthy and able in God's eyes to rule the world and fulfill God's purpose for the human race. And only one Man was found. Why do you and I look for another? And if God says this one Man is able to fulfill His purpose for the entire human race, He can work out to completion God's purpose in the details of your life.

This same Man Who alone is worthy in God's eyes to occupy the unequaled position of Lord and King of the universe is revealed also to be undisputed in power. His name is Jesus!

Finding Hope in the Undisputed Power of Jesus Christ

As John stifled his sobs and dried his tears, he looked where the elder must have been pointing. He "saw a Lamb, looking as if it had been slain, standing in the center of the throne" (Rev. 5:6a).

The Lamb looked as though He had been slain because He had scars on His brow where the thorns had been and prints in His hands and feet where the nails had been. While the world mocks the cross and man's need for a Savior, while the world insists there are other ways to God besides the cross of Christ, while the world criticizes and persecutes the minority of the godly who have been washed clean in the blood shed at the cross, the memories of Calvary are precious in heaven!

In the Old Testament, when someone sinned, the person was required to bring a lamb to the priest at the temple.[25] The sinner had to grasp the lamb with both hands and then confess his sin. It was as though the guilt of the sinner was conveyed through his arms, down to his hands, and transferred to the lamb. Then the sinner took the knife and killed the lamb, so the lamb died as a direct result of the sinner's action. Then the priest took the blood of the lamb and sprinkled it on the altar to make atonement for the person's sin. Based on the sinner's confession of sin, obedience to God's instructions, and faith in the blood sacrificed, the person was forgiven.

When John the Baptist observed Jesus of Nazareth walking beside the Jordan River, he exclaimed, "Look, the Lamb of God, who takes away the sin of the world!"[26] John was acknowledging that the sacrifices in the Old Testament—all the millions of animals that had been slaughtered and all of the oceans of blood that had been shed—were like audio-visual aids that pointed to Jesus Christ.

The sacrifices were like IOU notes. When someone sacrificed for sin, it was as though God said, "I owe you forgiveness. I owe you redemption. I owe you atonement." The blood of lambs and bulls and goats could never atone for man's sin,[27] because it was symbolic. They pointed to God's sending of Jesus. And when Jesus Christ died on the cross, His sacrifice for sin was accepted by God, and all the IOU notes were paid in full!

Today, when we grasp the Lamb of God with our "hands" of faith and confess our sin, the guilt of our sin is transferred to the Lamb. Although the Romans physically crucified Jesus, it was your sin and mine that was responsible for putting Him to death. He died as my personal sacrifice—and yours. His blood was sprinkled on the altar of the cross for my sin, and God accepted the sacrifice,[29] granting me atonement, redemption, and forgiveness through the substitutionary death of Jesus Christ.[30]

When John saw the "Lamb, looking as if He had been slain, standing in the center of the throne," He bore the marks of Calvary but was no longer lifeless on the altar! He was very much alive! John described Him as having seven horns representing His omnipotence and seven eyes representing His omniscience and seven Spirits of God representing His omnipresence. The number seven stands for perfection and completion. The horns symbolize strength, the eyes symbolize all-seeing and all-knowing, and the spirits symbolize the presence of God. The entire description of the Lamb is of One Who is perfect in strength, perfect in knowledge, and perfect in His presence simultaneously everywhere in the world. Isn't He magnificent!

John was describing the Creator of the heavens and the earth, the Lord God Almighty, as the Lamb Who died for me! The same Lamb Who died and rose from the dead and ascended into heaven and sat down at the right hand of the Father now stood up and "took the scroll from the right hand of him who sat on the throne" (Rev. 5:7). The Lamb simply walked over and *took* the scroll! He was asserting His right to rule the world! He had made it in creation, He had bought it at Calvary, and now He was claiming His right to rule it for Himself!

The reins of the government of the world passed into His nail-scarred palm! And no one said, "You can't do that!" No one said, "Who do You think You are?" No one said, "Let's discuss this for a moment." No one disputed His claim to be worthy to rule the world and to fulfill God's purpose for the human race, because He is worthy! And He was, and is, and forever will be undisputed in His power in the universe!

If He is undisputed in His power in the universe—and He is— why do we argue with Him, resisting His claim on our lives? He *created* you and me, He *bought* us at Calvary, and He is the *only* One Who has the right to rule our lives! Would you yield the reins of the government of your life to Him? You and I need to stop resisting His will, stop arguing about His purpose, stop complaining about His methods, and just submit to His authority!

How ashamed we will be one day to discover that we were the only ones in the entire universe disputing the authority of the Lamb. We need to change our arrogant attitude and fall in step with the rest of the universe that does not resist but praises Him!

Finding Hope in the Universal Praise of Jesus Christ

When the Lamb asserted His worthiness to rule the world and fulfill God's purpose for the human race, the four living creatures and the twenty-four elders fell down before Him in worship. They were "holding golden bowls full of incense, which are the prayers of the saints" (Rev. 5:8c). It was as though, after thousands of years of prayers ascending into heaven from the hearts, minds, and lips of God's people, He finally had enough. The bowls were full. Now human history could be brought to its conclusion.

Following World War II and the building of the Berlin Wall, as well as the forming of the Iron Curtain, Christians around the world began to pray. Stories of harassment, persecution, poverty, human-rights abuse, and depression slipped through the curtain and over the wall. God's people prayed for Him to intervene and deliver Eastern Europe from the tyranny of atheism and oppression. At times, triggered by world events, the prayers of believers around the world intensified. And in November 1989, the Berlin Wall fell, and the Iron Curtain came tumbling down! There was no logical explanation for this dramatic series of events except that "the bowls full of incense which are the prayers of the saints" had filled up! I wonder whose prayer was the last one to come in before God said, "I have all I need in order to proceed to accomplish My purpose." Prayer is necessary, not only for daily events to fit in with God's plan for the ages, but for the final fulfillment of His plan as well!

Often my vision in prayer is too small. I neglect to see the part my prayer has in the overall, big picture of what God is doing. If more Christians prayed for the Lord to claim His right to rule the world, we would actually hasten the day of His coming!

As the four living creatures and the twenty-four kings fell down in worship before the Lamb, John noted, "each one had a harp" (Rev. 5:8b). In the Old Testament, when Israel came under the judgment of God and was carried off into captivity, she hung up her harp.[30] When the Babylonians asked her to sing, she could not. She had lost her song—she had lost her *joy*—because she was living outside of God's will and separated from Him.

Counselors of all types are seeing a tidal wave of depression today, even within the church. The world wants to hear us sing! The world wants to see our joy! The world wants to observe the difference Jesus Christ makes in our lives. But instead of hearing a song, the world is seeing many Christians hang up their harps. In some instances, it is because Christians have allowed sin to separate them from God. A noted psychologist has observed, "We need to see ourselves as more sinful than wounded."[31] To live outside of God's will is to lose His blessing in life and along with it, real joy.

When did you hang up your harp? When you resist God's will for your life or for your loved ones, when you insist on your own way and get it, you can lose your joy. Even within the church you can become so deeply discouraged by the minority of the godly who seem to be swept away in the tide of wickedness permeating the world today that you can lose your joy. When you move your eyes off of Jesus and onto the world around you or onto your circumstances or onto yourself or onto others, you hang up your harp simply because you lose your focus. The key to regaining your harp is to focus on Christ in worship. Submit to and embrace His authority in your life by confessing your sins one by one, then yield all to Him.

When the four living creatures and the twenty-four elders fell down before the Lamb, focusing on Christ alone, prostrate in genuine worship of the One Who was asserting His authority to rule, each of them had a harp! Although they sang together, their song was an individual expression that arose from each of their own hearts! They were so filled with joy, they overflowed in praise to the Lamb Who alone is worthy!

John recorded, "They sang a new song" (Rev. 5:9a). It was new because it wasn't about Israel's deliverance from Egypt or the birth of Christ in Bethlehem or even about our Lord's death and resurrection. The new song was about His rightful claim to rule the world because He alone is worthy in the eyes of God the Father! It proclaimed, "You are worthy to take the scroll and to open its seals, because you were slain, and with your blood you purchased men for God from every tribe and language and people and nation. You have made them to be a kingdom and priests to serve our God, and they will reign on the earth" (Rev. 5:9–10).

There is no greater cure for discouragement than a new song about the power and glory of the One Who has the right to rule! When we feel we need a new song, perhaps what we really need is to fall down and worship the Lord Who is the Lamb upon the throne, surrendering our hearts and lives afresh to Him! As the universe worships the One Who is Lord they sing a new song. Those who lift their voice in praise were "from every tribe and language and people and nation" (Rev. 5:9b).

For those who think Jesus is a "white man's god" or "a Western god," for those who resist the mission of the church to share the gospel with those of other cultures and nations and religions—one day their voices will be drowned out by the universal praise of the One Who is the universe's Lord and King! Those who belong to Him represent every family, tribe, ethnic group, culture, language, and nation! Heaven's courts will ring with united, universal praise! There will not even be a *shadow* of racial prejudice, racial division, or even racial tension.

Will that day catch you by surprise? While you may be shocked to discover that you are surrounded by African Americans, Arabs, Chinese, Japanese, Koreans, Russians, Jews, Africans, Mexicans, South American tribesmen, Fiji Islanders, Eskimos, Indians, Gypsies, as well as Europeans and Anglo-Saxon Americans, someone else may be shocked to discover he or she is standing beside *you!* Today it is a joy as well as a responsibility to reflect the praise that one day will resound throughout the universe by maintaining the unity within the multinational, multicultural, multiracial, multitribal body of Christ!

With the song of the multitudes ringing in his ears, John "looked and heard the voice of many angels" (Rev. 5:11a). The same eyes that had seen Jesus spat upon, slapped, scourged, stripped, and crucified were now the eyes that were seeing millions of angels encircling the throne of the King of kings in adoration and worship. The same ears that had heard Jesus blasphemed, falsely accused, mocked, and convicted of blasphemy were now the ears that heard the four living creatures and the twenty-four elders join the millions of angels in thunderous praise of the Lamb Who alone is worthy!

If Jesus alone is worthy of all praise—and He is!—why do we seek praise for ourselves? Why are we offended when others don't give us credit for what we have done?

I once observed a beautiful, articulate woman who spoke dynamically and with humor for one hour and forty-five minutes— about herself! When she concluded, the tired audience politely applauded as she went to her seat. The master of ceremonies stepped into the pulpit, motioning with her hands for the audience to rise for the benediction. The speaker did not see the MC's gesture, and thought the audience had risen to give her a standing ovation! So she stepped back up to the pulpit to take her bows!

How many times do we do privately what that speaker did publicly? We seek to bask in the limelight, craving the applause of men, accepting an ovation that in reality is not ours.

Corrie ten Boom, the Dutch woman who was interned in a Nazi concentration camp for hiding Jews during World War II, shared her testimony on many occasions following her release. After speaking, people would line up to tell her what a blessing she had been to them. Corrie said she accepted each compliment as she would a flower. Then, at the end of the day, she offered her "bouquet" to the Lord!

Are you hording the "bouquet" until the flowers wilt because you are clutching some of the credit for yourself? It has been said that we don't seem to mind giving God the glory as long as we can take a 10 percent commission! But God warns He does not yield His glory to anyone else.[32]

When Elijah challenged the priests of Baal to a contest that would reveal whether the Lord or Baal was God, he told them to build an altar, and he would build an altar. He told them to make a sacrifice, and he would make a sacrifice. Then they were to call on Baal to send down fire to consume the sacrifice, and he would call on the Lord to do the same. The God Who sent down the fire would be acknowledged as the one, true, living God.

The priests of Baal prayed all day, dancing, chanting, slashing themselves with knives, only to wind up exhausted, with no "answer" from Baal.

Then Elijah ordered a trench to be dug around the altar he had built. He commanded water to be brought and poured on the altar three times until the sacrifice, wood, and stones were soaked. The water that had run onto the sacrifice and down the altar filled the trench that surrounded the altar. What was Elijah doing? He was making sure everyone knew the impossibility of the situation! If the sacrifice was even singed, it would be supernatural! Elijah was guaranteeing that if and when the fire fell, all the glory and credit would go to the Lord alone! He was refusing to touch God's glory! Is it any wonder, in answer to his simple prayer of faith, that the fire fell?!

When we touch God's glory, when we take for ourselves some of the credit and praise that are His alone, we rob God of what is rightfully His, hindering His work in the process. Those who "cash in" on God's glory will experience a "power shortage" and ultimately wind up cheating themselves and others of the fullness of His blessing.

John not only gave God the glory, he saw the glory of God in Jesus Christ and described what he heard as the entire universe gave a thunderous, thrilling response of praise:

> "Worthy is the Lamb, who was slain,
>   to receive power and wealth and wisdom and strength
>   and honor and glory and praise!"
> Then I heard *every* creature in heaven and on earth and
> under the earth and on the sea, and *all* that is in them,
> singing:
> "To him who sits on the throne and to the Lamb
> be praise and honor and glory and power,
>   for ever and ever!" (Rev. 5:12–13, emphasis mine).

The entire universe rocked in praise! The entire universe roared in acclamation of the Lamb Who alone is worthy! Because the One Who is unequaled in position and undisputed in power also receives universal praise!

I wonder, down on planet earth where the majority of the ungodly were blaspheming the Name of Christ and engaged in all manner of ungodliness and wickedness, did the world suddenly become quiet? Did those living on planet earth in some way hear what was taking place in the rest of the universe? John specifically testified that "every creature in heaven and on earth and under the earth and on the sea, and all that is in them" were singing praise to the Lamb. Because "God exalted him to the highest place and gave him the name that is above every name," was it at this moment that "every knee should bow, in heaven and on earth and under the earth, and every tongue confess that Jesus Christ is Lord, to the glory of God the Father?"[33]

When the Roman soldiers went to arrest Jesus in the Garden of Gethsemane, He stepped forward to meet them. When they said they sought Jesus of Nazareth, He replied, "I am he."[34] The phrase He used is the same one used throughout the Old Testament as God's identification of Himself.[35] The soldiers were confronted by Jesus, Who revealed Himself to them as God in the flesh! At that moment, whether they suddenly glimpsed His majesty or felt the impact of His power or were awe-struck by His glory, they all fell at His feet!

What individual do you know who has set himself or herself against Christ? What school or business? What organization? What nation? One day the entire world will set itself against Christ! But sooner or later, those who set themselves against Him will find themselves on their faces before Him, because God gives you and me the right to choose Jesus as Savior—or reject Him. But He gives us no right to choose whether or not we will acknowledge Him as Lord. One day, everyone will acknowledge Him, whether they want to or not, and the entire universe will resound with thunderous praise of the One Who alone is worthy as the sovereign Lord and the all-sufficient Lamb!

Are you discouraged by the minority of the godly? Would you give Jesus His rightful, unequaled position as Lord of your life and stop disputing His power and authority? Then fix your eyes on Jesus and tune your heart to worship Jesus and open your mouth to praise Jesus. The vision of His glory gives us hope that one day, the godly minority will join the rest of the universe and become a majority of those who praise and worship the Lamb forever and ever and ever!

Hope When You Are Distressed . . .

But the eyes of the Lord are on
those who fear him,
on those whose hope is in his
unfailing love,
to deliver them from death
and keep them alive in famine.

Psalm 33:18–19

7

Hope When You Are Distressed
by Evil Actions

Revelation 6–12

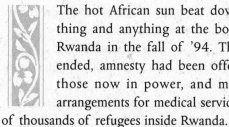 The hot African sun beat down unmercifully on everything and anything at the border between Uganda and Rwanda in the fall of '94. The Rwandan civil war had ended, amnesty had been offered to the losing side by those now in power, and my brother had just made arrangements for medical services to be given to hundreds of thousands of refugees inside Rwanda.

As he prepared to cross the border, guarded by soldiers who lazily lounged at their posts, passing the time by smoking cigarettes and flicking the ashes onto the sun-parched earth, he noticed a little Rwandan girl. She was seated in the back of a pickup truck, clutching a blanket, rocking back and forth, and quietly singing to herself. In reply to his inquiry, my brother was told she was one of the thousands of children whose parents had been killed during the war. This little girl in particular had seen her family hacked to death with machetes until not one family member was left. She was all alone in the world.

When my brother asked a nearby soldier what she was singing, the soldier shrugged indifferently and said he didn't know because she was singing in French. A soldier was found who spoke French, and when he was taken to the little girl, he listened casually then said, "She is singing something about God's love." My brother asked the soldier to listen more carefully and tell him exactly what she was singing. This time the soldier listened intently then said, "She is singing 'Jesus loves me, this I know; for the Bible tells me so.'"

The evil actions of others had stripped the little girl of everything except what her parents or missionaries apparently had given her—her faith in Jesus! In a deeply moving way, the little girl was clinging to all she had left in the world, which was her hope in God's love for her.

Such stories read in the newspaper, such scenes of cruelty observed on televised newscasts, such violence witnessed in our streets and schools and homes could cause any caring person to be deeply distressed over the evil actions of wicked people in our world. I find myself at times avoiding the local and world news because of the outrage I experience at such reports.

But sometimes the evil actions of others become very personal, and we cannot avoid them because they are committed against us or against our loved ones. In such instances, the outrage can become a root of deep-seated anger, hatred, frustration, and bitterness that festers until our lives are filled with distress.

Have you been stripped of everything? Stripped materially, emotionally, financially, socially, intellectually, physically? Stripped of your marriage, your health, your family, your home, your friends, your reputation, your youth? Are your days filled with distress because of the evil actions of others? Does your future look bleak and barren because your present is so bitter?

If you have been stripped of anything—or everything—look up! The vision of His glory gives you and me the same hope for the future as the little Rwandan refugee. What hope did she have for the future? None—*except for the hope she had in Jesus.* In Him, each of us has a glorious future—a glorious hope—because one day God will straighten the crooked, right the wrong, humble the proud, judge the wicked, and vindicate the righteous! Why? Because God is just!

By Evil Actions

Finding Hope in Knowing God Is Just

The apostle John had just witnessed the dramatic moment for which God's people yearn—the moment when the Lamb Who is the Lord Jesus Christ asserted His right to rule the world and fulfill God's purpose for the human race. At long last, the world would be ruled rightly and justly. The entire universe must have still been reverberating from the thunderous acclamation of the worthiness of Christ when John "watched as the Lamb opened the first of the seven seals" (Rev. 6:1). He watched as the Lamb began to take charge of a wicked world filled with evil actions.

The opening of the first of the seven seals apparently began a time in human history that Jesus described in Matthew 24:21–22 when He said, "For then there will be great distress, unequaled from the beginning of the world until now—and never to be equaled again. If those days had not been cut short, no one would survive, but for the sake of the elect those days will be shortened."

The Bible refers to this period of great distress as Jacob's trouble,[1] Daniel's seventieth week,[2] and the Great Tribulation.[3] In essence, the Great Tribulation is a time when God's wrath is poured out upon the world in response to man's evil actions. Because God is just, judgment is coming. And the principles with which He will judge the world in the future are the same principles with which He judges you and me today.

God Judges with Patience

One of the first principles of judgment that becomes apparent in Revelation 6 is that God judges with patience. John "saw under the altar the souls of those who had been slain because of the word of God and the testimony they had maintained. They called out in a loud voice, 'How long, Sovereign Lord, holy and true, until you judge the inhabitants of the earth and avenge our blood?' Then each of them was given a white robe, and they were told to wait a little longer" (Rev. 6:9–11a). God is patient in judgment.

When we read of a mother deliberately drowning her two young sons . . .

When we read of a wealthy, famous celebrity charged with nearly decapitating his beautiful young wife . . .

When we read of drive-by shootings that claim the lives of innocent children . . .

When we read of young children kidnapped for pornographic purposes . . .

When we read of babies born to be sacrificed in occult practices . . .

When we read of a thirteen-year-old boy brutally raping and beating to death a young mother in front of her children . . .

When we read of a government building occupied by hundreds of adults and dozens of children blown to bits in a fanatical protest of government . . .

When we read of murder, extortion, sadism, perversion, cruelty, and blasphemy, we want to scream, "God, holy and true and righteous! How can You stand it? Why do You allow such evil actions to take place? Why don't You strike such evil people with lightning? Or open up the ground and swallow them? Or just drop them dead in their tracks?"

Have you experienced injustice at the hands of someone else? Have you been the victim of evil actions by someone who seemed to get away with his or her wickedness? Like Jeremiah of old, did you cry out, "You are always righteous, O LORD, when I bring a case before you. Yet I would speak with you about your justice: Why does the way of the wicked prosper?"[4] Did you want to say, "If You are loving and good, why don't You *do* something about the evil actions of others?"

In the midst of our heated, passionate distress comes the quiet answer: "The Lord is not slow in keeping his promise, as some understand slowness. He is patient with you, not wanting anyone to perish, but everyone to come to repentance."[5]

God is patient because He understands how long eternity is! He knows that when an unbeliever dies, that person is not only separated from God and barred from heaven, he or she is condemned to live for all eternity in hell, a place of physical, emotional, mental, and spiritual torment that lasts forever and ever and ever and ever.

And God, Who so loved the world that He created it . . .

Who so loved man that when he sinned He planned for his redemption . . .

Who so loved the world that He sent His only, beloved Son to be the Redeemer, paying the price of redemption with His own blood . . . .

. . . so *loves* the world still, even with all of its evil actions, that He is not willing for *any* to perish! Therefore, He is patient. He withholds His wrath as He seeks *all* to come to repentance, that they might be saved from the judgment to come! What a magnificent God we worship!

In what way are you aware of God's patience? Have you misunderstood it, mistaking His patience for tolerance of evil?

On August 3, 1990, Saddam Hussein marched his Iraqi army into Kuwait, seizing that tiny, oil-rich emirate for himself. The United Nations subsequently issued twelve warnings to Saddam Hussein to get out, to withdraw. The first warning condemned the invasion, demanding a withdrawal. The following warnings included trade, sea, and air embargoes. Each warning was more severe than the one preceding it until finally, on November 29, the ultimate warning was given: "Get out, or we will forcibly remove you." In essence, Saddam Hussein was being told, "turn around, change your course of action, repent, or judgment is coming!"

Only God knows what was going through Saddam Hussein's mind at the time, but it appeared he did not take the warnings seriously. It seemed as though he was mistaking the patience of the United Nations and the United States for tolerance. He was wrong! On January 16, 1991, judgment fell on Saddam Hussein, and he was forcibly removed from Kuwait at great cost to his own people.

God's patience is a wonderful thing, but it is not to be toyed with or abused. There are many people today who resist the cross, believing the blessings in their lives—good health, loving family, relative security, financial independence—are evidence that God loves them and will therefore not judge them. Do you know someone who says, in effect, "I'm happy, healthy, good, and moral. God has been good to me. He answers my prayers and has blessed my life. I know a loving God will not send me to hell"? To that person Paul said, "Do you show contempt for the riches of his kindness, tolerance and patience, not realizing that God's kindness leads you towards repentance?"[6]

God's goodness should drive us to our knees in gratitude. Instead of resisting the cross because we think God's blessings in our lives prove we don't need it, we should fling ourselves at its foot, claiming the blood that was shed there for our sin, surrendering our lives to the One Who loved us so much He died for us. God's patience should provoke a deep debt of gratitude in us so that we live our lives for the One Who gave His life for us. When we mistake God's patience for tolerance, it is to our own destruction.

It took Noah 120 years to build the ark. The Bible tells us he was a preacher of righteousness.[7] One reason the ark took so long to build was that Noah preached to his generation, warning of judgment to come. God did not want anyone to perish; He wanted all to come to repentance. But Noah's generation mistook God's 120 years of patience for tolerance. Their attitude was, "God has not judged us yet; therefore He is not going to judge us." So they "were eating and drinking, marrying and giving in marriage, up to the day Noah entered the ark; and they knew nothing about what would happen until the flood came and took them all away. That is how it will be at the coming of the Son of Man."[8]

Peter said we must understand that in the days preceding the judgment of God there will be those who say, "Where is this 'coming' he promised? Ever since our fathers died, everything goes on as it has since the beginning of creation."[9] There is a generation yet to come—it may be our generation—that will make the fatal error of mistaking God's patience for tolerance of sin and evil, and as a result that generation will fall under His final wrath and judgment.

God Judges with Progression

Because there is a limit to God's patience, there will come a time in your life and mine, in the life of our nation, and in the life of the world, when, if there is no repentance, He will proceed with judgment.

When He begins to judge the world, as described in Revelation, He does so progressively. This progression is symbolized by the seals, trumpets, and bowls of wrath.[10] Each seal is opened one at a time, then the seventh seal gives way to the first trumpet. Each trumpet is sounded one at a time until the seventh trumpet announces the emptying of the first bowl of wrath. Each bowl of wrath is poured out until God's judgment is completed by the return of the Judge.

The entire progression is such that if at any point, mankind would repent of their sin and turn to God, God would stop the judgment! God's reluctance to judge can be felt in this deliberate progression of His judgment. It's as though God can hardly bear to send another disaster into the human race, and so He proceeds slowly, one judgment at a time, using these judgments to warn the human race: "Repent! Change your course! It's going to get worse if you do not turn around and turn to Me. Judgment is coming!"

God could judge us all at once. He could just blink His eye and send planet earth spinning out of control, flinging the human race off into the oblivion of the universe. But He doesn't. He seems to judge slowly, by degrees, giving us every opportunity to turn away from sin and return to Him.

We tend to think of God's judgment as fire falling from heaven, or as the ground opening up and swallowing evil men, or as lightning striking the offensive party. But Paul said in Romans 1 that God's wrath also is revealed in His *abandonment* of the wicked! And this abandonment occurs by degrees.

Paul describes God's progressive abandonment of the wicked in Romans 1. When the wicked reject the truth that has been revealed to them through their conscience, God takes one step back and gives them over to sexual immorality.[11]

When the wicked refuse to repent, God takes another step back and gives them over to sexual perversity.[12]

When they further harden their hearts and refuse to repent, God takes another step away from them and gives them over to sexual depravity.[13] At that point, the wicked, who are far from God, are still invited to repent, but they very seldom do because their hearts are hardened against Him.

In Romans 1 and in Revelation 6, we're told the drumbeat of judgment would cease—as it would in your life and mine—any time it is heeded. But in Revelation 6 it was not heeded. The drumbeat began with a series of six very carefully controlled natural disasters that were revealed when the seals were opened one at a time: "I watched as the Lamb opened the first of the seven seals. Then I heard one of the four living creatures say in a voice like thunder, 'Come!' I looked, and there before me was a white horse! Its rider held a bow, and he was given a crown, and he rode out as a conqueror bent on conquest" (Rev. 6:1–2).

One view interprets the white horse as symbolizing peace, but the rider holds a bow, which symbolizes war. The contradiction seems to indicate someone or something that promises peace but brings destruction instead. This could possibly describe a philosophy or a form of government that fills the whole world, promising peace when there is no peace because the philosophy or government does not bring man into a right relationship with the Prince of Peace. Communism, humanism, materialism, capitalism, and the New Age seem to fit this description.

Another view sees Jesus Christ as the Rider since Revelation 19 describes Him as entering the world on a white horse. In this case, the white horse would indicate the peace He will ultimately establish while the bow speaks of the destruction He uses to purge the world of sin and evil. Everything that followed the white horse would then be seen as under the control of the Rider, and the disasters described would come from the bow in His hand. This view seems to underscore Revelation 14:1, which emphasizes the Lamb has taken charge and His judgment has commenced.

The opening of the second seal revealed a world war: "When the Lamb opened the second seal, I heard the second living creature say, 'Come!' Then another horse came out, a fiery red one. Its rider was given power to take peace from the earth and to make men slay each other. To him was given a large sword" (Rev. 6:3–4).

The opening of the third seal revealed the consequences of the world war: "When the Lamb opened the third seal, I heard the third living creature say, 'Come!' I looked, and there before me was a black horse! Its rider was holding a pair of scales in his hand. Then I heard what sounded like a voice among the four living creatures, saying, 'A quart of wheat for a day's wages, and three quarts of barley for a day's wages, and do not damage the oil and the wine!'" (Rev. 6:5–6).

Global war's natural consequences are famine and a bankrupt world economy. With the modern stock markets in New York, Tokyo, Hong Kong, Paris, London, and others now tied together, it is easy to see how the crash of one would lead to the crash of others in a domino effect. And when they crash, ushering in worldwide depression, a day's wage will be required to buy one loaf of bread, leaving no money for clothes, medicines, rent, or paying bills in general. But while daily necessities will be unavailable to the average person, luxury items will abound for the rich—the worldwide depression does "not damage the oil and wine."

And then the fourth seal was opened: "When the Lamb opened the fourth seal, I heard the voice of the fourth living creature say, 'Come!' I looked, and there before me was a pale horse! Its rider was named Death, and Hades was following close behind him. They were given power over a fourth of the earth to kill by sword, famine and plague, and by the wild beasts of the earth" (Rev. 6:7–8).

This fourth seal reveals the inevitable consequence of the world war: famine and bankruptcy. The result is death on a scale the human race has yet to see.

The world that will go through all of these judgments apparently looks for a scapegoat. Just as Nero set fire to Rome then blamed the early Christians, so the world yet to come will self-destruct then blame Christians for it. And so the opening of the fifth seal reveals an outpouring of persecution upon believers: "When he opened the fifth seal, I saw under the altar the souls of those who had been slain because of the word of God and the testimony they had maintained" (Rev. 6:9).

It has been estimated that since 1950 over ten million believers have been put to death because of their faith in Jesus Christ. Whether or not that statistic, which came out of the Manila Conference on World Evangelism, is accurate, the persecution yet to come will be much worse—in fact, it will be the worst persecution the world has ever known. The world that has witnessed in this century the Jewish Holocaust in Nazi Germany; the "killing fields" in Cambodia; the machete-style butchery of Hutus and Tutsis in Rwanda; the eradication of the intellectuals, the educated, and the wealthy during the Cultural Revolution in China; and the ethnic cleansing in Bosnia-Herzegovina has yet to see its most evil days. The persecution of Christians yet to come will make all other bloodletting combined seem pale in comparison.

The opening of the next seal seems to be God's terrifying response to the persecution of those who belong to Him: "I watched as he opened the sixth seal. There was a great earthquake. The sun turned black like sackcloth made of goat hair, the whole moon turned blood red, and the stars in the sky fell to earth, as late figs drop from a fig tree when shaken by a strong wind. The sky receded like a scroll, rolling up, and every mountain and island was removed from its place" (Rev. 6:12–14).

Through television, we have witnessed devastating earthquakes in this century. Major earthquakes like those in Japan, California, Russia, and Armenia leave the viewer as well as the victim speechless with horror in the face of such total devastation. Man, machinery, technology, and wealth are rendered completely impotent before the power that rips apart the earth as though it were a rotten garment. But Revelation tells us the "big one" is yet to come! And it will hit not just California, but in some way it will impact the entire planet. One can imagine the dust level in the air from such an earthquake that would cover the earth and cause the sun to turn black "like sackcloth." Even the sky will roll up, referring perhaps to the ozone layer that will finally disintegrate.

When the sixth seal ends, it is apparent God's judgment has progressed in a repetitive cycle of disasters, troubles, and problems as God seeks to turn the evil, wicked, rebellious world to Himself before it's too late.

Have you experienced a cycle of problems? Are you always having financial crises? Do you always seem to have trouble with your child's teacher at school, regardless of who the teacher is? Or perhaps you always have difficulty with your neighbor, no matter where you live or who your neighbor is. Or maybe you always have trouble holding a job.

Could God be saying to you through the repetition of difficulty that the problem is not just with your finances, your child's teacher, your neighbor, or your job? Could He be saying the problem is inside you? Could it be God is trying to get your attention concerning an attitude or a relationship or a habit or a lifestyle that needs to be changed? Anytime you or I get that pattern of problems repeating itself in our lives, we need to ask the Lord if He is trying to get our attention. And if He is, we need to ask why.

Perhaps you haven't experienced a pattern of difficulty but a potential disaster that left you weak, shaking, and wondering. For instance, have you been in an accident that totaled your car, and yet you walked away? Have you lived through a violent storm that toppled a tree onto your house, narrowly missing the room in which you were sleeping? Have you had a brush with cancer that is now in remission? Has an earthquake or tornado struck, leveling every house on the block, including yours, but sparing your life? Could God be trying to get your attention through these natural disasters? What has been your response?

Revelation 6 describes how, through His progressive judgment, God will get the attention of planet earth. By the end of the sixth seal, the world knows it is coming under the judgment of the Lamb. But instead of repenting of sin and turning to God, the world runs from God! The world would rather die than submit to the Lamb. And so the rich and the poor, the great and the small, the educated and the ignorant, the powerful and the impotent, the influential and the insignificant all turn to created things for deliverance, rather than to the Creator. John sadly witnessed, "They called to the mountains and the rocks, 'Fall on us and hide us from the face of him who sits on the throne and from the wrath of the Lamb! For the great day of their wrath has come, and who can stand?'" (Rev. 6:16–17).

It's almost as though the people on planet earth all bury their heads in the sand, hoping God's judgment will not fall near them! In response to their paralyzing fear, God exercises His third principle of judgment.

He pauses.

God Judges with a Pause

Revelation 7 describes how God sends the angels to hold back the winds of the earth, stopping the circulation of air:
Suddenly there will be no mountain breezes,
no rustling of leaves in the forests,
no waves crashing on the shore,
no storms raging in the atmosphere,
no clouds moving through the sky.
Everything will be absolutely still!

While people on planet earth will surely be watching the Weather Channel and checking in with the local and national meteorologists for some logical explanation, John reveals the supernatural reason for the eerie stillness: "I saw four angels standing at the four corners of the earth, holding back the four winds of the earth to prevent any wind from blowing on the land or on the sea or on any tree" (Rev. 7:1).

The first verse of chapter 8 says not only will planet earth be completely still, heaven will be totally silent. There will be no rumbling peals of thunder from the throne, no new songs being sung by the four living creatures and the twenty-four elders, no angelic chorus of praise to the One Who alone is worthy, no roaring acclamation of the Lamb. Heaven will be silent! Awesomely, fearsomely, pregnantly silent!

God's pause in judgment is like the eye of a hurricane, a lull that gives the world time to reflect on its rebellion, blasphemy, sin, and evil actions. God gives the human race time to think things over.

Has God "paused" in your life? In the midst of all your health difficulties, do you find you are feeling better? In the midst of all your financial struggles, do you feel you can now make ends meet? After the cycle of problems, difficulties, and disasters has repeated itself in your life, are you able to cope today? What is your response to the pause?

In John's vision, planet earth responds by rationalizing what had taken place! The rebellious human race decides things haven't been as bad as had been thought. It's possible that educational institutions, research analysts, and government commissions studied the cycle of events and concluded they were the result of natural disasters, not the judgment of God after all! Like Pharaoh arguing with Moses, mankind just hardens its heart toward God and refuses to repent.

Perhaps the pause also gives time to believers to read their Bibles and come to an understanding of what is taking place. Certainly a worldwide concert of prayer takes effect as thousands of prayers ascend toward heaven. One reason for heaven's silence is perhaps that God Himself is waiting for His people to pray before He proceeds to act on their behalf and judge the wicked. Because—as at Pentecost, when the fire of the Holy Spirit fell as a result of prayer[14]—in the last days, the fire of judgment will also fall in answer to prayer.

The same John who witnessed the fire fall from heaven at Pentecost[15] is the same John who saw another angel, with a golden censer, [come] and stand at the altar. "He was given much incense to offer, with the prayers of all the saints, on the golden altar before the throne. The smoke of the incense, together with the prayers of the saints, went up before God from the angel's hand. Then the angel took the censer, filled it with fire from the altar, and hurled it on the earth; and there came peals of thunder, rumblings, flashes of lightning and an earthquake" (Rev. 8:3–5).

As the prayers rise to heaven from believers who are being persecuted unmercifully on earth, the heavenly silence and earthly stillness are broken by a terrifying, worldwide electrical storm. The storm is all the more shocking in its suddenness, contrasted with the silence and stillness that had preceded it. It is as though God takes planet earth by the shirt collar, shakes it, and shouts, "Wake up! Repent! If you do not turn from your evil actions you will experience My wrath!"

When we hear of the evil actions of others reported in the news or see wickedness on television, I wonder what the impact would be if we spent as much time praying as we do clucking our tongues, joining a demonstration, boycotting a product, or even writing a letter to the editor! On earth, we are distressed by the evil actions of others. When we get to heaven, will we be distressed over our own earthly prayerlessness?

In response to the united prayer of believers, God supernaturally intervenes in the rebellion of planet earth. Who do you know who is hellbent for destruction? Someone who is in rebellion against God? Pray! If God would move heaven and earth, literally, to warn planet earth, what will He do for your loved one if you just pray? This scene from heaven reveals that in response to the prayers of His people, God moves in powerful ways!

God Judges with Precision

The series of judgments John described as being announced by the sound of the seven trumpets following the seven seals are supernatural. The striking characteristic of these judgments is the precise way in which they are carried out.

During the Persian Gulf War, the United States Air Force deployed weapons referred to as "smart bombs." Although dropped from planes flying thousands of feet above the earth, these bombs could be computer-programmed to fall within inches of a target's center. Much was said about the precision of the bombing raids, which kept the loss of civilian life to a minimum while maximizing the destruction of the intended target. Despite the sophisticated accuracy of these "smart bombs" dropped on Baghdad during the Persian Gulf War, their precision is primitive compared with the judgments announced by the seven trumpets: "Then the seven angels who had the seven trumpets prepared to sound them.

"The first angel sounded his trumpet, and there came hail and fire mixed with blood, and it was hurled down upon the earth. A third of the earth was burned up, a third of the trees were burned up, and all the green grass was burned up.

"The second angel sounded his trumpet, and something like a huge mountain, all ablaze, was thrown into the sea. A third of the sea turned into blood, a third of the living creatures in the sea died, and a third of the ships were destroyed.

"The third angel sounded his trumpet, and a great star, blazing like a torch, fell from the sky on a third of the rivers and on the springs of water—the name of the star is Wormwood. A third of the waters turned bitter, and many people died from the waters that had become bitter.

"The fourth angel sounded his trumpet, and a third of the sun was struck, a third of the moon, and a third of the stars, so that a third of them turned dark. A third of the day was without light, and also a third of the night" (Rev. 8:6–12).

The first trumpet sounds, and something like Agent Orange defoliates one-third of the grass and trees. The second trumpet sounds, and something like burning oil destroys one-third of the sea water, sea life, and sea lanes. The third trumpet sounds, and something like chemical and biological warfare pollutes one-third of the fresh water supply. The fourth trumpet sounds, and something like the twilight that results from the smoke of battle or burning oil wells occurs. Light from the sun, moon, and stars is dimmed by one-third.

One-third! One-third! One-third! One-third! The trumpets announce a carefully controlled series of disasters designed to let the world know they are not random or circumstantial but the precise judgments of God.

Again and again, without realizing it, news commentators today report the precision of God's judgment. Recently, when an earthquake hit a major city, news reports spoke of the "luck" in that the quake hit one hour before rush-hour traffic, when it would have increased the death toll many times over. Or we read of a forest fire, raging out of control for days then suddenly dying out as it approaches the suburbs of a town. Or we watch as a hurricane, with the power to destroy anything or anyone in its path, brushes land then spins off to sea. Or we hear of a tornado touching down, demolishing homes that for some reason were vacant at the time.

When major disasters hit, invariably those who report them remark on how much greater the loss of human life could have been. Yet we seem to miss the message! God may be warning us through these carefully controlled disasters that He will hold us accountable for our sin and rebellion against Him.

Often His message of warning comes through the environment, as it did in the first four trumpets. In the Old Testament, when the people refused to listen to God's spoken Word through His prophets and when they rejected His written Word, He spoke to them through their environment. He sought their attention by sending a plague of locusts or a drought or a flood, warning them in precise judgments that if they did not repent of their sin and turn to Him, they would come under His wrath.

Jesus said the generation that would be the last to live on earth and would experience His second coming would also experience drastic changes in the environment. He said, "There will be famines and earthquakes in various places. All these are the beginning of birth pains."[16]

When I gave birth to each of my children, I went through long periods of labor pains that felt like a giant hand was gripping my waist and slowly squeezing. Although painful, when they began the contractions were not unbearable. At the onset of labor, the pains were four or five minutes apart and merely uncomfortable. As the birth of the baby drew near, however, the pains increased in frequency until they ran together and the intensity was so great it was excruciating at the time of actual delivery.

When Jesus said the generation at the end of the age would experience birth pains, He meant that certain "signs" in the spiritual, national, environmental, and personal world would begin to increase in frequency and intensity. For instance, the world has always had earthquakes. But they are coming more frequently now, and very often they are reported as the worst in recorded history. We have always had floods, fires, hurricanes, droughts, and storms of every description, but they seem to be growing in frequency and in intensity.

Although we may not be living in the time period described in Revelation 8, the environmental changes and disasters cause us to feel God is once again seeking to get our attention. I have great sympathy for some of the environmentalists of our day. Instinctively they seem to know what the Bible says in Genesis 1: that man has been given dominion over the earth. But rather than have dominion, exercising care and concern for our environment, we have abused and used it for selfish, greedy gain, paying the price in the depletion and even destruction of many natural resources. But the long-term solution to such abuse is not passing more laws; it is in repenting of our sin, turning to our Creator, and surrendering our lives to Him.

The greatest threat to our environment is not fluorocarbons or carbon monoxide or chemical plants or nuclear reactors or bulldozers or arsonists. The greatest threat to our environment is *sin!*

When Adam and Eve sinned in the Garden of Eden, one of the consequences was God's curse on the environment.[17] The apostle Paul explained, "The creation waits in eager expectation for the sons of God to be revealed. For the creation was subjected to frustration, not by its own choice, but by the will of the one who subjected it, in hope that the creation itself will be liberated from its bondage to decay and brought into the glorious freedom of the children of God. We know that the whole creation has been groaning as in the pains of childbirth right up to the present time."[18] While committed

Christians should be very conscientious in the way we care for the environment, creation will not be truly liberated and restored to its original state until all of mankind is right with God.

While the first four trumpets reveal something of the ultimate impact our sin will have on our environment the last three trumpets directly affect man himself: "The fifth angel sounded his trumpet, and I saw a star that had fallen from the sky to the earth. The star was given the key to the shaft of the Abyss. When he opened the Abyss, smoke rose from it like the smoke from a gigantic furnace. The sun and sky were darkened by the smoke from the Abyss. And out of the smoke locusts came down upon the earth and were given power like that of scorpions of the earth. They were told not to harm the grass of the earth or any plant or tree, but only those people who did not have the seal of God on their foreheads. They were not given power to kill them, but only to torture them for five months. And the agony they suffered was like that of the sting of a scorpion when it strikes a man. During those days men will seek death, but will not find it; they will long to die, but death will elude them" (Rev. 9:1–6).

The fallen star would appear to be Satan, who is allowed to release hordes of demons on earth. The resulting demonic activity causes worldwide depression, delusion, discouragement, distress, defeat, dissatisfaction, and despair. We could even say the entire human race becomes dysfunctional!

Have you ever been deeply depressed? Have you ever been around someone who was deeply depressed? Can you imagine how deeply depressing it would be to live in a world where everyone is deeply depressed! And before these miserable people even have time to really get settled in with a counselor, who himself would be deeply depressed, the sixth trumpet blows: "The sixth angel sounded his trumpet, and I heard a voice coming from the horns of the golden altar that is before God. It said to the sixth angel who had the trumpet, 'Release the four angels who are bound at the great river Euphrates.' And the four angels who had been kept ready for this very hour and day and month and year were released to kill a third of mankind. The number of the mounted troops was two hundred million. I heard their number" (Rev. 9:13–16).

If the fourth seal described a world war, the sixth trumpet may describe yet another world war! Or perhaps John is describing in a symbolic way the destruction of the human race through a plague such as AIDS or a virulent form of cancer or an uncontrollable virus such as the Ebola virus. However it is accomplished, the result is the annihilation of one-third of the human race.

We have seen pictures of the dead and dying in Bosnia and Somalia. We have seen pictures of dead bodies floating down the rivers from mainland China during the Cultural Revolution until the water itself turned red from their blood. We have seen pictures from Vietnam and Cambodia of massacres and mass graves. And who can ever forget the pictures of the death camps run by Nazi Germany? But all those together are *nothing* compared with the destruction of life resulting from the blast of the sixth trumpet!

Have you ever had a close brush with death? Perhaps in a car crash or a hunting accident? Or just standing at the grave of a loved one, have you been confronted with eternity? When I have those experiences, it gives my life a new perspective and a new seriousness. I deeply desire to be right with God and live in such a way that my life counts for something.

In John's vision, when the human race is confronted with death on every side in such a massive way, how do they react? Do they readjust their priorities? Do they get serious about God? Do they repent of their sin?

You would think each and every human being would cry out, "Lord, I am miserable! I'm no longer enjoying my rebellion! There is no more pleasure in sin, even for a season! I repent! Please forgive me of my sin! I want to know joy in my heart, and peace in my mind, and contentment in my life! I want to get right with You so that when my time to die comes, I will be ready!"

Instead, the people's reaction is much like shaking their fist in God's face! You can almost hear John's stunned incredulity: "The rest of mankind that were not killed by these plagues still did not repent of the work of their hands; they did not stop worshiping demons, and idols of gold, silver, bronze, stone and wood—idols that cannot see or hear or walk. Nor did they repent of their murders, their magic arts, their sexual immorality or their thefts" (Rev. 9:20–21).

Then, while rebellion, blasphemy, sin, and every kind of evil action are destroying the earth's environment and mankind in general, the seventh trumpet gives us a glimpse into what is taking place in heaven:

> The seventh angel sounded his trumpet, and there were loud voices in heaven, which said:
> > "The kingdom of the world has become the
> > > kingdom of our Lord and of his Christ,
> > > and he will reign for ever and ever."
> And the twenty-four elders, who were seated on their thrones before God, fell on their faces and worshipped God, saying:
> > "We give thanks to you, Lord God Almighty,
> > > the One who is and who was,
> > because you have taken your great power
> > > and have begun to reign.
> The nations were angry;
> > and your wrath has come.
> The time has come for judging the dead,
> > and for rewarding your servants the
> > > prophets
> and your saints and those who reverence your name,
> > both small and great—
> and for destroying those who destroy the
> > earth." (Rev. 11:15–18)

There will come a time when all heaven will rejoice that . . . wrong is set right . . .
> > and justice prevails . . .
> > > and righteousness rules . . .

and truth triumphs . . .

> and God's people are vindicated once and
> for all, forever!

The little Rwandan refugee girl can lift up her head! The same Jesus Who loves her is Lord and King and Judge of those wicked men who so brutalized her family! He will hold them and all sinners who are not under His blood accountable for their evil actions!

Thinking of this time to come reminds me of the story about an old farmer who worked hard in his field, which was bordered by his neighbor's field. Out of respect and reverence for the Lord's day, the old farmer never worked on Sunday, while his neighbor always did. Although he worked hard to make up for it, the loss of time cost the farmer. His soil was not plowed on time, his crops were not planted on time, and in the end, his fall harvest was not as full and profitable as his neighbor's. When the neighbor pointed out the difference and told the farmer God seemed to have blessed him more even though he had not honored the Lord's day, the old farmer replied, "God doesn't settle all of His accounts in October."

Are you distressed by the actions of evil men and women? Especially when they seem to get by with their sin and wickedness? Remember what the old farmer said. God doesn't settle all of His accounts in October! There will be an accounting—if not today, then tomorrow! Judgment is coming! When Jesus Christ "takes His great power and begins to reign," whether on planet earth or in your heart, there will be judgment of sin. Because God is just!

However, God is not only just, He is merciful. As Habbakuk prayed, "In wrath remember mercy."[19]

Finding Hope in Knowing God Is Merciful

At the same time God warns the people on planet earth in patient, progressive, paused, and precise judgments that they need to repent, He makes provision for them to turn to Him. Again and again, during the first three and a half years of the seven-year period of the Great Tribulation, God reaches out to the human race in mercy.

God's Merciful Provision of 144,000 Preachers

Even as the world reels in chaos as the result of rebellion against God, in His great mercy God still makes provision for the human race to hear the gospel. He seals 144,000 Jewish evangelists who are supernaturally preserved to proclaim the gospel of Jesus Christ: "Another angel . . . having the seal of the living God . . . called out in a loud voice to the four angels who had been given power to harm the land and the sea: 'Do not harm the land or the sea or the trees until we put a seal on the foreheads of the servants of our God.' Then I heard the number of those who were sealed: 144,000 from all the tribes of Israel" (Rev. 7:2–4).

God's sealed protection ensures that
armies cannot touch them,
floods cannot drown them,
fires cannot burn them,
famines cannot starve them,
torture chambers and concentration camps cannot hold them, and
the secret police cannot hinder them!

They will be a constant reminder to Satan and the wicked world that Jesus Christ is in control.

These evangelists will be so effective in what they do they will be able to permeate the entire world with the gospel, producing a worldwide revival. Thousands will respond to their invitation to receive Christ as Savior and commit their lives to Him as Lord!

All through history, the times of greatest human suffering have seemed to produce the greatest revivals. The pressure of pain and persecution and suffering seems to drive man in desperation to God. And desperation is one of the prerequisites for revival!

How thrilling it will be as the 144,000 Jews pick up the privilege of world evangelization! Remember, God chose the Jews because He loved them.[20] But increasingly, as He revealed Himself to them, they rejected Him. Their rejection climaxed when they instigated the crucifixion of Jesus Christ.[21] For the last two thousand years, although a remnant of Jews has believed in Jesus Christ as their Messiah, Savior, and Lord, the majority have not. But in the future, the majority will not only believe in Jesus Christ, they will lead others to a saving knowledge of Him, to the glory of God![22]

This unique, unparalleled revival yet to come will be a time of ecstasy and agony. The ecstasy will be experienced as thousands come to faith in Christ. The agony will be experienced as these new believers will be put to death for their faith: "After this I looked and there before me was a great multitude that no one could count, from every nation, tribe, people, and language, standing before the throne and in front of the Lamb. They were wearing white robes and were holding palm branches in their hands. . . . Then one of the elders asked me, 'These in white robes—who are they, and where did they come from?'

"I answered, 'Sir, you know.'

"And he said, 'These are they who have come out of the great tribulation; they have washed their robes and made them white in the blood of the Lamb'" (Rev. 7:9, 13–14).

The solemn truth John reveals is that not only worldwide revival breaks out but deadly persecution as well! These young believers will almost immediately have to put their faith on the line. As they give their lives for their Lord they will put to shame many of us who have lived in an easier time.

God's Merciful Provision of Two Prophets

While neither the majority of the population nor even the leadership of the world will turn to Christ, thousands of people will! John said they will respond to the 144,000 Jewish evangelists and to the testimony of those martyred for their faith, as well as to the two witnesses: "And I will give power to my two witnesses, and they will prophesy for 1,260 days, clothed in sackcloth" (Rev. 11:3). While the names of the two witnesses are not given, educated guesses conclude that one of them is Elijah.

Elijah was a very powerful prophet. As we considered earlier, Elijah prayed, and rain was withheld for three years in Israel.[23] He prayed again, and the three-year drought ended.[24] Because he did not die but was caught up to heaven in a whirlwind[25] and is prophesied to return to earth in his prophetic role immediately preceding the physical return of Jesus Christ to earth,[26] he is thought to be one of the two witnesses who "have power to shut up the sky so that it will not rain during the time they are prophesying" (Rev. 11:6a).

The other witness is thought to be Moses, the great deliverer of God's people.[27] When he relayed God's Word to Pharaoh, commanding him to release the Hebrews from slavery, Pharaoh refused. Moses was then given power and authority by God to strike Pharaoh and Egypt with a series of supernatural plagues that eventually forced Pharaoh to comply with God's command. The first of those plagues occurred when Moses stretched out his staff and turned all the water of Egypt to blood.[28] Because his burial was disputed when he died,[29] and because he appeared with Jesus and Elijah on the Mountain of Transfiguration,[30] he is thought to be one of the two witnesses who have "power to turn the waters into blood and to strike the earth with every kind of plague" (Rev. 11:6b). If the two witnesses are Moses and Elijah, then they would represent the law that revealed God's standards of righteousness and justice and the prophets who revealed God's love and grace.

Regardless of the identity of the two witnesses, they are enabled to preach the gospel to the entire world! The message they preach is demonstrated by the lives they live. Every aspect of their ministry and lives is carefully scrutinized, leaving the world without excuse!

I wonder how I would bear up under such scrutiny! Do I dare preach what I practice? These two witnesses will not only preach what they practice, they will practice what they preach.

And their testimony will rock the world!

Eventually, the two witnesses have nothing more to say, so God allows them to be slain. John records that the authorities refuse to permit the burial of their bodies, so they remain on the public streets of Jerusalem, where they had fallen. The entire world gloats over their deaths, displaying ghoulish delight by exchanging gifts as though celebrating a perversion of Christmas. The world seems greatly relieved to have these two negative doomsayers eliminated. "After all," they might say, "we all have our own gods. And if there is one God Who is supreme, He isn't as angry as they say. He is loving and good and would never send us to hell. Good riddance to those two old men who were always talking about judgment and repentance."

But the celebration is short-lived. The entire world (which watches, perhaps, through round-the-clock televised news coverage), is jolted when, after three and a half days, the two witnesses come back to life, rise up in their physical bodies, float up through the air, and disappear into heaven!

At the same moment the witnesses arise and ascend into heaven, a gigantic earthquake destroys a tenth of the city of Jerusalem, and seven thousand people are killed! Silas and Paul's Philippian jailer could identify with the reaction of those in the city who survive.[31] John bore witness that they will give glory to God, and we assume many will turn to Him in repentance for salvation.

If it took an earthquake to bring the Philippian jailer to salvation in Christ in the past, and if it takes an earthquake plus the death, resurrection, and ascension of the two witnesses to bring Jerusalem to salvation in Christ in the future, what will it take for you? For your loved ones? Praise God! There is no depth to which He will not stoop, no height to which He will not ascend, no lengths to which He will not go to save the lost from His own wrath for their sin! Because our God Who is just is also merciful!

God's Merciful Provision of Transformed People

However, there are people who cannot be moved by—and refuse to even attend—evangelistic rallies such as those the 144,000 evangelists very probably will hold. There are other people who find logical explanations for supernatural events such as the death, resurrection, and ascension of the two witnesses. There are many people who can only be won to Jesus Christ by the neighbor next door or the coworker in the adjoining office or their tennis partner or their college roommate or a friend through what we think of as lifestyle evangelism. And so God, in His mercy, provides the wicked, rebellious world with the witness of ordinary men and women whose lives have been transformed in Christ and who bear faithful witness to Him even unto death.

John wrote, "They overcame him [Satan] by the blood of the Lamb and by the word of their testimony; they did not love their lives so much as to shrink from death" (Rev. 12:11). The world sees friends, neighbors, coworkers, and family members who had been in rebellion against God *suddenly changed!* They are no longer deeply depressed as everyone else is! They have peace and joy! They are:

patient when confronted with rudeness,

kind when confronted with meanness,

loving when confronted with hatefulness,

considerate when confronted with thoughtlessness!

Some who will observe the witness of these ordinary people surely will respond by inquiring how they, too, can experience such a transformed life. How thrilling it will be, then, for the ordinary people to tell them the secret is a personal relationship with Jesus Christ. How delighted they will be to lead almost-lost loved ones to place their faith in Him alone!

But, sadly, the vast majority of those living in the world will not be changed; instead they will be enraged by these "nonconformists," and they will maneuver to put them to death.

In a world where the role models are entertainers, athletes, and politicians, many of whom lack morals, integrity, and even common decency . . .

In a world where no one seems to stand for anything unless it is to stand for self . . .

In a world where anything is compromised if it impedes success . . .

In a world where pleasure takes priority over principle . . .

In a world where there are no absolutes, where what is right is what works or what feels good . . .

In a world where character no longer seems to count . . .

In such a world, think how powerful the testimony of *one life* lived for Christ will be! *One life* that has been cleansed through faith in the blood of the Lamb . . . *One life* that confesses "with [the] mouth, 'Jesus Christ is Lord'"[32] . . . *One life* that has the courage to stand for godly convictions in front of the world, paying the supreme price with a life laid down for the One Who is Lord . . . *How I pray I might be one life like that!*

God's Merciful Provision of Angelic Proclamation

Finally, for those who will not respond to the 144,000 evangelists or to the two supernatural witnesses or to the thousands of ordinary witnesses, God will use one more means of presenting the gospel to a world gone insane. John wrote: "Then I saw another angel flying in midair, and he had the eternal gospel to proclaim to those who live on the earth—to every nation, tribe, language and people. He said in a loud voice, 'Fear God and give him glory, because the hour of his judgment has come. Worship him who made the heavens, the earth, the sea and the springs of water'" (Rev. 14:6–7).

Have you ever wondered why God left the evangelization of the world up to you and me when we seem so prone to failure? Since we are so inadequate for such a crucial task, why doesn't He do it Himself? Why doesn't He just give the gospel to the angels who could proclaim it from the skies perfectly, simply, and powerfully in a universal language everyone could understand? In the end, He does! It's as though God pulls out all the stops to call the world to Himself! He does not want "anyone to perish, but everyone to come to repentance."[33]

But the world's ears will be deaf, and the world's eyes will be blind, and the world's heart will be hard. The world that was made by Him and for Him in the end will totally reject Him and come under His wrath.

What evil actions against you or against someone you love are even now tormenting your spirit? What is causing you to cry bitterly between clenched teeth, "It just isn't fair! It's not right! How can they get by with that?"

Would you place the evil actions and evil people before the throne of God—before the One Who is keeping the books? Ask Him to take responsibility for setting things right. And remember, God doesn't settle all of His accounts in October, but He *does* settle all of His accounts! Then release your attitude of hate and bitterness, replacing it with an attitude of love and forgiveness. Why? Because "to this you were called, because Christ suffered for you, leaving you an example, that you should follow in his steps. 'He committed no sin, and no deceit was found in his mouth.' When they hurled their insults at him, he did not retaliate; when he suffered, he made no threats. Instead, he entrusted himself to him who judges justly."[34]

Like the piercing rays of the sun penetrating through dark storm clouds, the vision of His glory penetrates our distress over the evil actions of others, setting us free to place our hope in the One alone Who is absolutely just and merciful!

Why are you downcast, O my soul?

Why so disturbed within me?

Put your hope in God,

for I will yet praise him,

my Savior and my God.

Psalm 42:5

8

Hope When You Are Distressed by Evil Alliances

Revelation 13:1–19:21

 In our generation, the evil alliance known as the Union of Soviet Socialist Republics, which was atheistic at heart and repressive by nature, was considered by many to be the cause of more distress in the modern world than any other single source. It enslaved entire nations, kept its citizens in poverty while the leaders lived like czars, fostered and funded world terrorism, and unmercifully persecuted Jews and Christians alike. With a world-class army and an arsenal that included nuclear weapons, it was a formidable enemy that seemed unstoppable once it determined a course of action.

Then, due in part to a collapsing economy, in the winter of 1989, the Berlin Wall fell, and the USSR began to disintegrate. To the astonishment of the world, the entire Soviet Union unraveled!

The capital of the former Soviet Union was Moscow. A large, gray building there once housed the KGB—the dreaded secret police who symbolized the brutal repression of the entire USSR. During the seventy years of Communist rule, a statue of the founder of the KGB had stood imposingly in the square in front of the building.

When the peaceful revolution took place that caused communism to crumble, the statue in front of the KGB building was toppled. In its place, the Cossacks, a rugged Russian clan known for its fighting ability, erected a replica of the cross of Christ. The old KGB loyalists immediately removed it.

The Cossacks re-erected the cross, and again the KGB loyalists took it down. For the third time, the Cossacks erected the cross. But this time, twenty Cossacks formed a ring around the statue twenty-four hours a day, saying if the cross was removed, they would set themselves on fire.

And so, in front of the old KGB building in Moscow, on the pedestal that had once lifted up the statue of the founder of the KGB, stood the cross. Underneath it was this inscription: "In this sign we conquer."

What evil alliance is causing you distress? Perhaps it is not as massive as the former Soviet Union, but it probably seems just as formidable to you personally. Is it an alliance between your spouse and your mother-in-law? Or an alliance between your spouse and another companion? Or is it a distressing alliance between your boss and the chairman of the board of directors? Or an alliance between your pastor and a business consultant? Or an alliance between your child and someone else?

No matter how powerful the alliance confronting you now seems, the Bible reveals that an evil alliance is yet to come that will cause all others to seem insignificant in comparison. It will ultimately dominate the world, giving Satan unbridled freedom to work out his blasphemous plan of rebellion and destruction.

But the vision of His glory gives us hope when we are distressed by evil alliances, regardless of the size or scope, because it reveals Jesus Christ asserting His power, avenging His people, and in the end, appearing in Person to break up all evil alliances and establish His kingdom on earth!

Finding Hope in Knowing Jesus Christ
Will Assert His Power

God is a merciful God, but there is a limit to God's patience.

After two thousand years of seeking to teach the world about Himself through the family of Abraham . . .

After thirty-three years of revealing Himself visibly and physically in the person of His own Son sent to dwell among men on earth . . .

After demonstrating His love to an unrepentant, unresponsive human race through nine hours of trials, six hours on a Roman cross, and three days in a borrowed tomb . . .

After at least two thousand years of displaying His grace through the church . . .

After three and a half years of seeking to warn the world of impending, final judgment and woo the world to Himself, God ultimately restrains Himself no longer: "The wine of God's fury . . . has been poured full strength into the cup of his wrath."[1]

When God's patience ends, His fury is unleashed full-strength in that it is no longer mixed with mercy or grace. This is the beginning of the end!

As the Lord Jesus Christ proceeds to assert His power, cleansing the world of its sin and rebellion against Him, He uses three primary instruments—the same instruments He uses today, although not to the extent He will use them during the Great Tribulation.

Jesus Asserts His Power through Political Leaders

The first instrument He uses to assert His power is political leaders in the world, along with the governments these leaders establish. "There is no authority except that which God has established. The authorities that exist have been established by God."[2]

One of the most dramatic examples of God's use of political leaders is that of King Nebuchadnezzar of Babylon, a pagan despot. God referred to King Nebuchadnezzar as "my servant Nebuchadnezzar."[3] When Judah forsook God and went after pagan gods of stone and wood, refusing to heed the prophets or any of God's warnings, God asserted His power through Nebuchadnezzar, who laid waste the nation of Judah, destroyed the city of Jerusalem, turned the temple into a pile of rubble with not one stone left standing on top of another, and drove the Jews eight hundred miles east, into captivity in Babylon. Through Nebuchadnezzar, God asserted His power to purge Israel of her idolatry.

In the New Testament, when the Jews rejected His only begotten Son, God asserted His power through the Romans, who so devastated Israel that the nation was not only destroyed but its people were dispersed all over the world.

As leaders rise and fall, as nations disappear and develop, as armies march and retreat, instead of becoming distressed over the evil alliances, we would do well to look carefully for the hand of our God, asserting His power in the world.[4] God has used, He is using, and He will use political leaders for His own purposes.

During the last three and one half years of the Great Tribulation, God will assert His power through one political leader in particular to judge the world and purge it of sin. This leader is described in Revelation 13 as the "beast coming out of the sea." He is also known as the Antichrist, described by Paul as "the man of lawlessness,"[5] because his primary characteristic will be that of rebellion against God. He will be an almost-exact counterfeit of Christ, but instead of bringing peace and righteousness he will usher in war and a flood of evil such as the world has never known.

When the Antichrist first appears on the world scene, he will emerge suddenly, very probably during a period of great crisis. He will look so attractive, brilliant, able, and wise, the world will acknowledge and submit to his leadership. He will have brilliant executive and administrative ability, but he will be morally proud and profane. He "will do as he pleases. He will exalt and magnify himself above every god and will say unheard-of things against the God of gods."[6] He will have a scientific mind that will "honor a god of fortresses"[7]—science, technology, and military might. His reign in the world will be characterized by splendor and brilliance and supernatural power. In fact, the same terms are used in 2 Thessalonians to describe the power of the Antichrist as the letter to the Hebrews uses to describe the power of God in affirming the apostles when it says he will do "all kinds of miracles, signs and wonders."[8] At the beginning of his reign, he will use religion to help him subject the world to himself. Yet he will become so antagonistic to religion in the end,[9] he will seek to eliminate every religious holiday from the calendar,[10] destroying all religions as he declares himself to be god, demanding to be worshiped.[11]

At some point in his political career he will be assassinated. He will physically die then be supernaturally raised from the dead as the very incarnation of Satan![12] The entire world will be astounded, surrendering their sovereignty, their economies, their military, their treasuries, their *all* to him "until the time of wrath is completed, for what has been determined must take place."[13]

If we are as close to the second coming of Jesus Christ as many Christians believe we are, then this Antichrist may already be somewhere in the world today. Revelation 13 describes him as a beast emerging on the political scene and subsequently controlling the world:

"And I saw a beast coming out of the sea. He had ten horns and seven heads, with ten crowns on his horns, and on each head a blasphemous name.

"The beast I saw resembled a leopard, but had feet like those of a bear and a mouth like that of a lion. The dragon gave the beast his power and his throne and great authority. One of the heads of the beast seemed to have had a fatal wound, but the fatal wound had been healed. The whole world was astonished and followed the beast. Men worshiped the dragon because he had given authority to the beast, and they also worshiped the beast and asked, 'Who is like the beast? Who can make war against him?'

"The beast was given a mouth to utter proud words and blasphemies and to exercise his authority for forty-two months. He opened his mouth to blaspheme God, and to slander his name and his dwelling place and those who live in heaven. He was given power to make war against the saints and to conquer them. And he was given authority over every tribe, people, language and nation. All inhabitants of the earth will worship the beast—all whose names have not been written in the book of life belonging to the Lamb that was slain from the creation of the world" (Rev. 13:1–8).

While the "sea" apparently represents the Gentile nations from which the Antichrist will emerge,[14] the heads and horns refer to the nations he will rule and the kings who will submit to his authority. His empire will reflect past world empires symbolized by the leopard, bear, and lion[15] but will surpass them all in power because the dragon, who is Satan,[16] will give the Antichrist supernatural power and authority. This ultimate evil alliance between Satan and the Antichrist will last for forty-two months, which is the last three and one-half years of the Great Tribulation.

It will be as though every evil alliance in world history has combined, and at the head is the Antichrist. As difficult as it may be for us to comprehend, this dreadful "beast coming out of the sea" who rises up to rule the world in blasphemy is an instrument in the hand of God. God uses the Antichrist to reveal the depths of the depravity and wickedness of the human race while also purifying the saints[17] and preparing the way for Christ's visible return to earth.

Jesus Asserts His Power through Preachers and Prophets

In addition to political leaders, Revelation 13 says God also uses religious leaders to assert His power to purge the world of sin. For instance, in the Old Testament, when Israel had drifted so far away from God that she was living in rebellion and sin, refusing to heed or even hear the prophets, God sent a famine of His Word.[18] In other words, there were still preachers in every pulpit and prophets on every street corner, but God's Word was not given out. Instead, the religious leaders gave out their own opinions or they talked about social issues, or they just gave the people what they wanted to hear. The prophets were all false. So although Israel was very religious, she had no real Word from the Lord and no real truth.

Much of the world today that has refused God and His Son Jesus Christ is very religious. For example, most people in India consider it part of their own identity to be Hindu while the Chinese define themselves in terms of Buddhism and the Arabs are fanatical about Islam. Their rejection of the truth can be traced all the way back to Genesis 11 at the Tower of Babel, which we will discuss in detail a little later in this chapter. And because they have the truth as revealed through their conscience and through creation, they are without excuse for their rejection. Therefore, God has given them over to the delusion of false prophets who have led them in exchanging "the truth of God for a lie."[19]

The apostle Paul said that in the end, the rebellious people on planet earth refuse "to love the truth and so be saved. For this reason God sends them a powerful delusion so that they will believe the lie and so that all will be condemned who have not believed the truth but have delighted in wickedness."[20]

The "strong delusion" God sends is not only the leadership of the Antichrist, which the world is deceived into thinking is the answer to all of its problems, but the leadership of a world-renowned religious leader who gives credibility and respectability to the Antichrist:

"Then I saw another beast, coming out of the earth. He had two horns like a lamb [he appeared to be a religious leader], but he spoke like a dragon [his spirit and words came from Satan]. He exercised all the authority of the first beast on his behalf, and made the earth and its inhabitants worship the first beast, whose fatal wound had been healed. And he performed great and miraculous signs, even causing fire to come down from heaven to earth in full view of men. Because of the signs he was given power to do on behalf of the first beast, he deceived the inhabitants of the earth" (Rev. 13:11–14).

The false prophet will perform many supernatural signs and wonders on behalf of the Antichrist. We need to wake up! Not all miracles, signs, and wonders come from God! Satan has produced a talking snake,[21] sticks that turn into snakes,[22] and slaves that predict the future,[23] to name just a few of his miracles recorded in Scripture.

In our day, the world is becoming more and more fascinated with the supernatural. The popularity of Steven Spielberg's movies that primarily deal with the supernatural, the general acceptance of New Age philosophy, the increasing credibility of ESP, seances, channeling and such services as "dial-a-psychic," as well as other things give evidence that the world is being prepared to believe the ultimate lie. We, as believers, should not be fooled by someone who can concentrate intensely and cause a piece of paper to burst into flame or cause a table to lift in the air several inches or who can more or less accurately reveal some piece of hidden information. Satan is alive and well and can do many signs and wonders!

Satan's display of supernatural power climaxes in the work of the false prophet. And the whole world is deceived into thinking that because he can do signs and wonders, he must be good. The false prophet deceives the world into following the Antichrist, then he allies with the Antichrist to enslave the world:

"He ordered them to set up an image in honor of the beast who was wounded by the sword and yet lived. He was given power to give breath to the image of the first beast, so that it could speak and cause all who refused to worship the image to be killed. He also forced everyone, small and great, rich and poor, free and slave, to receive a mark on his right hand or on his fore-head, so that no one could buy or sell unless he had the mark, which is the name of the beast or the number of his name" (Rev. 13:14b–17).

At this point in the revelation, the Holy Spirit inspires John to insert a word of encouragement to the reader: "This calls for wisdom" (Rev. 13:18). Job tells us that wisdom is reverential and worshipful fear of the Lord.[24] As the entire world is mesmerized by signs and wonders and led by the false prophet to worship the beast, it will still be wise to fear, reverence, and worship God because, after all, the beast is just a man—although he's a *very evil* man: "If anyone has insight, let him calculate the number of the beast, for it is man's number. His number is 666" (Rev. 13:18). With all of their spectacular, supernatural, political, economic, and military powers, both the beast and the false prophet are mortal men, accountable to their Creator, and headed for judgment!

Jesus Asserts His Power through Plagues

Jesus Christ asserts His power, using political and religious leaders as His instruments of wrath poured out on a wicked world. Toward the end of the Great Tribulation, He also uses a series of plagues preceded by a solemn announcement:

"I looked, and there before me was a white cloud, and seated on the cloud was one 'like a son of man' with a crown of gold on his head and a sharp sickle in his hand. Then another angel came out of the temple and called in a loud voice to him who was sitting on the cloud, 'Take your sickle and reap, because the time to reap has come, for the harvest of the earth is ripe.' So he who was seated on the cloud swung his sickle over the earth, and the earth was harvested" (Rev. 14:14–16).

The angel comes "out of the temple," to reveal that the plagues that follow come directly from God. Just as He used plagues to judge Pharaoh and Egypt when they refused to heed His command, God once again will use plagues to judge the world at the end of the age.

Today, when we are stricken by plagues such as the worldwide outbreak of AIDS, while we pour billions of dollars into research for cures and preventative vaccines, we would do well to cry out to God, confess and repent of our sin, and plead for His mercy! There is no cure on the face of this earth for a plague that is an instrument of the wrath of God except the blood of Jesus Christ shed at the cross of Calvary!

The awesome scene described in Revelation 15 is not one of rage or passionate anger but of solemn, holy judgment. From this historic moment on, God will no longer tolerate sin, rebellion, or blasphemy among men on earth: "I saw in heaven another great and marvelous sign: seven angels with the seven last plagues—last, because with them God's wrath is completed" (Rev. 15:1).

As the plagues, represented by the bowls of wrath, are poured out on earth, those who had overcome the beast and had been faithful to Christ, even unto death, sing a song of victory. They are each given a harp by God. After days and weeks and months and perhaps years of torture, suffering, and unspeakable persecution, they have a song! They are filled with joy! Why? Because the unrepentant wicked and their evil alliances are finally held accountable by God:

> Great and marvelous are your deeds,
>   Lord God Almighty.
> Just and true are your ways,
>   King of the ages.
> Who will not fear you, O Lord,
>   and bring glory to your name?
> For you alone are holy.
>   All nations will come
> and worship before you,
>   for your righteous acts have been revealed.
>   (Rev. 15:3–4)

The redeemed in glory affirm, with joy in their hearts, that God is just and true and holy and right as He pours out His wrath on earth: "Then I heard a loud voice from the temple saying to the seven angels, 'Go, pour out the seven bowls of God's wrath on the earth'" (Rev. 16:1).

The first bowl is poured out, and a plague results that destroys human health. We are troubled today by the increase in heart disease, cancer, venereal disease, and other human health problems. But this first plague does not just *increase* disease; *it totally erases health altogether!* All human beings on planet earth who have rebelled against God will personally suffer in their physical bodies for their sin.

The second bowl is poured out, and the sea turns to blood, killing *all* sea life. One can only imagine the smell of death that would permeate the globe as a result. Notice that God does not destroy things by one-third this time, as He did when His judgment was tempered by mercy. His wrath now brings total destruction.

The third bowl is poured out, and *all* fresh water is contaminated as it, too, turns to blood. As the angel pours out the third bowl of wrath, he notes God's justice in forcing those who had shed the blood of God's people to have nothing to drink but blood. If the world is so bloodthirsty, God will give it to them—fountains of blood, springs of blood, rivers of blood, oceans of blood!

The fourth bowl is poured out, and it is as though the sun explodes! It is God's scorched-earth policy! The intense heat will boil the oceans dry and melt the polar ice caps as well as affect the people, unless what is described has more to do with ultraviolet rays that do not affect plant and animal life so drastically but do affect man. If you have ever been overexposed to the sun, perhaps getting a painful sunburn at the beach, you know a little of the agony the inhabitants of the earth will feel as their skin is *seared* by the intense heat!

In the event anyone feels sorry for the "poor, helpless" inhabitants of planet earth at this point, we are given insight into their reaction to God's wrath: "They were seared by the intense heat and they *cursed* the name of God, who had control over these plagues, *but they refused to repent* and glorify him" (Rev. 16:9, italics are mine). *No one* on the entire planet accepts responsibility for the consequences of sin and repents! *Every single person* on the planet curses God and hardens his or her heart in rebellion against Him!

The fifth bowl of wrath is poured out, and the world is plunged into darkness. Even a healthy person can grow morose and miserable after days and weeks of gray, gloomy skies. But remember the people on planet earth during these plagues are extremely unhealthy. Some of the worst nights of my life have been spent when I was ill and unable to sleep. The darkness seems to intensify the suffering and misery because there is no distraction from it. Yet like Pharaoh of old, the people harden their hearts against God even more as the plague of darkness and misery spreads: "Men gnawed their tongues in agony and cursed the God of heaven because of their pains and sores, *but they refused to repent* of what they had done" (Rev. 16:10–11, italics are mine). The *entire population* of planet earth will have a victim's mentality with *no one* accepting responsibility for the outpouring of God's wrath on the human race!

Then the sixth bowl is poured out, and the last world war commences. Because at this point the Antichrist is ruling a world that is disintegrating under the wrath of Almighty God, the nations of the world decide they will no longer tolerate his leadership. The armies of the East, which would presumably involve everything east of

Israel, including China, Japan, and Korea, march against the armies of the West, which would include Europe and possibly the United States. "Then they gathered the kings together to the place that in Hebrew is called Armageddon" (Rev. 16:16).[25] The stage is now set for the last battle on earth that will climax in the physical return of Christ.

Finally the seventh bowl of wrath is poured out, accompanied by "a loud voice from the throne, saying, 'It is done!'" (Rev. 16:17). As a result of this seventh plague, the cities of the world are destroyed, and a global storm changes the topography of the earth: "Then there came flashes of lightning, rumblings, peals of thunder and a severe earthquake. No earthquake like it has ever occurred since man has been on earth, so tremendous was the quake. The great city split into three parts, and the cities of the nations collapsed. God remembered Babylon the Great and gave her the cup filled with the wine of the fury of his wrath. Every island fled away and the mountains could not be found. From the sky huge hailstones of about a hundred pounds each fell upon men" (Rev. 16:18–21a).

Notice in what quick succession these bowls of wrath are poured out! There is no patience or provision or pause—just a steady outpouring of the wrath of a holy God judging a wicked, rebellious world. And what is the world's response? "They cursed God on account of the plague of hail, because the plague was so terrible" (Rev. 16:21b).

As the world hardens its heart in rebellious defiance against Him, God declares, "It is done!" (Rev. 16:17). Jesus Christ had asserted His power to purge the earth of sin and rebellion and evil alliances. With this final plague, all was accomplished that was necessary to prepare for the visible return and reign of Jesus Christ.

But before John was given the vision of the sky unfolding and the Rider on the white horse standing in heaven poised to return, he was given details concerning the fall of Babylon. It's as though he had been looking at the future through a wide-angle lens. Now he zooms in on one important aspect of God's judgment that gives hope to those who are distressed by evil alliances, especially evil alliances that dishonor and defame and destroy God's people. Because the day is coming when Jesus Christ will avenge His people!

Finding Hope in Knowing Jesus Christ Will Avenge His People

Has someone persecuted you? Caused you to suffer unjustly? Abused you for your faith in Jesus Christ and the word of your testimony? Have you repeatedly been humiliated, made to feel inferior and stupid because of your relationship and devotion to Christ? Or have you perhaps watched as a loved one or friend has been demoted professionally, destroyed personally, or devastated emotionally because of his or her stand for Christ? How have you responded? Lee Iacocca, the former chairman of the Chrysler Corporation who is highly regarded in the corporate world, said he taught his children to respond to those who wrong them, not by getting mad but by just getting even!

Vengeance can take many forms. It can be expressed by withholding forgiveness, refusing to speak, seeking a divorce, initiating a lawsuit, slashing with a sharp tongue, destroying someone's reputation through gossip, or just returning like measure. Yet it may be that if we take vengeance into our own hands, God will step back and allow us to substitute our vengeance for His! In other words, if you take vengeance, the offending party may get off much lighter than if you left the vengeance to God!

Jesus said, "Shall not God avenge his own elect, which cry day and night unto him, though he bear long with them? I tell you he will avenge them speedily."[26]

The Bible teaches that while hatred of wickedness, evil, sin, and unrighteousness is right, taking vengeance into our own hands is wrong.

Paul admonished us, "Do not take revenge, my friends, but leave room for God's wrath, for it is written: 'It is mine to avenge; I will repay,' says the Lord."[27]

Revelation 17 and 18 give details concerning the righteous

vengeance of Jesus Christ on behalf of His people. Thousands, if not millions, of people come to faith in Jesus Christ during the first three and one-half years of the Great Tribulation as they respond to God's merciful provision discussed earlier. Once they have received Jesus Christ as their Savior and confessed Him as their Lord, they will then live in a world that is in blasphemous rebellion against Christ. The society in which they live and work and go to school and shop and play and raise their families will be in direct opposition to them. Every citizen on the planet will be required to bear the "name of the beast" so that no one can buy or sell unless he or she has the mark.[28]

To wear the mark would be an outward acknowledgment of loyalty to the beast and would invoke the wrath of God (see Rev. 14:9–12). But without the mark of the beast, they will be effectively severed from all means of support. They will literally be "non-persons," unable to hold a job, buy food or clothing, pay for housing, transportation, or medical care. Those who do not die through starvation, exposure to the elements, or lack of medical attention will be put to death in every conceivable way.

This unparalleled persecution will be orchestrated by an age-old political and religious system referred to in Revelation 17 and 18 as "Babylon." Babylon symbolizes the rebellion of the entire human race throughout all of history against God and His people. The roots of Babylon can be traced back to Genesis 11.

Following the flood, God had twice commanded Noah to "be fruitful and increase in number and fill the earth."[29] But instead of scattering out to fill the earth as God had commanded, Noah's descendants clung together, moving in mass until they came to the plain of Shinar in what is now Iraq. "Then they said, 'Come, let us build ourselves a city, with a tower that reaches to the heavens, so that we may make a name for ourselves and not be scattered over the face of the whole earth.'"[30]

Notice the city was conceived in rebellion. There is nothing wrong with building a city, but the Babylonians emphasized this city was *for themselves!* Their plan was to build a totally humanistic society, one that had no room or need for God.

But while being totally humanistic, they had a religious system symbolized by "a tower that reaches to the heavens." The Babylonians recognized they had spiritual needs; they just decided to meet those needs through a religious system they made up to suit themselves!

It was no wonder that this rebellious city with a rebellious religious creed produced a rebellious culture that wanted to "make a name" for themselves. Pride was their number one virtue! And the rebellious culture produced people with a rebellious conduct who decided to "not be scattered over the face of the whole earth" in direct defiance of God's expressed word.

In response, God, in a unique way, forced them to obey Him, scattering them out all over the world, and along with them, the seeds of rebellion that had taken root in their hearts. The city they were kept from completing was called Babel, and the people who had lived there were known as the "Babylonians."

When John saw the vision of Babylon described in Revelation 17 and 18, he was being given a closer look at a worldwide rebellion that had begun with that ancient city of Babel as depicted in Genesis 11. It is "Babylon" that will be responsible for the coming holocaust, when rebellion against God and His people reaches a boiling point during the Great Tribulation, with the Antichrist and the false prophet at the head of the insurrection. Babylon will be the culmination of the rebellion against God that has continued with every generation in all the ages, and it provokes the vengeance of Jesus Christ on behalf of His people because Babylon is drenched in the blood of the saints:

"One of the seven angels who had the seven bowls came and said to me, 'Come, I will show you the punishment of the great prostitute, who sits on many waters. With her the kings of the earth committed adultery and the inhabitants of the earth were intoxicated with the wine of her adulteries.'

"Then the angel carried me away in the Spirit into a desert. There I saw a woman sitting on a scarlet beast that was covered with blasphemous names and had seven heads and ten horns. The woman was dressed in purple and scarlet, and was glittering with gold, precious stones and pearls. She held a golden cup in her hand, filled with abominable things and the filth of her adulteries. This title was written on her forehead:

MYSTERY

BABYLON THE GREAT

THE MOTHER OF PROSTITUTES

AND OF THE ABOMINATIONS OF THE EARTH.

"I saw that the woman was drunk with the blood of the saints, the blood of those who bore testimony to Jesus" (Rev. 17:1–6).

John uses the symbolism of a prostitute to describe a worldwide religious system that is totally unfaithful to God, His Son, His Word, His gospel, and His truth! Yet this false religious system is embraced by the entire human race and thus becomes responsible for the martyrdom of millions of believers.

It is said that coming events cast long shadows before them. There are times when we can see the shadows of just such a world religion today. Astrology and horoscopes seem to be increasingly accepted as ways to find wisdom and guidance. This fascination with the stars has led to an eastern mysticism that is a mixture of Buddhism and Hinduism called the New Age philosophy. And the New Age has produced hard-core nature worshipers with pagan beliefs who seek a goddess mother as the source of all life![31] The coming world religion may well be a blend of all these beliefs, and much more, as it turns the hearts of the people to pagan practices that match man's more base instincts, resurrecting the ancient Babylonian expression of religious rebellion. As the world surrenders to the embrace of the "prostitute," she will become more and more hostile to God's truth and less and less tolerant of God's people until the worldwide Babylonian religious system seeks to eradicate all Christians from the face of the earth.

In our nation today, there are "reasonable" discussions concerning the validity of abortion and euthanasia, the elimination of unwanted life at both ends of its existence. While abortion is legal in every state and is even funded and protected by the government, euthanasia now seems to be gaining acceptance by the public. The trend seems to be that just as a fetus can be eliminated when unwanted by the mother, an elderly person, or crippled person, or sick person, can be eliminated by consenting parties. In other words, society seems to be paving the way for the elimination of any life deemed unwanted or unproductive—and in the future, those deemed unwanted and unproductive will be believers of any age, any gender, any nationality, any race, any language, any culture, any people who place their faith in Jesus Christ as Savior and Lord!

But when that dreadful day comes, Jesus Christ will intervene to avenge the blood of His people. He will use the Antichrist and his evil alliance with other kings to bring this worldwide Babylonian religious system to ruin. As the Antichrist sets himself up to be god, demanding to be worshiped, he destroys the "prostitute": "They will bring her to ruin and leave her naked; they will eat her flesh and burn her with fire. For God has put it into their hearts to accomplish his purpose" (Rev. 17:16b–17a).

In John's vision, Babylon not only represents a worldwide rebellious religious system but also a worldwide rebellious political system. And the capital of this political system, from which world trade is apparently conducted, is destroyed along with the false religious system: "Fallen! Fallen is Babylon the Great! She has become a home for demons and a haunt for every evil spirit. . . . The kings of the earth committed adultery with her, and the merchants of the earth grew rich from her excessive luxuries. . . . Woe! Woe, O great city, O Babylon, city of power!" (Rev. 18:2–3, 10).

The Babylonians may have believed, as the ship's officer said as the *Titanic* was setting out for her maiden voyage, "Not even God can sink this ship." Babylon was so strong, formidable, and seemingly invincible that she boasted, "I sit as queen; . . . I will never mourn" (Rev. 18:7). But "in her was found the blood of prophets and of the saints, and of all who have been killed on the earth" (Rev. 18:24). And that blood cried out for vengeance!

The city that was indestructible, the power that was "invincible," and the haughty, self-assured people who thought they were superior are destroyed in just one hour as Jesus Christ avenges His people! "Her sins are piled up to heaven, and God has remembered her crimes. Give back to her as she has given; pay her back double for what she has done. . . . She will be consumed by fire, for mighty is the Lord God who judges her. . . . In one hour she has been brought to ruin! . . . Rejoice, saints and apostles and prophets! God has judged her for the way she treated you. . . . He has avenged on her the blood of his servants" (Rev. 18:5–6, 8, 19–20, 19:2b).

God keeps thorough, meticulous accounts. When you are treated wrongly by others, He sees, He cares, and He will avenge in His own time and in His own way.

Not one evil alliance . . .

    No matter how great or small . . .

    No matter how broad or limited . . .

    No matter how powerful or weak . . .

    Whether in the past, present, or future . . .

No one will escape the vengeance of our just, holy, righteous God.
One day, all the rebellion will be crushed.

    All the wrong will be set right.

        All the righteous will be exalted.

One day,

"He who sits on the throne will spread his tent over
    [you].
Never again will [you] hunger;
    never again will [you] thirst.
The sun will not beat upon [you],
    nor any scorching heat.
For the Lamb at the center of the throne will be
    [your] shepherd;
he will lead [you] to springs of living water.
And God will wipe away every tear from [your] eyes."
        (Rev. 7:15–17)

One day, Jesus Christ will appear in person, and He will bring you blessed relief from your tormentors, from those whose evil alliances have caused you to suffer!

Finding Hope in Knowing Jesus Christ Will Appear in Person

As the spectacular, indomitable hub of the world—the city of Babylon—falls, the roar of that destruction and the cries of the dying will impact the entire world. But above the deafening din of weeping and mourning as the splendor of Babylon goes up in smoke, beyond the sound of the world's eulogies for the capital city that in one hour went from glory to the grave, the apostle John becomes aware of another sound.

The Saints Rejoice over the Destruction of the Wicked

The sound John hears is the triumphant roar of approval and praise that goes up in heaven over the destruction of the great enemy of God's people! Greater and louder even than the expressions of blasphemy on earth are the sounds of victory in heaven!

Some may read this and be repulsed by it, thinking, "I don't like this! I don't think this is fair! And I don't think God is right to do this!" But remember: Our sense of rightness and fairness comes from God. In fact, the strongest sense of justice and fairness and rightness we possess is just a shadow of His! And remember also: "God has judged her for the way she treated you" (Rev. 18:20b). As God pours out His wrath on earth, the entire universe is united in thunderous approval: "Salvation and glory and power belong to our God, for true and just are his judgments" (Rev. 19:1b–2a). God, You are fair! God, You are right! God, You are just!

The celebration of the saints must have seemed to John like a swelling tidal wave of joyous triumph sweeping through the universe:

> After this I heard what sounded like the roar of a
> great multitude in heaven shouting:

"Hallelujah!
Salvation and glory and power belong to our God,
    for true and just are his judgments.
He has condemned the great prostitute
    who corrupted the earth by her adulteries.
He has avenged on her the blood of his servants."
And again they shouted:
"Hallelujah!
The smoke from her goes up for ever and ever."

The twenty-four elders and the four living creatures fell down and worshiped God, who was seated on the throne. And they cried:

"Amen, Hallelujah!"

Then a voice came from the throne, saying:
    "Praise our God,
        all you his servants,
    you who fear him,
        both small and great!"

Then I heard what sounded like a great multitude, like the roar of rushing waters and like loud peals of thunder, shouting:

"Hallelujah!
    For our Lord God Almighty reigns." (Rev. 19:1–6)

Even today, saints rejoice on earth in the destruction of the wicked. When we hear news of a drug czar who has been seized, or a serial killer who has been apprehended, or a pornography king who has been imprisoned, or a Mafia boss who has been arrested, we rejoice. We can only imagine, when the entire world is filled with such wicked people in alliance with each other for the purpose of massacring the people of God, how great will be the rejoicing in heaven when the wicked are destroyed!

By Evil Alliances

Saints Rejoice at the Celebration of the Wedding

The saints will not only rejoice at the destruction of the wicked, they will also celebrate the wedding between the Lamb and His bride: "Let us rejoice and be glad and give him glory. For the wedding of the Lamb has come, and his bride has made herself ready" (Rev. 19:7).

The bride is every person since the cross, resurrection, and the ascension of Jesus Christ Who has confessed his or her sin, asked for forgiveness, claimed the blood of Jesus Christ to make atonement for sin, invited Christ into his or her life as Savior and Lord, and is therefore indwelt by the Holy Spirit of the Living God.

The bride is you and me!

It may help us understand the depth of Jesus' feelings toward us when we think of a young adult, perhaps your child, who is looking for that one special person who will be his or her true companion. Perhaps you can remember when you were looking for your life's true companion. How indescribably wonderful it is to find that one person in all the world and have that one person find you! I will never get over the wonder that out of all the women Danny Lotz had met, gotten to know, and dated, he chose me! No one forced him into the relationship. I certainly had no property, position, or prominence that would attract him. He simply chose me because he loved me!

The apostle Paul said that in a similar way the Lord Jesus Christ searched the entire world over and chose you and me to belong to Himself as His bride![32] There was nothing to attract Him to us except His love for us! That is not a problem, as some people would suggest; *it is a blessing!* What a supreme privilege to be the chosen bride of Christ! All other marriages, no matter how sincere and devout and passionate they are, are dim shadows of this exalted relationship!

Paul said that Jesus Christ loved me so much, He gave Himself up for me. He laid down His life for me even before I said my vows of commitment to Him! But when I did say my vows of commitment at the "marriage altar" of the cross, He began working in my life through His Spirit and His Word to make me holy and clean so that on the day of the wedding feast, I might be presented to Him as a radiant bride, without the stain of sin or the wrinkle of guilt or any other blemish of shame![33]

Yet I continue to sin! Although I am deeply assured that I have been washed and cleansed and forgiven by the blood of Jesus, and I am confident I am growing in my faith, and I know my personal relationship with Christ is developing day by day, I still sin! I do not willfully sin. I do not deliberately sin. I do not consciously sin. *But I do sin!* The stronger I grow in faith, the closer I draw to Jesus, the more I learn to love and trust Him alone, the more disgusted, discouraged, depressed, and defeated I become over sin and failure in my life! I am *sick* of sin! *My* sin!

But there is hope for me! God's Word promises "that he who began a good work in [me] will carry it on to completion until the day of Christ Jesus."[34] What I will be like "has not yet been made known. But [I] know that when he appears, [I] shall be like him, for [I] shall see him as he is."[35] *Praise God!*

One day I will no longer struggle with sin.

> I will no longer be inconsistent in commitment.
>
> I will no longer stumble and fall.
>
> I will no longer falter and fail.
>
> I will no longer be tried and tempted.

One day this bride will be ready!!

Yes, there is hope for me—and for you. "Everyone who has this hope in him purifies himself, just as he is pure."[36] The deep desire to be ready at any moment to be ushered into the wedding feast of the Lamb, not as a friend of the family, not even as an honored guest, but as the bride herself, should drive us to purity!

"His bride has made herself ready" (Rev. 19:7b). What are you doing to make yourself ready? If you're like most brides, one of your first considerations is what you will wear for your wedding. John said the bride's wedding garment is made up of "fine linen, bright and clean . . . . [that] stands for the righteous acts of the saints" (Rev. 19:8). If you have ever shopped for a wedding gown, you know there are many different styles, many different qualities, and many different prices. If each of us, as the bride of the Lamb, is dressed in a garment made up of our own righteous acts, what type of gown will you be wearing? I wonder if some of us will look as though we are just wearing a slip because although we were saved we lived for ourselves. Perhaps others will wear gowns fit for Westminster Abbey, with yards and yards and yards of linen making up the spectacular wedding garment because they have lived totally for Christ.

Although I am not sure this is an accurate scenario, it would be interesting to see who was dressed in what. I wonder if some of the Christian celebrities of our day and some of the outstanding "pillars" in the church will be skimpily attired while a poor, unheard-of, unknown outcast from some faraway country will be magnificently clothed!

It will also be interesting, as we sit down to feast at the table, to look around and see the characteristics of the bride.

Black, yellow, brown, red, and white . . .

Rich and poor . . .

Young and old . . .

Male and female . . .

Wise and simple . . .

Educated and ignorant . .

Strong and weak . . .

Influential and ignored . . .

From every ethnic group, language, culture, generation, and nation . . .

The various traits will be like the facets of a priceless jewel, causing the bride to sparkle in all her radiant beauty as she reflects her Bridegroom!

As we gather around the table, the mood will be jubilant. Hallelujah! Hallelujah! Hallelujah! Hallelujah! Four times this great hallelujah chorus will thunder from the vaults of heaven, echoing throughout the universe. The wedding of the Lamb is an occasion of unsurpassed joy! "Hallelujah! For our Lord God Almighty reigns.

Let us rejoice and be glad and give him glory!" (Rev. 19:6b). If we are to fully enter into the joy of that moment in the future, we need to begin to prepare for it in the present. Get ready!

The vision of His glory reveals, in the end, the greatest joy the world has ever known. The saints rejoice over the destruction of the wicked. The saints rejoice at the celebration of the wedding. The saints rejoice as the Son returns!

The Saints Rejoice As the Son Returns

Jesus is coming! He is coming one day to appear on earth in person, visibly and victoriously!

John looks, and with the same eyes that had seen Jesus Christ alive on earth in ministry . . .

The same eyes that had seen Jesus Christ crucified, dead, and buried . . .

The same eyes that had seen Him raised from the dead and ascend into heaven . . .

The same eyes that had witnessed countless atrocities against those who bore His Name . . .

Now those very eyes see the sky split open, revealing the visible, physical appearance of Jesus Christ! He has kept His Word! He has come back to rescue His people and to rule the world: "I saw heaven standing open and there before me was a white horse, whose rider is called Faithful and True. With justice he judges and makes war" (Rev. 19:11).

He is coming, and He is angry! "His eyes are like blazing fire" (Rev. 19:12a) because He is filled with God's wrath against all sin and wickedness and rebellion against Himself. And "on his head are many crowns" (Rev. 19:12b). These crowns are not the ones given to you and me as rewards for our service; these are not the crowns we will lay at His feet in worship. These are the crowns the kings of the earth had dared to wear! In their presumption and arrogance, they thought they could rule the world without Him! But He will strip the crowns from the heads of the pretenders to the throne, and rightfully wear them Himself because He is King of kings and Lord of lords!

The people and leaders of planet earth have been cursing and blaspheming His Name. But when He returns, they are not allowed to even *know* His Name, much less speak it! John said, "He has a name written on him that no one but he himself knows" (Rev. 19:12c). From this point on, He is unapproachable by those who are not His!

"He is dressed in a robe dipped in blood" (Rev. 19:13a). The blood that stains His robe is not His own, shed at the cross. Nor is it from the millions of martyrs slain in His Name and for His sake! That blood is the blood of His enemies, and its appearance at the end was described thousands of years ago by the prophet Isaiah:

> Why are your garments red,
>   like those of one treading the winepress?
> "I have trodden the winepress alone;
>   from the nations no one was with me.
> I trampled them in my anger
>   and trod them down in my wrath;
> their blood spattered my garments,
>   and I stained all my clothing."[37]

The robe that was stripped from Him at the cross, the robe that was rudely gambled for while He hung dying, now drips in the blood of those who have dared to lift a hand against Him and His people! The sight is so terrifying, I don't know how John continued to look! Surely our fear of such a terrible, awesome God should drive us to our knees in repentance of sin that provokes such anger!

"His name is the Word of God" (Rev. 19:13b). The Bible that people even today deny, distort, dilute, defy, doubt, and disobey *is the same as His Name!* While the Bible is the written Word of God, and Jesus Christ is the living Word of God, both are revelations of God. Oh, how careful we must be concerning our attitude and our handling of the Book, which is the Word of God! He considers our reception or rejection of the Bible to be reception or rejection of Himself. Jesus Christ, the King of kings and Lord of lords, is so identified with it, it is His Name!

When Jesus appears, John sees that He is not alone: "The armies of heaven were following him, riding on white horses and dressed in fine linen, white and clean" (Rev. 19:14). The army of heaven is the bride of Christ, coming from the wedding feast, still robed in her wedding gown, to share in the glory of her Bridegroom—to rule and reign with Him on earth![38]

The next scene John describes is almost beyond comprehension. As the sky unfolds, revealing the Rider on the white horse wearing the crowns of the kings of the earth and dripping in the blood of His enemies, with the sharp sword of His Word coming from His mouth, "with which to strike down the nations" (Rev. 19:15a), there is no question as to His intention. He is returning to tread "the winepress of the fury of the wrath of God Almighty (Rev. 19:15a). He is returning to avenge and rescue His own. He is returning to totally destroy every evil alliance, rebellion, wickedness, and all that have set themselves against God, His truth, and His people.

There is *also* no questions as to His identity. But, in the event someone is in doubt, written on His robe and on His thigh is one of His titles:

KING OF KINGS AND LORD OF LORDS.

Then in stunning, unbelievable defiance, "the beast and the kings of the earth and their armies gathered together to make war against the rider on the horse and his army" (Rev. 19:19). How could One Who is so good and kind and gracious and loving and true and right and just be the object of such vicious, deep-seated hatred? How could it be that every single heart of every single person on planet earth is so depraved and wicked that although they had gathered to fight each other, they now unite in the ultimate evil alliance to make war against the Lamb? I know individuals with hate-filled, rebellious attitudes toward Christ, but an entire world like that? It defies imagination!

Yet John said he saw it! The people alive on earth look up and see Jesus! They know He is the Lamb, the Messiah, the Son of God, the Creator of the universe! They see Him! They know Who He is!

They know He is returning to rule the world! But their hearts are so hardened, instead of falling on their faces in repentance before Him, they unite in their rebellion against Him! The beast and the kings of the earth marshal the armies of the world. They line up their tanks! They aim their missiles! They poise their nuclear weapons! They position their battleships! All to make war against the One Who is Lord! Against the One Who is their Creator!

And while this is happening is there fear in heaven? Is there any cause for alarm? Are the King and His army in danger? No! No! No! A thousand times *No!*

The very hand of God reaches down and seizes the beast and the false prophet, throwing them into a place many people today say does not exist! But it does exist! It is a place prepared for all those who have hardened their hearts in rebellion against Christ! It is "the fiery lake of burning sulfur" (Rev. 19:20). And the first two to enter its torment are the two who had tormented God's people!

Following the capture and destruction of the beast and the false prophet, does the battle commence? Does the war rage? No! There is no war at all! The King simply speaks a word, and everyone else drops dead! "The rest of them were killed with the sword that came out of the mouth of the rider on the horse" (Rev. 19:21a) as every evil alliance is defeated and destroyed by the living Word of God Who is the King of Kings!

On June 2, 1995, while flying a mission for the United States Air Force in cooperation with the United Nations, Captain Scott O'Grady was shot down by a surface-to-air missile over Bosnian territory in Eastern Europe. When his plane exploded out from under him, he was able to safely eject. As he slowly parachuted down to earth, he did so with growing fear and dread as he saw people, including enemy soldiers, watching and waiting for him.

He landed in a grassy clearing slightly away from the gathering crowd, quickly shed his parachute, and dashed to hide in a small clump of bushes. There he plunged his face into the dirt, covering his ears with his green-gloved hands so that no bare skin would attract the attention of any searchers. Within four minutes of his landing, the area was swarming with Serbs who were furiously looking for him.

For the next six days, Captain O'Grady eluded his would-be captors by remaining frozen during the day with his face in the dirt, moving very cautiously only at night. Those searching for him with guns and bayonets often passed within three feet of where he lay hidden. Cows leisurely cropped grass around his legs while he lay prostrate beneath bushes. He survived by eating bugs, leaves, and grass and by drinking what little dew and rainwater he could collect. His days and nights were filled with the terror of possible capture by the enemy.

Listen to his own testimony: "I prayed to God and asked him for a lot of things, and he delivered throughout the entire time. When I prayed for rain, he gave me rain. One time I prayed, 'Lord, let me at least have someone know I'm alive and maybe come rescue me.' And guess what? That night T.O. [air force pilot Thomas O. Hanford] came up on the radio."[39]

On the sixth day, at 2:08 in the morning, he was hungry, lonely, cold, afraid, and the object of a massive enemy ground search. It was then, after a week of thwarted efforts, he made radio contact with a U.S. plane that relayed his message and location to the rescue team. When he shot off a yellow flare at 6:35 A.M. so that rescue helicopters could pinpoint his location, fog rolled into the valley, blinding the villagers to anything taking place above them. When the helicopters dropped out of the sky, Captain O'Grady ran for his life toward them.

As he scrambled across the threshold into one of the waiting helicopters, his chest was heaving, he was sobbing, and he kept repeating, "Thank you, thank you, thank you."

Captain Scott O'Grady was thrilled to be rescued from enemy territory!

But his thrill is only a shadow of the thrill Christians all over the world will one day experience at the end of the Great Tribulation. After not just six days, but seven years of being hungry and cold and lonely and hunted by a hostile, Antichrist-dominated society and after years of praying for deliverance and living in enemy territory, the sky will unfold to reveal their rescue team, led by the One Who is faithful and true!

Except for the vision of His glory, our distress over evil alliances would increase until that day, because the world will get progressively worse and more hostile to Christ and His people. But the vision of His glory gives us hope because it reveals that one day, Jesus Christ will assert His power. One day, Jesus Christ will avenge His people. One day, Jesus Christ will appear in person to rescue, to rule, and to reign on this earth. One day, oh, glorious day! Jesus Christ will come, just as He said He would!

Hope When You Are Defeated . . .

 *And hope does not disappoint us,*

because God has poured out his love

into our hearts by the Holy Spirit, whom he

has given us.

Romans 5:5

9
Hope When You Are Defeated by Life

Revelation 20:1–15

 The following letter was sent to a Christian leader in Croatia by a former Muslim who has come to Christ and now pastors a small church in war-torn Sarajevo. A missionary translated it into English, and I have left it, punctuation and all, exactly as it was written. It reveals one who would be totally defeated by life, except for his hope in Christ.

Dear Respected Brother,

I would like to inform you that yesterday on Sunday we held services in our dear church. For the first service there were eight of us, all new Christians. . . . I am worried how we can survive over this third cold winter. We are naked and barefoot! Our wardrobes are empty, there is no electricity or water. May God help us! My desire is to live normal for just one month, to eat until I am full, to take a bath, to just once feel human. This is only a dream which I dream. Here it is again dangerous to walk in the city because there is shooting once again. Our people are dying. Every time I leave the apartment, I am not sure if I will return.

I pray to God to protect us and to keep us from every evil. Only our God can help us.

My dear Brother, to me it is the greatest joy that our faith in Jesus can grow and that people get saved and turn to the Lord. These are great riches. Everything else is unimportant and passing away. My life is Christ. May Christ live in me! Amen a hundred times. My tears which now fall while I am writing this letter are of joy because I know that Christ lives in me. Oh thank you God for your joy because I worship you and I am your obedient servant and my faith whispers to me that I can call you my Father. My dear friend, I pray to God for you and for your fellowship. Let peace and love guide you. . . .

In closing I would like to ask if it is possible for you to save us from freezing this winter. . . .

Many greetings in Christ I give to you. . . .

As our hearts are moved in grief and compassion by the eloquence of this Christian brother describing the utter hopelessness of his daily life, we also rejoice! Praise God! There *is real hope* for those defeated by life! One day, the glory of Christ will no longer be just a vision! One day, this dear pastor—and you and I—will see and experience the glory of Christ!

Finding Hope in Knowing We Will Experience the Glory of Christ

No doubt the ground was still trembling and the smoke of battle from Armageddon was still clearing when John witnessed Satan being bound, then thrown into the Abyss, where he was locked and sealed for one thousand years. For one thousand years, Jesus Christ re-enters human history in His physical presence to rule and reign on planet earth without the evil presence, power, and influence of Satan. And He will rule the world as God has always intended the world should be ruled—in perfect righteousness and justice and grace and peace and love! John gives us his eyewitness account:

"And I saw an angel coming down out of heaven, having the key to the Abyss and holding in his hand a great chain. He seized the dragon, that ancient serpent, who is the devil, or Satan, and bound him for one thousand years. He threw him into the Abyss, and locked and sealed it over him, to keep him from deceiving the nations anymore until the thousand years were ended. After that, he must be set free for a short time.

"I saw thrones on which were seated those who had been given authority to judge. And I saw the souls of those who had been beheaded because of their testimony for Jesus and because of the word of God. They had not worshiped the beast or his image and had not received his mark on their foreheads or their hands. They came to life and reigned with Christ a thousand years. (The rest of the dead did not come to life until the thousand years were ended.) This is the first resurrection. Blessed and holy are those who have part in the first resurrection. The second death has no power over them, but they will be priests of God and of Christ and will reign with him for one thousand years" (Rev. 20:1–6).

Who can imagine what it would be like to live on planet earth with Jesus Christ as the visible Ruler of the world? There would be:

No more fear . . .
No more dishonesty,
No more secret deals,
No more land grabs and loan foreclosures,
No more pandering to big money and big corporations,
No more runaway inflation and trillion-dollar deficits,
No more contracts with "small print,"
No more clandestine operations,
No more organized crime—in fact, no more crime at all!
No more civil disobedience,
No more riots,
No more sexual harassment in the workplace,
No more racial prejudice,

No more discrimination for any reason,
No more "ethnic cleansing,"
No more civil wars,
No more wars at all!
No more homeless,
No more beggars,
No more poor,
No more starvation,
No more naked, hungry, barefooted pastors in Bosnia or any-where else!

Our imaginations could go on and on! And those who have suffered because of their identification with Jesus Christ will reign with Him! This honored, elite group of rulers will be made up of those who were "raptured," those who were raised from the dead at the Rapture, and those who had come to faith and been martyred during the Great Tribulation then raised to life at the beginning of the one-thousand-year reign of Christ. In other words, you and I will be among those who will be given authority to judge!

Experiencing His Glory through Service

It may be that the position of authority we will be given during the one-thousand-year reign of Christ will be determined by our previous faithfulness in service on earth. Jesus referred to this possibility in a parable when He said, "Well done, good and faithful servant! You have been faithful with a few things; I will put you in charge of many things. Come and share your master's happiness!"[1]

All through the Bible, we are encouraged and exhorted, commanded and compelled, to be faithful in life and in service. Jesus said repeatedly that we are to do our "acts of righteousness" so that our Father, "who sees what is done in secret, will reward you."[2]

My children were always expected to do their share of the housework when growing up. But on those occasions when I did more thorough cleaning, in order to motivate them to wash windows or clean out closets and drawers or polish silver, I offered them the reward of cash. It was amazing to see the difference the promise of a reward made, not only in their attitude, but in the quality of their work! They were much more pleasant in their attitude and much more conscientious in their tasks.

The same is true in the Christian life. The promise of a reward adds eagerness to our attitude and energy to our work. It changes our motivation from "I *have* to do this" to "I *want* to do this." It may be the reward of God's pleasure that motivates us, or the reward of a crown to lay at His feet, or perhaps the reward of a position of authority in His earthly kingdom. If the position of authority that you will be given one day is in proportion to your faithfulness in our Lord's service today, how much responsibility will you have during His future reign on earth?

I find even now, as my love for the Lord Jesus Christ grows, my desire to serve Him grows also. And I am not contented in small, part-time service. I want to serve Him fully and effectively. I want to impact the greatest number of people for Christ that I can. I want to feel that my service makes a difference and really counts for eternity. I want the entire universe one day to applaud Him for what they see in and through my life! If I feel like this when I am living by faith, I can only imagine the intensity of my desire when I see Him face to face! Part of my motivation to be faithful in "a few things" now is the reward of responsibility for greater things in the future.

Regardless of the extent of authority we are given, each of us will have a position of service. We will share in His glory as we serve the King of kings and Lord of lords!

Experiencing His Glory through Serenity

As we share in His glory by serving Him, the entire earth will also experience His serenity. Isaiah described it as the peaceable kingdom where "the wolf will live with the lamb, the leopard will lie down with the goat, the calf and the lion and the yearling together; and a little child will lead them."[3] It will be a time when people will be at peace with God, at peace with each other, and even at peace with the environment!

There will be no more poverty or prisons or hospitals or war.

There will be no more psychiatric wards or army barracks or bars or orphanages or divorce courts.

There will be no more homes for the elderly, no more crack houses, no more halfway houses, and no more houses of ill repute.

There will be no more detox centers, no more drug-rehab clinics, and no more abortion facilities.

There will be no more AIDS or cancer or heart disease or venereal disease or Parkinson's disease or arthritis or diabetes.

There will be no more pollution or crime or slums or roadside litter.

Experiencing His Glory through Satisfaction

As we experience worldwide, blissful serenity, we will also experience deep satisfaction. "Blessed . . . are those who have part in [this]" (Rev. 20:6). The word *blessed* means to be so deeply satisfied that you cannot be more satisfied.

What has been the most satisfying moment in your life? When you signed a contract that secured your financial future? When you sold a house everyone said you could never sell? When you received your diploma after having worked your way through school? When you scored the winning goal for your team in the championship game? When your child was born? When your gift made it possible for a handicapped child to walk? When your care made a sick person well or a sad person happy? When you hiked up a high mountain and made it to the top?

When John said we are blessed as we experience the glory of Christ in His earthly kingdom, it's as though the most satisfying moment of our lives is captured and becomes the eternal state of mind of each person living in the world!

As we serve the Lord in blissful serenity and with deep satisfaction, experiencing His glory on earth, we will begin to reflect Him in our lives, just as the "four living creatures" of Revelation 4 reflected Him.

Experiencing His Glory through Sanctification

In addition to our experiencing God's glory through service, serenity, and satisfaction during this one-thousand-year period, everyone living in the world will also be sanctified by the experience: "Holy are those who have part in [this]" (Rev. 20:6). To be holy is to be separate from sin, to be like Jesus—to be set apart from sin for God, for a unique purpose. The devil will be bound, and there will be no more temptations, no more struggle with sin and our old natures.

I long for the day when I see Jesus and everyone will be like Him![4]

I long for the day when I am no longer in the minority as a believer . . .

I long for the day when what I believe is what everyone believes . . .

I long for the day when I no longer have to endure the painful separation from the world that includes friends and loved ones.

I long for the day when everyone will agree and support and encourage and love and understand each other.

I long for the day when there will be no more criticizers, ostracizers, persecutors, gossips, or liars!

I long for the day when the entire world will be filled with His glory and every living person will be holy as He is holy!

We have been commanded to be holy;[5] we are growing in holiness now,[6] but one day we will be holy! God will complete what He has begun in your life and mine![7]

Experiencing His Glory in Security

Living in such a godly atmosphere, surrounded by such godly people, and engaged in such godly service, we will be absolutely secure! John said, "Blessed and holy are those who have part in the first resurrection.[8] The second death has no power over them, but they will be priests of God and of Christ and will reign with him for one thousand years."

Have you ever been paralyzed by fear? I consider myself to be a fairly strong person and not easily given to fear. But when our house was broken into and robbed, for months I was terrified by strange sounds in our home or strange people at the door. I felt vulnerable and violated, and I was afraid evil persons would come back and take, not just the rest of my things, but my children!

I also remember feeling paralyzed by fear when I went to visit a convicted murderer on death row in our state's maximum-security prison. I was so frightened by the barbed wire, the guards and guns, the heavy gates, and the clanging of the locks that when I tried to sign in with the guard, I could not write my name. I just made a squiggly line of ink with the pen.

What are you afraid of? Both in the prison and after the robbery, I was afraid of evil. Afraid of the power of sin and wickedness and the suffering it brings.

There have been other times when I have felt truly frightened, such as a brushing with death on the highway or losing a child at the state fair. I am afraid of being totally out of control and under the control of violence, such as in a car or plane accident. I am afraid of the devil and demonic activity.

While the second death John describes is hell and separation from God, it also represents our greatest fears in our present life. On the day we experience the glory of Christ as we reign with Him on earth, there will be no fear of evil or the devil or demons or dying or death or judgment or hell. Can you imagine it? There will be no fear. Period. We will be absolutely secure!

Praise God! The vision of His glory reveals hope for those who are defeated by life! We will experience the glory of Jesus Christ, even as we exult in His victory!

Finding Hope in Knowing We Will Exult in the Victory of Christ

For one thousand years, the world will be free from Satan's temptations, accusations, manipulations, deceptions, distortions, and lies. The one who is called Lucifer, son of the morning, the great blasphemer, the murderer from the beginning, the father of lies, the angel of light, the roaring lion, the evil one, the wicked one, the dragon, the serpent—Satan himself will be bound and imprisoned for one thousand years.

Why? Does it give him time to reflect on his sin and rebellion against God? Time even to repent? Is this evidence of God's patience and pause in judgment? Could Satan come out of his imprisonment when the one thousand years are over, fall on his face before Christ, and claim the cross as the basis for forgiveness of his sins? Would God, in His infinite mercy and grace, extend forgiveness and reconciliation to Satan?

We will never know because that is not Satan's reaction when he is released from prison! He does not use the pause as a time to reflect and repent; he obviously uses the time to plot his revenge! He isn't just mad; he wants to get even!

Exulting in His Victory over the Deception

At the end of Satan's one-thousand-year imprisonment that coincides with Christ's one-thousand-year reign on earth (called the Millennium), Satan will be released to deceive those on planet earth for one last time. God uses Satan one final time to reveal that the human heart is desperately wicked, incapable of ever being reformed or remade. If it could be remade, it would be under the one-thousand-year reign of Jesus Christ. But nothing will suffice except a new heart recreated in the image of Christ. Jesus clearly and emphatically pinpointed the solution: "You must be born again."[9]

At the end of the one-thousand-year period the earth will be populated by the believers who were Raptured, the believers who had died and were raised at the Rapture, and those who had come to faith in Christ during the Great Tribulation and been martyred then raised at the return of Christ. Each resurrected person will go into the Millennium in his or her resurrection body. Those who come to faith during the Great Tribulation and somehow miraculously survive will enter the Millennium in their natural bodies. The population will also include the descendants of these survivors.

And it is to these descendants, who will make up the majority of the population at the end of the Millennium, that Satan will turn his attention when he is released.[10]

When the one thousand years of Christ's millennial era are completed, Satan "will go out to deceive the nations in the four corners of the earth. . . . In number they are like the sand on the seashore" (Rev. 20:8). How could those who have lived under the perfect, righteous, just, compassionate reign of Christ on earth be deceived into rebelling against Him? It almost defies the imagination! Certainly the descendants believe in Jesus because He is the physical, visible Ruler of the world for one thousand years!

Is the rebellion made possible because the parents do not pass on to their children the necessity of a personal relationship with Jesus Christ? Have these descendants submitted to the authority of Christ merely because they have never been tempted to do otherwise?

Do these descendants worship Christ and work for Christ just because everyone else does and there is no opportunity to choose an alternative?

However it happens, somewhere along the line, worship of Christ becomes a ritual, work for Christ becomes a job, obedience to Christ becomes orthodoxy, a holy lifestyle becomes a culture, and a personal relationship with Christ becomes a religion. The majority of the population of planet earth go through the outward motions of worshiping and working for Christ. He will be on their lips, but their hearts will be far from Him![11]

When my brother Franklin was small, he was a handful. James Dobson's book entitled *The Strong-Willed Child* could be his autobiography! One morning when my mother called us all to come sit at the table for breakfast Franklin refused. My mother repeated her invitation, which had now become a command: "Franklin, sit down." Again, he refused emphatically: "No, I won't!" At that point my mother began to count to three. We all knew what that meant. If she got to three and Franklin had not obeyed, judgment would fall! So she began, "Franklin, one, two, th—" He quickly sat down then glared up at her defiantly and said, "I may be sitting down on the outside, but I'm standing up on the inside!" His attitude, like that of the descendants during the Millennium, was one of lawless rebellion!

At the end of the Millennium, the descendants of the outstanding men and women of faith who had survived the Great Tribulation (including, I would suppose, even some of the descendants of the 144,000 Jewish evangelists!), will harbor an inward attitude of lawless rebellion. They will be "sitting down on the outside but standing up on the inside!" And Satan knows it!

Have you given Satan an advantage in your life for the same reason? Are you outwardly sitting down, with the appearance of a "good Christian," but inwardly you are resisting the authority of Christ in some area of your life? The area may be small or large; it makes no difference. Your parents or grandparents may have been outstanding men and women of faith. You may even have been raised in the home of a missionary or evangelist or other full-time Christian worker. It makes no difference. Resistance to the Lordship of Christ renders you vulnerable to Satan's attack!

At this point the descendants of the survivors of the Great Tribulation will have never experienced temptation before. They will never have had to exercise their will in choosing right over wrong, good over evil, love over hate, because they will have never even been exposed to anything that was wrong, evil, or hateful!

Imagine how vulnerable these descendants will be to Satan's deception! And what will his deception be? Somehow, Satan will convince them, "Living under the lordship of Christ is bad for you! Submitting to the authority of Christ confines your personality and limits your potentiality! Surrender to His will is not as good for you as living according to your own will! Real freedom and fun are only experienced when you live for yourself!" Somehow, Satan will deceive practically everyone in the world into thinking they would be better off if Jesus Christ was not their Lord and King!

The great deceiver is using the same tactics today as he will then. Has he been working his deception on you? Watch out! Once you are saved, the father of lies will fight tooth and claw to keep you from submitting to the authority of Christ, deceiving you into thinking somehow that the lordship of Christ will make you miserable or at least less happy than you would otherwise be. Actually, the opposite is true! Living under the authority of Christ is where the fullness of blessing is experienced!

Exulting in His Victory over the Deceived

Tragically, at the end of the Millennium the people on planet earth will be deceived into repudiating the authority of Christ and embracing the authority of Satan. Their rebellion destroys the theory that if you can somehow make a perfect world, you can have a perfect people. It also destroys the theory that crime, depression, and dishonesty are the result of the environment in which we live. And it proves the fallacy of believing that if we could just order a new world with educational opportunities for all, with enough money for everyone to live comfortably, with enough food and housing for everyone, where peace and love ruled supreme, where truth and justice prevailed for the great and the small . . . then people would be perfectly happy, content, and good! The rebellion at the end of the Millennium proves otherwise!

This rebellion should serve as a warning to you and me. If we claim to be under the lordship of Christ and therefore feel safe from satanic assault, convinced we are so "mature" in our faith and relationship with Christ that we would never rebel, we need to watch out! If those living under the lordship of Christ for one thousand years will be capable of rebellion against Him, you and I are also capable of rebellion against Him.

Why is this so? Because, according to Jeremiah's insight, "the heart [of man] is . . . desperately wicked: who can know it?"[12] Each person born into the human race yesterday, today, tomorrow, or at the end of the Millennium is born with the seed of sin in his or her heart. Given time and the right opportunity, that seed sprouts and produces the fruit of rebellion against God and against Christ.

The majority of the descendants during the Millennium buy into Satan's deception. They march on Jerusalem, from which Jesus Christ rules the world, with the apparent intent of overthrowing the One Who is Lord of lords and King of kings! What pride! What arrogance! What presumption! What sin! What wicked deception to think they could defy the authority of Christ and get away with it! But they don't get away with it: "Fire came down from heaven and devoured them" (Rev. 20:9b).

There is no discussion, no argument, no hearing, no trial, no treaty, no terms of surrender. There is just immediate destruction and judgment!

Since the Garden of Eden, rebellion against the authority of Christ has always begun with the devil's deception, and it always ends in destruction. Only this time, it ends in the devil's destruction as well!

Exulting in His Victory over the Deceiver

"And the devil, who deceived them, was thrown into the lake of burning sulfur, where the beast and the false prophet had been thrown. They will all be tormented day and night for ever and ever" (Rev. 20:10).

I can almost hear the sigh of relief and the shout of victory that goes up from God's people as Satan disappears in the sulfuric inferno! The devil is destroyed! Forever! Praise God! Oh, that the day of his destruction would be hastened!

I once passed a little country church with this sign on the marquee on the front lawn: "When the devil seeks to remind you of your past, just remind him of his future!" That small congregation of believers was already exulting in the coming victory! They understood that the devil is used by God for His own purposes, but only temporarily. His days are numbered, and his time is short.

The vision of the glory of Jesus Christ gives hope to those defeated by life because it reveals that when all is said and done, ours is the victory! One day, we will share in the glory of Christ! One day, we will exult in the victory of Christ! One day, we will escape the penalty of Christ!

Finding Hope in Knowing We Will Escape the Penalty of Christ

Generally speaking, society today seems to be convinced there is no final penalty for sin. That seems logical since society also seems to be convinced there is no such thing as sin. And they have reduced *the* God to *a* god within themselves—or in rocks, in trees, or in crystals—who may be called by any name they care to give him. Many of these people have embraced a mechanical, godless evolution, which, when followed to its logical conclusion, teaches that we are all a mistake, that we are a great cosmic accident, that our lives therefore do not count, that we have no reason for existence, that there is no Creator to Whom we must give an account, that in the end we all just snuff out!

Even those who think there is something "out there" after death have been misled by stories of those who say they have died and come back from the dead to tell their experience. Usually they relate that when they died, they entered into a warm, bright light. They usually say they felt intense peace and love. In other words, they are saying, "Relax. Death is nothing to fear. There is no judgment or penalty to come. There is no accountability for life. There is no hell. Just warmth, light, love, and peace!" In fact, some of the most popular movies today have as their theme those who die then "come back" to continue their relationships or engage in some type of work in an outer-body experience or even to play baseball!

But the Bible says, "Man is destined to die once, and after that to face judgment."[13] Whatever else it may be, these persons' experience of death, bright lights, and resurrection is not truth, at least in its implication. The master of deception would appear to have dipped into his bag of tricks, giving the rebellious a sense of false security.

The Place of Judgment

We know there will be a final judgment—John said he saw the place, and he describes it in terrifying simplicity: "Then I saw a great white throne" (Rev. 20:11a). There was no sign of the cross, or the Lamb, or the human form of the Son of Man, or a rainbow encircling the throne, or thousands upon ten thousands of angels, or twenty-four elders, or the four living creatures, or the bride! There was only the blinding purity and holiness of the great white throne, the place of final judgment!

By Life

The Presence of the Judge

As John focused on the throne, he said he saw the presence of the Judge: "Then I saw . . . him who was seated on it. Earth and sky fled from his presence, and there was no place for them" (Rev. 20:11b). Someone was sitting on the throne! Someone Whose presence was so terrible, heaven and earth fled from Him! His Name was not given because He was unapproachable. There was nothing familiar about the Judge, yet we know Who He is. For "the Father judges no one, but has entrusted all judgment to the Son."[14]

The same One Who was Himself brought to the judgment hall and placed on trial . . .

The same One Who was falsely accused, cursed, mocked, blasphemed, slapped, spat upon, and scourged . . .

The same One Who was convicted and crucified for blasphemy for saying He is the Son of God . . . *IS the Son of God!* And now He sits on the great white throne as the Judge of all the universe—the Judge of all those who have rejected Him!

From His presence, heaven and earth will flee! Everything familiar will be gone! Every recognizable landmark will disappear! There will be no hiding place! There will be no means of escape! There will be only a vast eternal emptiness, a place of judgment, the presence of the Judge, and individual people to be judged.

The People Who Will Be Judged

Every unbeliever of every generation, of every age, of every family, tribe, nation, and language will be raised to stand before the Judge. One by one. Individually. You can almost hear the hushed horror in John's voice as he describes those who are brought before the Judge: "I saw the dead, great and small, standing before the throne. . . . Each person was judged" (Rev. 20:12a–13b). Those who were buried at sea or on land, those who were eaten by cannibals or who died peacefully in their sleep, those who were burned on some fiery pyre or embalmed in some Egyptian tomb, those who were laid to rest in satin-lined caskets or in primitive pine boxes, those who were buried in vaults, surrounded by treasure, and those whose bodies were left for the vultures—all will be raised to stand before the Judge! God knows every speck of human dust, and He calls it forth from deserts, caves, jungles, seas, tombs, ghettos, and palaces!

Those who were "great"—

    emperors,

      pharaohs,

        caesars,

          kings,

            queens,

              rulers,

            presidents,

        professors,

      CEOs,

      and internationally acclaimed prize winners—

Each stands alone before the great white throne and the Judge from Whose presence everything fled! Those who were great cannot escape!

Those who were "small"—

    the poor,

      the uneducated,

        the homeless,

          the street people,

            the boat people,

              the underprivileged,

            the illiterate

            the untouchables,

          the beggars

        the faceless masses of

        India and China and

          Africa and America—

Each stands alone before the great white throne and the Judge from Whose presence everything had fled! There is no escape for the small! One by one by one, those who have been good, moral, pagan, or religious, and those whose sin is big or small, black or gray or "little white" ones—all stand before the Judge!

The Proof of Justice

How do we know each of these millions and billions of people will get a fair trial? Because John said he also saw the proof of justice: "And books were opened. Another book was opened, which is the book of life. The dead were judged according to what they had done as recorded in the books . . . If anyone's name was not found written in the book of life, he was thrown into the lake of fire" (Rev. 20:12b, 15).

Each person's life has been carefully recorded in heaven. It may be that every person who has ever been born into the human race has his or her name recorded in the Book of Life. But when that person dies, having rejected God's gracious salvation, his or her name is blotted out of the Book of Life.[15] How utterly tragic to think that Jesus Christ died to reconcile the world to Himself,[16] yet as the pages of the book are turned, again and again blank spaces appear where the names of those who had been died for could have been recorded but instead were blotted out because they rejected Christ! Could it be? Each one, as he or she is thrown into the lake of fire, goes knowing his or her name had been recorded in the Book of Life but was blotted out by his or her own choice to reject God's gracious salvation through Christ! God does not send the rebellious to hell since sinners are already condemned to go there.[17] Instead, God so loved the world of sinners that He gave His own Son to die on the cross so all might be saved. In rejecting God's offer of salvation, the rebellious themselves choose to go to hell.

Each person is also judged according to his or her works, just as many people today believe. However, to be judged according to our works is to be condemned, because no one can do enough works or do them so well that we can please a holy, righteous God with standards of perfection. It is the final proof of justice that each person understands the Judge is fully acquainted with every detail of his or her life and reaches the verdict of "guilty" because he or she does not meet the Judge's standards.

One by one. . .

> *Each person* who said believing in the cross was not necessary . . .

> *Each one* who said there are other ways to God besides Jesus Christ . . .

> *Each one* who believed we all have our own gods, and as long as we are sincere it doesn't matter what we believe . . .

> *Each one* who charged it is legalistic and narrow-minded to think there is only one way to God . . .

> *Each one* who hoped their good deeds would out-weigh their bad deeds so that God would let them into heaven . . .

> *Each one* who decided to just take the chance, believing a loving God would never send anyone to hell . . .

> *Each one* who said there is no such thing as judgment and hell, that there is no such thing as God . . .

One by one, every single person who has stood before the great white throne is cast into the lake of fire. Each one is eternally condemned, not because this will be the desire of the Judge but because each one had rejected His offer of grace!

Who do you know who is determined to stand on his or her own record? To stand on your own record is to be cast into the lake of fire! And what is the lake of fire? It is hell. Perhaps it is best described in contrast to heaven.

Hell is a place of intense suffering—of gnashing of teeth and weeping.[18] The only time I remember gnashing my teeth and weeping was during the intense pain of childbirth. In other words, hell is a place of intense physical suffering and excruciating torment.[19] But *in heaven, there is "no more death or mourning or crying or pain."*[20]

Hell is a place of no security. It is described as a bottomless pit, the Abyss.[21] To be placed into a bottomless pit would be to have the sensation of falling, falling, with nothing to cling to, nothing to catch yourself on, nothing to break your fall. In contrast, *heaven is a city with high walls and strong gates.* Those within are absolutely secure.

Hell is a place where there is no stability. It is sometimes described as a "lake,"[22] a place having no firm foundation. There is nothing on which to stand. *Heaven is a city with twelve foundations.*[23] It is a place to stand, and walk, and live for all time.

Hell has no sunshine or light. Have you ever heard people say they won't mind going to hell because all of their friends will be there and they will just "party it up"? Well, all your friends may be there, and you may hear the screams of those in torment as they gnash their teeth, but you will never see even one of them, because hell is a place of total darkness.[24] *Heaven is a place where "there will be no more night."*[25]

Jesus spoke of "the fire of hell."[26] Again and again, it is described as a place of searing, burning fire.[27] *Hell is a place of intense dissatisfaction.* Those in hell consciously yearn for what they can never have. And it may well be that it is also a literal fire, where the flesh, like the burning bush of old, continuously burns but is not consumed. If you have ever even burned your finger, you can imagine what it would be like for your whole body to burn for all eternity! In contrast, *the river of life flows through the center of heaven from the throne of God,* bringing life and healing and deep, lasting satisfaction to the nations.[28]

And worst of all, *hell is a place of eternal separation* from the very One for Whom we were created.[29] What would it be like to never know the voice of God, to never feel the touch of God, to never feel the love of God, to never receive any blessing from God at all—to be totally without God forever and ever and ever! To be totally, absolutely, completely devoid of all hope—forever!

The best thing about heaven is that it is a place where God's servants "will see his face!"[30] We will no longer live by faith; we will see Him face to face and live in His presence forever!

God loves you! He loves you so much, in fact, that "he gave his one and only Son, that whoever believes in him shall not perish but have eternal life. For God did not send his Son into the world to condemn the world, but to save the world through him."[31]

If you were to die today and stand before the Judge, what would He say is your eternal destiny? Will you go to heaven or hell? The choice is yours to make. Now. If you were to die today, would there be a blank space where your name had been recorded in the Book of Life but was blotted out because you have never deliberately, consciously made the choice to receive Jesus Christ by faith as your Savior and Lord? If you would like to know that you will be saved from hell, that you will go to heaven when you die, would you take a moment now to quietly, earnestly, pray this prayer:

> *Dear God,*
>
> *I confess to You that I am a sinner. I am sorry for my sin and am willing to repent, to stop sinning. I believe that Jesus Christ died on the cross as the only acceptable sacrifice for my sin. God, I ask You, in Jesus' Name, to forgive me and cleanse me of my sin with the blood of Jesus. I believe that Jesus Christ rose from the dead to give me eternal life. So God, right now, would You give eternal life to me? I open up the door of my heart, my inner life, and invite Jesus to come live within me as my Savior and Lord. I surrender the control of my life to Him, and from this day forward, I will seek to live for Him. In Jesus' Name, Amen.[32]*

If you have just prayed this prayer, or if you have prayed a similar prayer in the past, praise God! Regardless of your present circumstances or condition, you have been saved from hell! Your name will never be blotted out of the Lamb's Book of Life!

Until October 25, 1994, Union, South Carolina, was just another small, sleepy, typically southern town unnoticed by the world at large. But on a warm fall evening, a young mother's heart-wrenching pleas thrust Union to the front and center of national and world attention, changing forever the lives of those who live there.

The woman was Susan Smith, who tearfully claimed her two young sons had been abducted in a car-jacking. The entire nation became caught up in the search for little Michael and Alex, only to be stunned nine days later by the shocking announcement that she herself had rolled her car into the John D. Long Lake with her two sons strapped to their car seats. Susan Smith had drowned her own sons!

In the weeks and months that followed, the intense media focus on Susan Smith and the citizens of Union revealed one sordid story after another as the private lives of ordinary townspeople were exposed for all to see. Men and women who were upstanding citizens of the community were publicly stripped of their carefully crafted images and exposed as adulterers, liars, and exploiters. Reputations were shattered by revelations of private abuse, immorality, dishonesty, selfishness, and greed.

Susan's stepfather was an outstanding, widely respected member of the town who was active in civic and church affairs. But as the investigative spotlight settled on him, the disclosures of his sexual molestation of Susan forced him to leave town, returning to furtively slip through the back door of the courthouse in order to give his testimony at her trial. The shameful revelations cost him his job, his family, his reputation, his leadership positions. He said, "I am at the point where I can hardly function."[33]

As the jury-selection process began, the lives of others came under scrutiny. At times the resulting revelations became poignant. One resident of the town was disqualified when it was discovered he was illiterate. Another potential juror was dismissed when she confessed to a hidden past of sexual abuse. One by one, the private lives of friends and neighbors were exposed, and many experienced deep shame and humiliation that will last long after the trial's conclusion.

The shockingly sordid revelations left the entire nation wondering about the private lives of their own neighbors and friends. But even worse, it left many people shuddering at the thought of local law enforcement officers, sheriff's deputies, the FBI and the state bureau of investigation, as well as investigative reporters from around the country, delving into the hidden nooks and crannies of their lives, publishing their findings for the world to read.

While recoiling at the thought of such painful public exposure of private sin, I can't help but wonder what difference it would make if people realized that one day they will stand alone before the Judge and listen as He reads to an attentive universe every private and public word, thought, and deed from the life of each one who appears before Him.[34] Individuals will be not just scrutinized by other sinners, as devastating as that in itself would be, but each life will be scrutinized by the sinless Son of God in the intense light of His holiness, measured against the perfection of His Holy Spirit.

Even as our minds shudder and our faces burn with shame and humiliation at the thought of such scrutiny, the heart of the believer should be filled with overwhelming gratitude for the blood of Jesus Christ that covers any and all sin! Because no one who has ever been to the cross and received the forgiveness of God through faith in Christ will ever be held eternally responsible for sin and guilt. "As far as the east is from the west, so far has he removed our transgressions from us."[35] Praise God! All of our sin, public and private, large and small, past, present, and future, is under the blood of the Lamb!

The vision of His glory gives hope when you are defeated by life because it reveals that . . .

One day you will experience the glory of Christ!

One day you will exult in the victory of Christ!

One day you will escape the penalty of Christ!

Instead of living a life of defeat, choose to live not *just somehow*, but *triumphantly* as you daily rejoice in the coming glory and victory and eternity that will be yours in Jesus Christ!

 *If only for this life we have hope in Christ,*
we are to be pitied more than all men.

1 Corinthians 15:19

10

Hope When You Are Defeated by Death

Revelation 21:1–22:5

 The story is told of an old missionary named Samuel Morrison who, after twenty-five years in Africa, was returning to the United States to die. As it so happened, he traveled home on the same ocean liner that brought President Teddy Roosevelt back from a hunting expedition. When the great ship pulled into the New York harbor, the dock where it was to tie up was jammed with what looked like the entire population of New York City! Bands were playing, banners were waving, choirs of children were singing, multicolored balloons were floating in the air, flashbulbs were popping, and newsreel cameras were poised to record the return of the president.

Mr. Roosevelt stepped down the gangplank to thunderous cheers and applause, showered with confetti and ticker tape. If the crowd had not been restrained by ropes and police, he would have been mobbed!

At the same time, Samuel Morrison quietly walked off the boat. No one was there to greet him. He slipped alone through the crowd. Because of the crush of people there to welcome the president, he couldn't even find a cab. Inside his heart, he began to complain, *Lord, the president has been in Africa for three weeks, killing animals, and the whole world turns out to welcome him home! I've given twenty-five years of my life in Africa, serving You, and no one has greeted me or even knows I'm here.*

In the quietness of his heart, a gentle, loving voice whispered, *But My dear child, you are not home yet!*

Home! What does the word mean to you? For me, it is synonymous with love, acceptance, comfort, and security. It is a place where my needs are met. It is a place where I can take my burdens and lay them down. It is a place not only where I can find answers but where my questions no longer seem to matter. Home for me will always be a log cabin nestled in the mountains of western North Carolina, with a light in the window, a fire on the hearth, and a welcome embrace at the door.

While I praise God for placing me in an earthly home that so clearly reflects my heavenly home, I am aware even now, when I visit that old log cabin, that I am not really "home" yet because of Jesus' promise to me: "In my Father's house are many rooms; if it were not so, I would have told you. I am going there to prepare a place for you. And if I go and prepare a place for you, I will come back and take you to be with me, that you also may be where I am."[1]

Has your entire life been a series of struggles?

Have you been more sick than well?

More defeated than successful?

More tired than rested?

More alone than accompanied?

More empty than satisfied?

More hungry than filled?

More sad than happy?

Do you feel defeated because after a lifetime of struggle, all you have to look forward to is death and a cold grave? Look up! The Lord Jesus Christ is preparing a heavenly home that "no eye has seen, no ear has heard, no mind has conceived . . . for those who love him."[2]

The vision of His glory gives hope to you and me and all those who are ultimately defeated by death as we glimpse the heavenly home our Bridegroom is preparing for those who love Him!

The Hope of a Beautiful Place

John's words describing the glorious vision of our heavenly home came to mind as I stood in front of a reflecting pool gazing at the spectacular beauty of the Taj Mahal in Agra, India: "Then I saw a new heaven and a new earth, for the first heaven and the first earth had passed away, and there was no longer any sea. I saw the Holy City, the new Jerusalem, coming down out of heaven from God, prepared as a bride beautifully dressed for her husband" (Rev. 21:1–2).

The Taj Mahal was built between 1632 and 1653 by Shah Jahan for his wife of fourteen years. Constructed of white marble, it glistens like a jewel on the bank of a wide river. It is framed by four minarets, each one placed at the corner of the red-sandstone platform on which the entire building sits. The exterior of the white-marble structure is inlaid with black onyx in flowing script depicting quotes from the Koran. The interior—including walls, ceiling, and caskets—is inlaid with semi-precious stones in floral designs.

How can one imagine the painstaking craftsmanship involved in completing a project that required over twenty thousand skilled workers and took more than twenty years to complete? How can one imagine the love that conceived such a project in the first place? In the end, the lavishly romantic and wealthy Shah was defeated by death—the death of his beloved wife as well as his own death. The Taj Mahal is a tomb! But if one Indian ruler could build something as exquisite as the Taj Mahal as a place *to bury* his wife of fourteen years, what must Jesus be preparing as a place *to live* with His bride of over two thousand years? The place He is preparing for us shines "with the glory of God, and its brilliance was like that of a very precious jewel" (Rev. 21:11).

Finding Hope in the Preparation of Heaven

John saw our heavenly home "prepared as a bride beautifully dressed for her husband" (Rev. 21:2). Have you ever been involved in wedding preparations? If you have, you know something of the intense effort that goes into getting ready for the big event. The bride spends hours selecting just the right dress. Then she must find the right headpiece to go with the dress. Next she searches for the right shoes to go with the dress and the headpiece, and after that she seeks out just the right jewelry and the right hairdo and the right flowers and the right church and the right music and the right bridesmaids and the right bridesmaids' dresses and the right groomsmen—and hopefully the right groom! And then there is the selection of the place for the rehearsal dinner, the menu for the rehearsal dinner, the place for the reception, the menus for the reception, the bride and groom's cakes for the reception, and the decorations for each event. Preparing for a wedding can be a full-time job for months preceding the actual wedding day! And all of this is just to prepare the bride for her husband!

Of all these elaborate plans, no part of the preparations receives more attention, thought, planning, and care, than the appearance of the bride herself! The morning of my wedding day, my mother brought me breakfast in bed, serving it on the new china and with the new silver I had been given as wedding gifts. After breakfast, I stayed in my bedclothes, resting and taking it easy, so I would be fresh for the marriage ceremony and the reception that would follow that evening. Several hours before I was to leave the house to go to the church, I began to get ready. I started with my makeup, carefully applying it in order to enhance any physical beauty I might have and hide the many flaws I did have! I worked on my hair, sweeping it up so it would stay under the veil yet be visible enough to frame my face. Finally my mother came to my room and helped me get into my wedding gown, fastening the dozens of small buttons up the back and adjusting the chapel-length veil. When I had done everything I knew to do to get myself ready, I just stood in front of the full-length mirror and gazed at the young woman enveloped in ivory silk and lace who was reflected in it. I was tense and eager as I wondered, after six and a half months of preparation, if I would be beautiful and desirable to my husband.

As elaborate as my preparations were as a bride seeking to be beautiful for my husband, they were feeble in comparison with the

Lord God's preparations for His bride, beginning with the very first earthly home. After at least five "days" of intensely creative work, He "planted a garden in the east, in Eden; and there he put the man he had formed. And the Lord God made all kinds of trees grow out of the ground—trees that were pleasing to the eye."[3] Genesis gives us the unforgettable picture of the Lord God, on His hands and knees, grubbing in the dirt, planting trees and flowers and shrubs and grass, watering and pruning and landscaping, preparing a place for Adam and Eve that was pleasing to the eye—beautiful! One can only imagine the joyful eagerness of the Gardener as He presented Adam with his lovingly prepared home that was not just adequate or sufficient to meet his needs but extravagant in its lush beauty and comfort.

But the preparations made for that first earthly home, like the preparations I made for my wedding, or like the shah made for his beloved wife's tomb, are nothing compared with the preparations being made for our heavenly home! Jesus promised, "I am going there to prepare a place for you."[4] That was approximately two thousand years ago! In Revelation 21:6 He proclaims, "It is done. I am the Alpha and the Omega, the Beginning and the End." What God begins, He always completes. God's purpose that began at creation will one day be finished. His preparations will be completed. Our heavenly home will be ready. With loving eagerness and anticipation of our joy, God will present the New Jerusalem—heaven—*to His children only:* "He who overcomes will inherit all this, and I will be his God and he will be my son. But the cowardly, the unbelieving, the vile, the murderers, the sexually immoral, those who practice magic arts, the idolaters and all liars—their place will be in the fiery lake of burning sulfur. This is the second death" (Rev. 21:7–8).

Heaven is not for everyone, just as my home on earth is not for everyone.

The place I call home in western North Carolina is secured by a tall fence, guarded by dogs, and situated on a mountain accessible only by a winding road. While many thousands of people have expressed interest in seeing it, it is off-limits to the general public. Only members of the family or specially invited guests are allowed.

Heaven is also off-limits to the general public! The invitation to come in has been extended to everyone through Jesus Christ at the cross, but when the invitation is refused, the door to heaven is closed. "Nothing impure will ever enter it, nor will anyone who does what is shameful or deceitful, but only those whose names are written in the Lamb's book of life" (Rev. 21:27).

Jesus said some people would try to just "show up," expecting to be admitted and saying to Him: "'Lord, Lord, did we not prophesy in your name, and in your name drive out demons and perform many miracles?' Then I will tell them plainly, 'I never knew you. Away from me, you evildoers!'"[5]

In his response to the would-be heavenly gate-crashers, Jesus described evildoers as those who "prophesied," who quoted Scripture and perhaps even taught Scripture. He described evildoers as those who "drove out demons," who got involved in service and in religious activities, who "performed many miracles," who even seemingly received answers to prayer! But evildoers are also those who never knew Christ! They may have been religious in their lifetimes—indeed, they "prophesied" and "drove out demons" and "performed many miracles"—but they never established a personal relationship with Jesus Christ through faith!

These evildoers will be kept outside and denied entrance into heaven along with the "cowardly," who cared more about what others thought of them than what God thought, and the "unbelieving," who refused to believe that Jesus Christ is the way, the truth, and the life and that no one would get into heaven without coming through faith in Him.[6] Standing outside heaven will also be the vile; the murderers (including those who insisted on and never repented from their "right to choose"); the sexually immoral who called their behavior "fooling around" or "an alternate lifestyle"; those who practice the magic arts of the New Age as well as the old witchcraft; the idolaters who sold their health, their families, their relationships, their integrity, their character, and their very souls, for material possessions;[7] and all liars.

Make no mistake about it! Heaven is a specially prepared place for a particular people! There will be those who will be received and invited to come in, and those who will be rejected and told to stay out. Will you be inside or outside? If you belong to God through faith in Jesus Christ, if you are His child, then your hope is found in heaven, where you will be welcomed into His heavenly home which He has prepared for you! And He has prepared heaven perfectly!

Finding Hope in the Perfection of Heaven

Apparently the fire that annihilates the rebellious at the end of the Millennium will also destroy heaven and earth as we know them today. Peter revealed, "The present heavens and earth are reserved for fire, being kept for the day of judgment and destruction of ungodly men. . . . The heavens will disappear with a roar; the elements will be destroyed by fire, and the earth and everything in it will be laid bare. . . . Everything will be destroyed in this way."[8]

As the old heaven and earth disintegrated, John stood in awed wonder of a "new heaven and a new earth" (Rev. 21:1). What he saw was confirmed by the words of the One Who was seated on the throne: "I am making everything new!" (Rev. 21:5). Imagine it: One day, *everything* will be brand-new!

We bought the house we live in when it was twenty years old, and we have been living in it now for twenty-four years. Because it is nearly forty-five years old, there are some stains I will never be able to remove, some cracks in the tile that can never be repaired, some wear and tear that can give the house a frayed, worn-out look. When I visit some of my friends in their brand-new homes, I look longingly at the fresh, unmarked woodwork and painted walls; the fresh, unstained carpet; the fresh, glistening tile and appliances; the fresh, unscratched windowpanes—it's all fresh! New! Unsoiled and unworn by age!

Planet earth is thousands of years old. Some think it may be millions of years old! And it is showing signs of age. It is getting frayed and worn out. The air is polluted, the water is polluted, natural resources like oil and coal and trees and fresh water are all running out. Some of it is damage man has willfully and selfishly inflicted on it, but some of it is simply due to age! It was not created to last forever!

In contrast, our heavenly home is going to be brand-new! Not just restored, but created fresh! It will not only *look* fresh and new, it will *feel* fresh and new! John gives us, not just a vision of heaven's fresh beauty, but a "feel" of heaven's serenity, which permeates the atmosphere because God is there: "And I heard a loud voice from the throne saying, 'Now the dwelling of God is with men, and he will live with them. They will be his people, and God himself will be with them and be their God. He will wipe every tear from their eyes. There will be no more death or mourning or crying or pain, for the old order of things has passed away'" (Rev. 21:3–4).

In this brand-new home there will be no more death
or pain
or hospitals
or funerals
or grief
or broken homes
or broken hearts
or broken lives
or broken dreams.

There will be no more mental retardation
or physical handicaps
or muscular dystrophy
or multiple sclerosis
or blindness
or lameness
or deafness.

Heaven will be perfect in its quality of life, not only because the life of Christ is lived out in redeemed men and women for all eternity, but because He is the center of it! Heaven is not only our home, it is *His* home! He is not only preparing this place as a heavenly home for you and me, but as a heavenly home for Himself!

We will live with Jesus Christ! Jesus Christ will live with us! We will live with each other! Forever! We will never again be separated from our loved ones or from our Lord. John alluded to this when he said, "There was no longer any sea" (Rev. 21:1).

By Death

I love the sea. Every summer, I spend as much time there as I am able. I love to see the vast expanse of sky and water. I love to hear the waves crashing on the shore. I love to walk along the beach and feel the sand beneath my feet and the breeze blowing gently in my face. But the sea separates families and friends and entire continents from each other! In heaven, there will be *nothing* that separates us from each other or from God. Ever!

No hard or hurt feelings,
    no unforgiving or critical spirit,
        no divorce,
           no fires or famines or floods,
             no business trips,
               no sickness or death,
                 no dangers or hardships,
                   no visible or invisible beings . . .
                     no natural or supernatural powers . . .

Nothing will separate us.

And in heaven there will be perfect health and harmony and unity and unbroken times together! There will not even be the natural separation between night and day, because, "The city does not need the sun or the moon to shine on it, for the glory of God gives it light, and the Lamb is its lamp" (Rev. 21:23). Our heavenly home glows and radiates with light from within.

I have been in some of the great cities of the world at night. I have looked out from Victoria Peak at Hong Kong during the Chinese New Year after sunset, and I have seen the lights transform the hills surrounding the harbor into a virtual fairyland. I have seen Capetown, South Africa, wrapped around Table Mountain at night with the lights looking like a jewel-studded skirt! I have seen Paris from Montmartre after dinner, stretched out for miles in an endless sea of light, with the lighted outline of the Eiffel Tower beckoning like a finger to those who love beauty!

But even in those great cities with their millions of lights, there are still pockets of darkness. In our heavenly home, there will be no darkness at all! No one will ever stumble or be lost or unable to find his or her way. Jesus said, "I am the light of the world,"[9] and He also said *we* "are the light of the world."[10] The sole light in heaven will be the light that comes directly from God through Jesus Christ, which will be reflected in the life of each believer! The entire city will be saturated with the glory and light of Christ! Praise God! Our hope is sure! John records, "Then he said: 'Write this down, for these words are trustworthy and true'" (Rev. 21:5). In other words, God says all of His promises are true, and you can count on the hope of heaven.

Finding Hope in the Physical Place of Heaven

As John goes on to describe our heavenly home, he seems to be emphasizing to us that what he saw was a literal, specific, physical place:[11] "The angel who talked with me had a measuring rod of gold to measure the city, its gates and its walls" (Rev. 21:15). Heaven is for real! It is a physical place that can be felt and seen and measured! As we progressively destroy planet earth, it is exciting to contemplate that somewhere in the universe at this very moment, our heavenly home is being prepared for us! As this world ends, a new world begins.

From time to time people have asked me, and I have wondered myself, what heaven will be like. With no sea, will it be less enjoyable than earth and its mighty oceans? With no sunsets or sunrises or full moons or shooting stars, will it be less beautiful than the vast expanse that spreads over our earthly home? I wonder . . . then I remember that Jesus knows exactly what brings me pleasure and joy! The Creator Who created all the earthly beauty we have grown to love—

The majestic snow-capped peaks of the Alps,

The rushing mountain streams,

The brilliantly colored fall leaves,

The carpets of wildflowers,

The glistening fin of a fish as it leaps out of a sparkling sea,

The graceful gliding of a swan across the lake,
The lilting notes of a canary's song,
The whir of a hummingbird's wings,
The shimmer of the dew on the grass in early morning,

This is the *same* Creator Who has prepared our heavenly home for us! If God could make the heavens and earth as beautiful as we think they are today—which includes thousands of years of wear and tear, corruption and pollution, sin and selfishness—can you imagine what the new heaven and new earth will look like? It will be much more glorious than any eyes have seen, any ears have heard, or any minds have ever conceived![12]

And John saw it! He said our future home has "a great, high wall . . . made of jasper" (Rev. 21:12, 18). The wall is described as being over two hundred feet thick! It is so strong that those within are eternally secure. As we discussed in chapters 3 and 5, jasper is a stone similar to a diamond. Can you imagine the beauty of two-hundred-foot-thick walls made of "diamonds" that reflect the light of the Lamb?

The city and its streets are made of pure gold[13] as transparent as glass (Rev. 21:18, 21). Everywhere we look, every step we take, will reflect the glory and light of the Lamb! In such a city, there will not be any shadows to mar the perfect purity and beauty.

We know the foundation of the heavenly city is Jesus Christ. He is described as the living stone, the cornerstone, and the capstone of the temple of God.[14] He Himself said He was the Rock on which He would build His church.[15] John describes the foundation in more detail: "The wall of the city had twelve foundations, and on them were the names of the twelve apostles of the Lamb. . . . The foundations of the city walls were decorated with every kind of precious stone" (Rev. 21:14, 19). The walls of our heavenly home are actually built on twelve foundations of Rock, each one decorated with a different gem representing the many facets of the character of Christ. And every facet is beautiful!

These twelve foundations of Rock have more than gems embedded in them. Each one is also engraved with the name of one of "the twelve apostles of the Lamb" (Rev. 21:14), who were responsible for revealing to the world the glory of the character of Jesus Christ! The entire outward appearance of the city from height to depth reflects Christ.

I wonder what John thought when he saw his heavenly home with his own name engraved on one of the foundations . . . What a thrill it must have been when he realized all of his work and witness for Christ on earth, for which he had been beaten, imprisoned, and now exiled, had been stored up for him in heaven as a glorious treasure![16] His life's work was all worth it because it had eternal value! His hope was found in heaven!

And I wonder, how will Abraham feel when he sees the city for the first time? About four thousand years ago, Abraham left Ur of the Chaldees, looking for "the city with foundations, whose architect and builder is God."[17] Can you imagine Abraham bursting through the gates, running into the heavenly city, shouting, "I've found it! I've finally found it! I've found what I was looking for! I've found what I have been hoping for! All the days and nights of wandering and living in tents were worth it! All of God's promises are true!" All of Abraham's goals and hopes and dreams—those things that were the driving motivational forces in his life—had been focused on his eternal home, and he will not be disappointed!

My husband has played basketball all of his life. He grew up playing in the streets of New York City, in backyard lots, on playground courts, and even in an old barn his father had converted for that purpose. One of his childhood dreams was realized when he was given a four-year scholarship to play at a major university. The second year he played at the university, his team went undefeated for thirty-two straight games. They not only won the NCAA national championship, but their season set an all-time record that still stands! It was the accomplishment of a lifelong goal that had consumed hours and hours of time, effort, and energy. My husband describes the experience of winning that final game for the national championship—in triple overtime!—as a thrill he had not experienced before or since. But within a few short hours, the thrill was gone, an emptiness set in, and he wondered, "Is that all there is?" A dust-collecting plaque, a few newspaper clippings that have grown yellow, and memories that have faded with time are all that are left of the thrill that was the dream and achievement of a lifetime.

When the game of life is over and we step into eternity, I wonder how many people will have that same empty feeling of, "Is that all there is? Is that all there is to my life's work and dreams and achievements?" I wonder what treasures we will have in heaven as evidence of our work and witness on earth.

Or like Abraham, will we shout, "I found it! I finally found it! Everything I dreamed of and worked for is here! All of the sacrifice I made on earth has been compensated a hundred times over in heaven! It was all worth it! I found all I hoped for—and more!"

I can hardly wait to walk through those heavenly gates!

And speaking of the gates . . . . they are perhaps the single most spectacular characteristic of our heavenly home. Incredibly, "the twelve gates were twelve pearls, each gate made of a single pearl" (Rev. 21:21). Can you imagine how large those pearls would have to be, to be set in walls that are two hundred feet thick?

Pearls are formed when a small grain of sand becomes embedded in an oyster, irritating it. To soften the irritation, the oyster coats the grain of sand with a smooth layer of what is called mother of pearl. As long as the oyster can feel the irritation, it continues to coat the sand with layers of pearl. What kind of irritation would have been necessary to form the pearls that make up the gates to our heavenly city when they are so large they can fit into a wall that is two hundred feet thick?! It must have been more than just irritation. It must have been horrendous, severe suffering!

I wonder . . . are the pearls a reminder, every time we enter our heavenly home, that we enter only because of the intense suffering of the Pearl of Great Price? Do those pearly gates reflect the cross of Jesus Christ? Will they be a continual reminder to us of what it cost Him personally to throw open the gates of that city and welcome us home? As we enter our heavenly home through portals of pearl, we will be enveloped by symbols of His sacrificial love for us.

Finding Hope in the Population of Heaven

And who will live within those gates? Heaven is the most beautiful place ever imagined, but it's not a mere showplace; it is a home! It is the home of the Lord God Almighty and the Lamb. John said, "I did not see a temple in the city, because the Lord God Almighty and the Lamb are its temple" (Rev. 21:23).

The Greek word for "temple" is, in this case, the same word used for the "Most Holy Place" that was the inner sanctuary of the ancient Israelites' tabernacle, and later the temple. It was the place where God dwelt. The high priest could only enter once a year to sprinkle the sacrificed animals' blood on the mercy seat in order to make atonement for the sin of God's people.[18] Hebrews teaches us that today "we have confidence to enter the Most Holy Place by the blood of Jesus, by a new and living way opened for us through the curtain, that is, his body."[19] In other words, through the death and broken body of Jesus Christ, you and I have been given access to the presence of God when we approach Him by faith and prayer.

In our heavenly home, we will not just have occasional access to the presence of God; we will *live* in His presence! Every moment! Every day! Every week and month and year! For all eternity!

Before I realized this truth, I was troubled by a crisis of spirit. I thought that when we get to heaven, you would live there, and I would live there, and Jesus would live there, and maybe one day He would come to visit me in my "mansion" then leave and go visit you in yours! In other words, I thought there would be moments when I would not be in His actual, visible presence! But then I realized that when John said "the Lord God Almighty and the Lamb are its temple," he was describing our entire heavenly home as the Most Holy Place. There will be *no place* in heaven where Jesus Christ is not physically, visibly present! Because He is omnipresent, He will live fully and completely with me every moment, as though I were the only resident of heaven! And He will live every moment fully and completely with you as though you were the only resident of heaven! What a wonderful place heaven will be!

Not only will the Lamb and His loved ones live in the heavenly city, but the leaders of the nations of the earth will also come in and out of it. John described his view of the procession: "The nations will walk by its light, and the kings of the earth will bring their splendor into it. On no day will its gates ever be shut, for there will be no night there. The glory and honor of the nations will be brought into it" (Rev. 21:26).

Who are these leaders of the nations of the earth? Since we are told the only ones who enter the heavenly city are those whose names are written in the Lamb's Book of Life, the leaders and kings who come and go must be redeemed humanity—you and me! Apparently we will be given positions of leadership and responsibility in the new earth so that we might uniquely serve Christ for all eternity. No matter where our service takes us or what our service is, it will ultimately be for the glory of Christ.

And as we enter our heavenly home, we will have the indescribable joy of laying at our Lord's nail-pierced feet any glory and honor we have received. There will be no hidden agendas, no ulterior motives, no secret ambitions, no selfish pride in heaven. Everyone— *every* single person—will live and serve for the praise and glory of Jesus Christ! It's no wonder our heavenly home is not only a beautiful place, it is a blessed place!

Our Hope of a Blessed Place

If heaven were a beautiful place only, it would not be enough. But heaven is also a blessed place—a place that receives the fullness of God's favor. A place that is completely, totally, absolutely, serenely, permanently happy.

Finding Hope in the Source of Blessing

We have already considered John's description of the throne as the authority of God and the lordship of Jesus Christ. Now John sees "the river of the water of life, as clear as crystal, flowing from the throne of God and of the Lamb down the middle of the great street of the city" (Rev. 22:1). The river symbolizes the eternal blessing of God. And it flows from the throne. The source of all blessing has been, is, and forever will be the throne, or the authority of God and the Lordship of Jesus Christ! Abundant life, rich blessing, deep satisfaction, permanent peace, all come from having a right relationship to the throne. That will be true in heaven, and that is true today.

When Jesus Christ is in full authority in your life . . .

When you have completely surrendered yourself to Him . . .

When His will is your will . . .

When you deeply desire what He wants more than what you want . . .

When you deny yourself, take up your cross daily, and follow Him . . .

When you live in a right relationship to the throne . . .

That's when the river flows!

Jesus promised us this when He said, "Whoever believes in me, as the Scripture has said, streams of living water will flow from within him." John explained, "By this he meant the Spirit, whom those who believed in him were later to receive."[20] When you receive Jesus Christ by faith as your Savior, the Holy Spirit comes to live within you. And when the Spirit of the Lord is Lord of your life, the river runs freely[21] within you to fill your life with blessing and to flow from you as a source of blessing to others! But the Spirit *must* be the Lord of your life!

Finding Hope in the Course of Blessing

On the bank beside the road going up the mountain where I grew up, there is a freshwater spring. My mother had it dug out, lined with rocks, and then had a pipe put into it. To this day, the water flows from the spring, through the pipe, into an old oak bucket that then fills up with fresh spring water, overflowing into a ditch beside the road.

On occasion, a small pebble or leaf or salamander gets lodged in the pipe, slowing or stopping the flow of the water into the bucket.

Mother then runs a slender stick through the pipe to dislodge the blockage so the water can once again run freely.

Our lives are like that oak bucket, connected to the living Water of the Holy Spirit by our personal relationship with God through faith in Jesus Christ. When the Holy Spirit lives within us and we are totally yielded to Him, we are filled with living Water to the extent we overflow into the lives of those around us.

But if something hinders our relationship with God, the flow of the Holy Spirit in and through our lives is blocked. And the hindrance does not have to be large. It can be a "small" sin or "minor" resistance to the will of Christ in some area, or it can be a grudge held silently or lustful thoughts or an unkind, selfish attitude or a lie or an angry retort. Like the blockage in the pipe, the sin must be removed, confessed specifically, then we must repent of the sin before the Holy Spirit is free once again to fill us up to overflow.

Do you feel spiritually dry? What is damming up the flow of the river in your life? Would you confess it by name, repent, and ask the Holy Spirit to fill you with Himself?

As the Holy Spirit fills your life, the vision of the glory of Christ promises you will be fruitful: "On each side of the river stood the tree of life, bearing twelve crops of fruit, yielding its fruit every month. And the leaves of the tree are for the healing of the nations" (Rev. 22:2).

If the river of life (the Holy Spirit and the blessing He brings), is filling you and me, there will be outward evidence of His fruit: love, joy, peace, patience, kindness, goodness, faithfulness, gentleness, and self-control.[22] We don't struggle to produce this fruit, just as a tree doesn't struggle to produce buds, then blossoms, then leaves, then fruit; it all happens as the natural result of the free-flowing sap that rises automatically in the spring.

Are you trying too hard to be Christlike? Are you constantly taking inventory of the "fruit" in your character? Instead of focusing on the fruit and struggling to be loving or kind or good, just focus on your relationship with Christ. Are you maintaining an unhindered relationship with Him? If so, you *will* bear fruit.

Not only will His fruit be evident in our character but also in our service. John's statement, "The leaves of the tree are for the healing of the nations" (Rev. 22:2b), implies that heaven will be a place of ministry and service. Our heavenly home will be a blessed place, where the outward evidence of the Holy Spirit is revealed in every person's character and service as we live and serve to the glory of God.

Have you ever wondered if you will get bored in such a beautiful, blessed place? Have you ever wondered if you will get tired of being good and serving the King and living in your heavenly home? I'll admit that I have. But the presence of water indicates I will still get thirsty, and the presence of fruit indicates I will still get hungry, and the leaves that are for healing indicate I will still have needs to be met. In other words, I will continue to face constant challenges, each of which will instantly be met in Christ. I will be continuously thirsty and continuously satisfied. I will be continuously hungry and continuously filled. I will have continuous needs and be continuously healed of those needs. The hunger and thirst and needs will keep me abiding close to the river in constant, joyful activity.

The course of the river of blessing not only brings fruit, it brings freedom: "No longer will there be any curse" (Rev. 22:3). When Adam and Eve sinned, they suffered the consequences, which the Bible refers to as a "curse." The consequences involved Adam and Eve as well as their descendants and all of creation, including animals and plant life. They were cursed to live in separation from God, cursed to die physically and spiritually, cursed to struggle through life, only to be defeated in the end by death.[23] Now John tells us the course of the River will bring final, permanent freedom from the curse to all creation! No longer will leaves fall, plants die, grass wither, flowers fade, and birds sing in minor key![24]

We will be free from sin and suffering and death. No one will age or deteriorate. No one will be tired or ignorant or selfish or sick or weak. For the first time in your life, you will be totally free from the memories of guilt and the scars of sin.

I talked with one dear woman who was abused while growing up, and in turn she had become an abusive parent. Although she had received Christ as her Savior and was forgiven of her sin, and although she had, for Christ's sake, made the choice to forgive those who had sinned against her, the memories of her years of abuse were like demons that tormented her. I prayed with her and did all I could to share God's love and grace with her, but in the end, I knew she would never be completely free of sin's scars and memories until the "curse" is finally and permanently removed.

One day we will be free from sin and its curse—free to serve the Lord in power and joyful abandonment. We will serve Him as we have always longed to serve.

Surely our joy will cause heaven's portals to ring with songs of praise to the One Who sits on the throne, and to the Lamb, as we have already seen. I can't wait to be able to hit the high notes!

And surely our joy will permeate heaven with our words of praise as we tell others what our great God has done for us. I do hope we will see a video of Genesis 1! I can already guarantee you it will not start with a big bang! And what will it be like to hear Mrs. Noah's testimony? To pray with Daniel? To see Enoch walk? To hear David sing? To watch Elijah call on the Name of his God? To listen to Paul preach and Peter say anything he feels like saying?

I would like to hear the testimony of missionaries seeking to spread the gospel in the jungles of South America whose lives were threatened—and even taken—by drug lords.

I would like to hear the testimony of pastors in Africa who encouraged their starving congregations, and testimony of Christians in Eastern Europe who chose to love their neighbors as themselves, and testimony of those living under atheistic regimes who chose to love the Lord their God with all their heart, soul, mind, and strength regardless of the earthly consequences.

And I would like to hear the testimony of ordinary believers. I would like to hear *your* testimony! I want to hear the testimonies of businessmen and women who maintained their integrity when confronted with greed . . .

And of young people who maintained their purity when confronted with immorality . . .

And of marriage partners who maintained their unity when confronted with divorce . . .

And of housewives who maintained their families when confronted with careers . . .

And of single parents who produced godly children while, out of necessity, maintaining jobs and homes . . .

I want to hear the testimony of the sufficiency of God's grace!

I want to hear the thrilling stories of how His strength was made perfect in weakness when a spouse suddenly walked out, when a child was killed, when a parent died, when a business was lost, when tragedy struck!

It will take an eternity for us to hear all the testimonies we want to hear! And every single testimony will be a story of God's mercy and great faithfulness that are new every morning and fresh every evening! The entire universe will resound with our praise to His glory!

But make no mistake about it! Our priority will not just be singing His praise or sharing His goodness, as blessed as that will all be—and it will be *blessed!* Instead, our priority will be to worship the Lamb and serve the King forever and ever and ever!

John states, "The throne of God and of the Lamb will be in the city, and his servants will serve him. . . . And they will reign for ever and ever" (Rev. 22:3, 5). We will rule with Him in the universe, we will convey knowledge of Him everywhere, and we will *never* grow weary in well-doing! Our work will flow from our worship, and we will serve Him perfectly!

And as we serve Him, we will experience blessed fellowship. We will "see his face, and his name will be on [our] foreheads" (Rev. 22:4). His Name will be our name! His face will always be turned toward us because we will never again be separated from Him! It will be as Paul described to the Corinthians: "Now we see but a poor reflection as in a mirror; then we shall see face to face. Now I know in part; then I shall know fully, even as I am fully known."[25]

The entire goal of my life is to know God. Therefore, I put time into prayer and Bible reading. I put effort into Bible study and application. I seek to live obediently and serve humbly, sensitive to the leading of the Holy Spirit. I do all this in the hope and for the purpose of growing in my personal knowledge of God! Yet after a lifetime of pursuing this goal, my knowledge will only be partial, frustratingly incomplete. But one day, when I see and serve Him face to face, I will know Him fully, even as He knows me. And that will indeed be heaven for me!

Every person born into the human race, no matter how wealthy, powerful, or knowledgeable he or she becomes, no matter how small and insignificant he or she feels, will ultimately be defeated by death. Death is the great equalizer. But the vision of His glory gives hope to you when you are defeated by death. It gives hope to you because you have placed your faith in Jesus Christ; your name has been written in the Lamb's Book of Life! The vision of His glory gives you hope because it reveals that this world is not your home, that death does not have the final word, that one day your faith will become sight and you will see the gates of pearl flung open for you.

And then, best of all, you will hear your King say,
"Welcome home!"

The Vision of His Glory . . .

Hope That Ignites Our Hearts!

 *[The grace of God] teaches us to say "No" to all ungodliness and worldly passions, and to live self-controlled, upright and godly lives in this present age, while we wait for the blessed hope—the glorious appearing of our great God and Savior, Jesus Christ.*

Titus 2:12–13

Hope That Ignites Our Hearts

Revelation 22:6–21

 The church in Liberia, Africa, was cut off from the rest of the world during that country's bloody civil war. The pastor of a church in the capital city of Monrovia, writing his Christmas letter by candlelight to the leaders of his denomination, expressed the hope of his heart: "My candle is soon to go out, but the sun is rising. And who needs a candle when you have the Son?"

What has caused you to feel that the candle of hope in your life is soon to go out? Bloody civil war in your home? Discord in your marriage? Turmoil in your business? Is the source of your hopelessness nothing you can really pinpoint, just a general feeling of depression, of disillusionment, of discouragement, of distress, and of defeat? After reading Revelation, are you convinced Jesus Christ will reign in the world at some future time, but you don't know what difference that makes in your life today?

The vision of His glory concludes with a challenge to us to experience the difference hope does make today. We are challenged not to place our hope in the things of this world but to keep our focus on the rising Son in every aspect of our lives.

The Old Testament describes how, for approximately fourteen years after David was anointed by God as king over God's people, he did not sit on the throne. His enemy, Saul, was in power, and during that time, Saul desperately did all he could to destroy David and those who were loyal to him.

Four hundred men from all walks of life became terrified of Saul. To them, he seemed invincible in his power and immovable from his position of authority. Faced with Saul's seemingly permanent rule over them, the four hundred men became discontented, distressed, and discouraged in their daily life. Their candle of hope went out.

Then they heard about David. They heard that he was God's anointed king. They heard that one day he would rule from the throne in Jerusalem. They heard of his victory over Goliath and the Philistine army, and of his repeated skirmishes with Saul and other enemies. They heard he was a courageous, compassionate leader who was undefeated in battle. So these four hundred men forsook everything and put all their hope in David. "All those who were in distress or in debt or discontented gathered around him, and he became their leader."[1]

David, as a king in exile, became a rallying point for God's people. His leadership in their lives, even before he ruled from the throne in Jerusalem, radically changed their perspective of the present as well as of the future. David gave them hope!

The four hundred men who lived with him and fought for him and placed all their hope in him became David's mighty men. And when he was crowned king of Israel, they reigned with him.

In one sense, the Lord Jesus Christ is God's anointed King in exile. The enemies—Satan, self, and sin—reign supreme on His earthly throne of authority. Often these "kings," like King Saul, seem to be invincible in their power and immovable in their position, causing our candle of hope to flicker and falter.

But we have heard of the King! We have heard of God's anointed One! We have heard of His courageous and compassionate leadership! We have heard of His amazing exploits and His victories in battle! When our candle flickers, our hope in Him ignites the fire of our hearts in devoted faithfulness to Him. Perhaps our candle of hope has almost gone out, "but the sun is rising. And who needs a candle when you have the Son?"

The vision of His glory is the King's rallying cry to His people, challenging us to place all our hope in Him. Make Him your priority! Give Him your loyalty! Fan the flame of your love for Him! Live for Him! Serve Him! Be faithful to the King in exile! One day, you will reign with Him!

Hope Ignites Faithfulness to His Word

The story is told of an acrobat who walked on a tightrope over Niagara Falls. A crowd gathered, oohing and aahing at his remarkable feat. Then, to their amazement, he pushed a wheelbarrow across the tightrope over Niagara Falls and back! As the crowd applauded wildly, the acrobat picked up a bag of sand, placed it in the wheelbarrow, and again pushed the wheelbarrow across the tightrope and back. There was a moment of stunned silence, then the crowd erupted in cheers, whistles, and more applause. As the viewers quieted down to see what the acrobat would do next, he said in a loud voice, "I have walked by myself across the tightrope, I have pushed an empty wheelbarrow across the tightrope, and I have pushed a loaded wheelbarrow across the tightrope. How many of you believe I can push a person in the wheelbarrow across the tightrope?"

The entire crowd shouted enthusiastically, "We do! We believe you can do it!"

Then the acrobat challenged, "Who will volunteer to climb into the wheelbarrow and let me push you across?"

Suddenly the crowd became deathly silent. People shuffled their feet, averted their eyes, and hung their heads. Finally, from the back, a little old man worked his way through the crowd, and said, "I'll do it."

To the shocked consternation of the onlookers, the man climbed into the wheelbarrow, and the acrobat pushed him across the tightrope over Niagara Falls and safely back again to a thunderous ovation from those watching!

All the people had *said* they believed. But the little old man was the only one who was willing to *commit himself* to what he said he believed. He was willing to risk everything to demonstrate his faith. Keeping that story in mind, the angel's words to John are a personal challenge as the vision of the glory of Christ draws to a close: "The angel said to me, 'These words are trustworthy and true. The Lord, the God of the spirits of the prophets, sent his angel to show his servants the things that must soon take place.' [Jesus said,] 'Behold, I am coming soon! Blessed is he who keeps the words of the prophecy in this book'" (Rev. 22:6–7).

Do you believe what the angel told John? That not only these words, but God's Word in its entirety, is trustworthy and true? That all the things described in His Word *must* take place, if for no other reason than because God said so?

If you have not done so before, would you make the decision at this moment to *believe* God's Word? You may not understand everything in it, but take it by faith as the truth because it is *God's Word*, and He does not lie! He is a Gentleman! You can take Him at His Word!

Do you *really believe* what the angel told John? If you do, then would you demonstrate your faith by committing yourself to reading and heeding God's Word—to keeping it, as Jesus Himself commands us to do?

The promise of blessing to those who "keep the words of the prophecy in this book" is given directly by Jesus Christ. The promise specifically regards Revelation, but generally it applies to the entire Bible. By keeping the Word, He does not mean we buy a Bible and keep it on the shelf or on the bedside table, dusting it off once a week for church. To *keep* the Word means we make the time to read it, study it, apply it, and obey it. We keep it on our hearts, keep it on our minds, and keep it on our lips. And the blessing we receive is a growing, confident, fully committed hope in Jesus Christ! He alone is our hope![2]

The vision of His glory ignites our faithfulness to the Word because increasingly we will experience its firm stability as everything else in the world around us seems to collapse. There is no other foundation on which to build our lives, no other Rock on which to stand, no other purpose to live for, no other Lord Who is able to rule our lives so that we live victoriously in a world that is increasingly defeated and hopeless—only Jesus! And He is revealed by God through His Word! Therefore, you can do nothing more important than to make time for the Word every day! Keep the Word! Read the Word! In light of the vision of His glory, be faithful to the Word!

Hope Ignites Faithfulness in Worship

To worship God literally means to attribute worth to Him. We attribute worth to God by being preoccupied with Him, by making Him our first priority, by focusing on Him, by obeying what He says, by praising Him for Who He is and what He has done, by prostrating ourselves at His feet as though dead.

Following the vision of the glory of Christ, you might expect John to be so enthralled with what he had seen that it would be impossible for him to even consider worshiping anyone or anything except the one true God. But, as unlikely as it seems, John humbly confesses: "I, John, am the one who heard and saw these things. And when I had heard and seen them, I fell down to worship at the feet of the angel who had been showing them to me. But he said to me, 'Do not do it! I am a fellow servant with you and with your brothers the prophets and of all who keep the words of this book. Worship God!'" (Rev. 22:8–9).

Can you believe it? At the conclusion of the vision of the glory of Christ, John fell down to worship someone or something other than God! How could that be?

How could one who had heard the voice that commanded him to record the glorious vision . . .

Who had heard the accurate evaluation of the hearts of seven churches . . .

Who had seen the Lamb upon the throne at the center of the universe and heard millions and millions of angels joined by every living creature give "praise and honor and glory and power" to the One alone Who is worthy . . .

Who had witnessed the Lord's judgment executed in mercy . . .

Who had trembled at the wrath of God poured out upon a rebellious, blaspheming human race . . .

Who had thrilled at the triumphant return of the King to set up His rule on earth for one thousand years . . .

Who had seen Satan cast into the lake of fire and all unbelievers judged at the great white throne and the New Jerusalem come down from heaven as a dwelling place for God and His people . . .

How could *John*, who had seen the vision of the glory of Christ *firsthand*, worship an angel? Yet he did! And if he did, are you and I, who have seen the vision of the glory of Christ secondhand, in danger of the same sin?

If we do not make a conscious effort to be faithful in our worship of God as a result of the vision of His glory, we may find ourselves doing the same as John!

When you have completed this book, what will be your focus? Will you set it aside and allow yourself to become preoccupied with your circumstances? Will you allow business obligations and family responsibilities and church activities and the accumulation of possessions and the care of the possessions you have accumulated or just your daily routine to crowd Christ from His preeminent position in your life? Instead of seeking first the kingdom of God and His righteousness, will you try to squeeze them into your spare time?

The vision of His glory ignites our faithfulness in worship by exalting the uniqueness of Jesus Christ! No one else, nor anything else, is worthy of our worship. Only Jesus Christ! In light of the vision of His glory, be faithful to worship Him!

Hope Ignites Faithfulness to His Work

Finally, the angel told John, "Do not seal up the words of the prophecy of this book, because the time is near. Let him who does wrong continue to do wrong; let him who is vile continue to be vile; let him who does right continue to do right; and let him who is holy continue to be holy" (Rev. 22:10–12).

At the end of the book of Revelation, at the end of the Bible, God has nothing more to say! If salvation is rejected, the only alternative is judgment. If heaven is refused, the only alternative is hell. If the revelation of Jesus Christ from Genesis to Revelation has not brought the reader to a humble confession of sin and repentance from sin and conversion to Christ through faith, nothing will. If God's message is rejected, there is none other. Charles H. Spurgeon said at this point, "There is no hope of change of character. Where death leaves us, judgment finds us, and eternity keeps us."[3]

Time is running out! There is coming a day when not only *unbe-*lievers will lose any chance to repent and be saved from judgment, but believers will lose any opportunity to work for the Lord on earth! Jesus said, "As long as it is day, we must do the work of him who sent me. Night is coming, when no one can work."[4] When the night comes—either death or the Rapture—our work on earth will cease. Five minutes before that takes place, what will you wish you had done differently in your life? Will you wish you had taught Sunday school, or opened your home for a neighborhood prayer group, or started a Bible study over your lunch hour with your coworker who had seemed so interested, or gone on that mission trip, or made yourself available to your church for any service your pastor needed, or written those notes of encouragement to missionaries you always meant to write, or started a worship service in the rest home where you visit your elderly parent, or _____. You fill in the blank. What will you wish you had done at that too-late time? Whatever it is, "just do it!" *Now!*

When I was growing up, my father traveled a lot. To help us focus on his "comings" instead of his "goings," whenever he returned from a trip he always brought a surprise for each of us children. It was usually something he had picked up in some airport or hotel gift shop, but it could have been the Hope diamond judging by our response! We had to restrain ourselves from digging into his suitcases before he even got through the front door! We couldn't wait to see what he had brought us. My childhood experience seems to relate to our Lord's promise: "Behold, I am coming soon! My reward is with me, and I will give to everyone according to what he has done" (Rev. 22:12). Your Lord is returning from a long "trip," and He has a "surprise" for each and every one of His children who have been faithful to His work. When He is passing out His surprises, will there be one for you?

The vision of His glory ignites faithfulness in our work for Him because it motivates us to make use of every moment we have left. It keeps our focus on the big picture lest we grow "weary in doing good."[5] In light of the vision of His glory, we live for the crowns given as rewards for service to Christ—crowns that one day we can lay at His nail-pierced feet in the ultimate expression of devotion to Him. In light of the vision of His glory, be faithful to work for Christ!

Hope Ignites Faithfulness to Wash

Be faithful to *wash?* Isn't that one of the last-minute instructions your mother gave you as you went off to camp or college?

"Be sure to eat a good breakfast."

"Be sure to take an umbrella."

"Be sure to button up your overcoat."

"Be sure to brush your teeth."

"Be sure to wash behind your ears."

One of the last-minute instructions our Lord gives us as He comes to the conclusion of the Bible, an entire book of instructions, is a summary of the challenge the vision of His glory should be to our daily lives: "Blessed are those who wash their robes, that they may have the right to the tree of life and may go through the gates into the city. Outside are the dogs, those who practice magic arts, the sexually immoral, the murderers, the idolaters and everyone who loves and practices falsehood" (Rev. 22:14–15).

Our robe is our right-standing before God, given to us at the cross of Christ in exchange for the filthy garments of our own righteousness. When we receive that robe, we are forgiven for all our sin.[6] Since Jesus died on the cross for my sin two thousand years ago, and since at that point all my sin was future to Him, when I claim the cross by faith for forgiveness, all my sin is covered by His blood. This includes past, present, and future sins. It includes sins we consider small, like gossip and little white lies; it also includes sins we consider medium-size, like losing our temper. And it includes what we think of as great big sins like murder, adultery, and stealing. All are forgiven at the cross of Christ!

I was trying to explain this to a woman convicted of murder, as we talked together on death row the night of her execution. I asked her if she had ever gone to the beach, and she said yes. Then I asked if she had seen small holes in the sand, the kind that crabs make, and she had. I asked if she had seen medium-size holes that perhaps had resulted from a child digging out a sand castle, and she nodded her head affirmatively. Then I asked if she had seen huge holes, where perhaps a dredger was digging out a waterway, and again she said yes, she had. Then I asked, "What happens when the tide comes in? The water covers all the holes equally, doesn't it?"

"Yes!" she said. And she smiled with radiant relief and understanding.

The blood of Jesus is like the tide. When we claim it as a covering for our sin, it covers *all* our sin. Big sins and little sins and medium sins. Past sins, present sins, and future sins. They are all forgiven through the blood of Christ!

If we continue to ask for forgiveness, we imply we do not believe in the sufficiency of the cross to cleanse us of any and all sin. Once we have truly been forgiven, to pray again, "Lord, forgive me . . ." is really saying, "Lord, I don't believe You forgave me of everything when I asked before, so I am asking You again . . ." It reveals unbelief in the power of the blood of Christ. Knowing we don't have to repeatedly ask for forgiveness, we can just live, enjoying our forgiven-ness! We never have to ask for forgiveness again because we cannot be more forgiven than we already are!

Although His love for us demonstrated at the cross causes us to hate sin, we still sin! Once we are forgiven, sin will never cause us to stop being the Father's child, but it will break our fellowship with Him. So we are told, "If we confess our sins, he is faithful and just and will forgive us our sins and purify us from all unrighteousness."[7]

The word *confess* means to say the same thing about our sin that God says about it. Sometimes we switch the labels we give sin to make it seem less like sin!

We call unbelief "worry."

We call lying "exaggeration."

We call pride "self-esteem."

We call adultery a "love affair."

We call murder "the right to choose."

We call homosexuality "gay."

The list could go on and on. To confess your sin means to stop playing games with the labels and to say the same thing about it that God says about it. Name it for what it is. It is anger, jealousy, pride, lying, hate, selfishness, stealing, lust . . . Only when we confess our sin will we be cleansed and washed in order to maintain right fellowship with God.

When one of my children was in her first year of college, we had a disagreement concerning her classes for the next semester. Since she went to school about fifteen hundred miles away, we were having our discussion on the telephone, and she hung up on me. I tried to call her back, but she did not pick up the phone. For four days, I tried unsuccessfully to reach her. She had not ceased to be my child, but we definitely had a broken relationship!

As it so happened, the next week my travel schedule took me to a city near her, and I made arrangements to swing by to see her. When I confronted her, she confessed her wrongdoing. We cried, prayed, and set things right. Immediately, our fellowship was restored! In the same way, when we sin against God we do not cease to be His children, but we must go to Him in prayer and confess our sins—sincerely say we are sorry for them—in order to set things right.

When Jesus told John, "Blessed are those that wash their robes" (Rev. 22:14a), He was saying, in effect, blessed are those who are not only forgiven but who daily confess their sin that they might be cleansed, maintaining right, sweet, loving fellowship with the Father. When He continued, "They . . . have the right to the tree of life" (Rev. 22:14b), He was promising they would be deeply satisfied as they enjoy their eternal life. And when He said they "go through the gates into the city" (Rev. 22:14c), He was acknowledging they have found hope as they lived in an awareness of their acceptance by God and their welcome in His presence, with nothing to hide or fear.

The vision of His glory ignites our faithfulness to wash our robes—confess our sins daily—because we never know when we will suddenly find ourselves standing face to face before the One Who is Lord of lords and King of kings! And we don't want that moment to come when we are living out of fellowship, in a broken relationship, with Him.

In light of the vision of His glory, isn't it time you did a load of wash?

Hope Ignites Faithfulness to Witness

I have always loved to read. One of my favorite books when I was growing up was entitled *A Little Princess* by Frances Hodgeson Burnett. In the plot, the heroine, Sara Crewe, is condemned to be a scullery maid for an exclusive girls boarding school in London. One Christmas she was running errands for the cook through the snow-covered streets, dressed in threadbare rags and wearing shoes with holes in them. She was freezing cold, physically exhausted, and weary of spirit. She had no money, no family, no friends, and no hope for anything better in life.

As Sara was making her way back through the dusk to the boarding school, she passed a home with light flooding from the windows. She paused and looked into a warm, cozy room complete with crackling fire, where children were talking and laughing as their parents were giving them presents from under a beautifully decorated Christmas tree. The entire scene was one of warmth and love and security and happiness. When little Sara turned away to continue her journey alone down the cold, snowy streets, there were big tears running down her grimy cheeks. Because Sara was on the outside, looking in.

As a girl, I wondered why that family didn't look up and see Sara peering longingly through the window. Why didn't they run to the door, fling it open, and say, "Won't you please come in and join us?" Why were they so preoccupied with their own happiness and celebration that they were oblivious to Sara's misery? Why?

Why are you and I so preoccupied with our own happiness and celebration in Christ that we are oblivious to a lost and dying world? Jesus clearly states He has given us this testimony, not just for our own blessed hope but *also* for others: "I, Jesus, have sent my angel to give you this testimony *for* the churches. I am the Root and the Offspring of David, and the bright Morning Star" (Rev. 22:16, italics are mine).

John immediately accepts the challenge as he passes on the invitation that rings down through the ages: "The Spirit and the bride say, *'Come!'* And let him who hears say, *'Come!'* Whoever is thirsty, let him *come;* and whoever wishes, let him take the free gift of the water of life" (Rev. 22:16–17, italics are mine).

While you and I rejoice in the love and security and blessedness of belonging to the family of God, why are we oblivious to the misery of others? Why don't we see the lonely, hungry, thirsty expressions on the faces of those on the outside, looking in? Why don't we run to our loved one, our neighbor, our friend, our coworker, or our business associate and fling open the "door," extending to that person the Spirit and the bride's invitation to "Come!"?

To the woman seeking love in multiple marriages and relationships, the Spirit says, "Come! Come to the well of living water that satisfies so you will never thirst again!"[8]

To the man who is a workaholic, striving so hard to achieve the good life and provide comfortably for his family yet never seeming to have enough, the Spirit says, "Come! Come to the Bread of Life and eat until you are filled!"[9]

To the one who is burdened with a heavy load of sin and guilt, the Spirit says, "Come! Come to the Savior Who died to cleanse you of all sin and absolve you of all guilt."[10]

To the one who has been abused, abandoned, attacked, and takes pills to get up in the morning and pills to make it through the day and more pills again at night to sleep, He says, "Come! Come to the Light of the world, who can turn your dark night of depression and despair into day!"[11]

To the one who is consumed with worry, suffering from panic attacks, He says, "Come! Come to the Prince of Peace, Who will give you peace that passes all understanding!"[12]

To the one who is terrified by the diagnosis of a terminal illness or who cannot cope with the loss of a loved one, He says, "Come! Come to the resurrection and the life that you might live forever!"[13]

Come to the cross! Come to Christ!

Who relayed the invitation to you? When did you respond? To whom have *you* issued the invitation? The vision of His glory helps us to be faithful in our witness because it makes us aware that any moment, the One Who is Lord and King may return for His bride! And those who do not belong to Him will be left to endure His judgment!

How many people do you know who would come under the judgment of God if Jesus were to return today? Name them!

How many people will be saved from judgment because you were faithful to extend to them His invitation to "come!"?

Would you make it a priority to lengthen the second list? In light of the vision of His glory, be faithful to witness!

Hope Ignites Faithfulness to Warn

At the very beginning of human history, God clearly told Adam, "You must not eat from the tree of the knowledge of good and evil, for when you eat of it you will surely die."[14]

A short time later, Satan, in the disguise of a serpent, asked Eve, "Did God really say, 'You must not eat from any tree in the garden'?"

As Satan cast doubt on God's Word and God's goodness, notice how Eve responded: "God did say, 'You must not eat fruit from the tree that is in the middle of the garden, *and you must not touch it*, or you will die.'"[15] What had Eve done? She had *added to* God's Word! Eve's seemingly harmless exaggeration was rooted in rebellion against God's command and had devastating impact on herself, her husband, her children, her grandchildren, for every generation since! Eve's tampering with God's Word led, not only to her own disobedience and destruction, but also to that of myriads of others! To add to God's Word is to invite His judgment on yourself and to lead others into it as well!

At the very end of God's revelation of human history, He warns against repeating the same sin. His Word conveys His thoughts and ways and will, and not one word is to be tampered with: "I warn everyone who hears the words of the prophecy of this book: If anyone adds anything to them, God will add to him the plagues described in this book. And if anyone takes words away from this book of prophecy, God will take away from him his share in the tree of life and in the holy city, which are described in this book" (Rev. 22:18–19).

While we think of cults today as groups who add to God's Word, I wonder if there are others who do so less obviously. When people say they have "a word of knowledge," or a "prophecy," and what they say is held in the same regard as Scripture, does God view that as adding to His Word?

Some people are considered deeply spiritual by their friends. Their conversation is peppered with comments such as, "God told me . . ." and "God said to me just this morning . . ." and "God spoke to me and said . . ." They seem to be impressed, and they impress many others, that they have unique revelations from God that they respond to as they would His Word. Often when someone suggests that they say instead, "God *seemed* to say to me . . ." or "I felt impressed God was leading me to do such and such . . . ," they imply that person doesn't understand because he or she isn't on their spiritual level! Does God view such comments as adding to His Word?

We are not to add to God's Word as though it is insufficient in itself, and we are not to take one word away from it as though it is irrelevant or unreliable or unimportant or untrue!

Jeremiah was one of the greatest of the Old Testament prophets. He served the Lord in Judah during a time of great moral wickedness and spiritual rebellion. God told him to "take a scroll and write on it all the words I have spoken to you. . . . Perhaps when the people of Judah hear about every disaster I plan to inflict on them, each of them will turn from his wicked way; then I will forgive their wickedness and their sin."[16]

Jeremiah faithfully wrote down the Word of the Lord as it was revealed to Him. A copy of his scroll was given to the king of Judah, Jehoiakim, who had it read to him one winter evening while he was sitting by the fire. As God's Word was read, Jehoiakim took his penknife and shredded the scroll, burning the scraps of paper in the fire! He gave a dramatic illustration of the attitude of countless people down through the centuries who cannot tolerate the truth and therefore seek to deny, discard, and destroy it.

But man's attitude and actions do not affect God's truth. The very Word Jehoiakim had despised came to pass. The very judgment he said would not fall, did! Not only did Jehoiakim come under the judgment of God when he was shackled and taken off to Babylon by Nebuchadnezzar, but he was influential in leading his entire nation into judgment as well! It wasn't long after that, that Judah was carried off into captivity in Babylon! To take away from God's Word is to not only invite judgment on yourself but to lead others into it also!

Who do you know who does not necessarily use a penknife to slice up God's Word but whose critical attitude toward it has the same effect? Who do you know who says this part of the Bible is true but that part is not? Who do you know who says the Bible "contains" the Word of God but is not the Word of God entirely? Who do you know who picks and chooses what they will and will not believe in the Bible? The tragedy is that many people with this attitude are in responsible positions of leadership, and they influence others with their destructive views.

Jesus revealed His attitude toward tampering with God's Word when He said, "I tell you the truth, until heaven and earth disappear, not the smallest letter, not the least stroke of a pen, will by any means disappear from the Law until everything is accomplished."[17] Would you be faithful to warn others that God's Word is not to be tampered with? Would you heed the warning yourself?

The vision of His glory ignites our faithfulness to God's warning by giving us a holy fear of His displeasure, judgment, and wrath. Those who destroy, dilute, deny, despise, and defy God's Word ultimately disobey it—to their own personal destruction, and the destruction of others! In light of the vision of His glory, be faithful to His warning!

Hope Ignites Our Faithfulness to Watch

My husband leaves for work around seven forty-five in the morning, and returns home somewhere between five and six o'clock in the evening. He likes for me to have his dinner prepared and ready to go on the table as soon as he steps through the door. So starting around five o'clock in the evening, I begin to watch for him. I am usually occupied in the kitchen, preparing for his return, but also keeping one eye on the window from which I can glimpse the first sight of his car coming down the road. That one hour is filled with anticipation, as I know he is coming home, but he just has not arrived yet!

The vision of His glory ends with the thrilling promise of hope: "'Yes, I am coming soon'. Amen. Come, Lord Jesus. The grace of the Lord Jesus be with God's people. Amen." (Rev. 22:20–21).

He is coming!

HE IS COMING!

HE IS COMING!

We *know* He is coming soon; He just has not arrived yet. Hope wakes us up and keeps us awake! In light of the vision of His glory, be faithful to watch!

Hope ignites our hearts to live:
    Faithful to His Word,
        Faithful to worship,
            Faithful to His work,
                Faithful to wash,
                    Faithful to witness,
                        Faithful to warn,
                            Faithful to watch!
What has diverted your focus from Christ? What is lulling you into complacent sleep? What has caused you to drift into faithlessness? Refocus! Wake up! Be faithful! Live your life in the light of the vision of His glory!

The vision of His glory gives hope to the hopeless:
    all those who are depressed by the smallness of their lives and the greatness of their problems . .
    all those who are deluded by their own importance and by their own insignificance . .
    all those who are discouraged by the majority of the ungodly and by the minority of the godly . .
    all those who are distressed by evil actions and by evil alliances . .
    all those who are defeated by life and defeated by death . .
Do you know hope? Do you really believe in Hope? If so, would you buy into what you believe by claiming the hope of the vision of His glory as your own, then living your life in the light of it?

The Vision of His Glory

The vision of His glory ignites our hearts with passionate anticipation, challenging us to live faithfully every day, every hour, every moment in the light of the imminent return of the One Who alone is worthy as . . .

THE ALPHA AND THE OMEGA

THE SON OF MAN

THE SON OF GOD

THE GREAT HIGH PRIEST

THE LIGHT OF THE WORLD

THE EVERLASTING FATHER

THE COMMANDER OF THE LORD'S ARMY

THE AVENGER OF HIS PEOPLE

THE LION OF JUDAH

THE LAMB WHO WAS SLAIN

THE RIDER CALLED FAITHFUL AND TRUE

THE WORD OF GOD

THE FINAL JUDGE

THE LORD OF LORDS

and

THE KING OF KINGS . . .

THE ONLY HOPE OF THE WORLD!

To the glory of God!

Appendix

Hope That Helps

 Jesus Christ is our Hope! What a thrilling privilege as well as awesome responsibility to present Him to a hopeless world! The following is a sampler, in alphabetical order, of nonprofit organizations of exceptional quality that seek to offer the hope of Jesus Christ in a variety of unique ways:

BEE International (Biblical Education by Extension) helps give hope to men and women in Eastern Europe and the former Soviet territories by offering seminary-level curricula, discipleship, and leadership training through biblical education by extension in the hope that churches might be multiplied.

> *President: James Mugg*
> 8111 LBJ Freeway, Suite 635
> Dallas, Texas 75251
> USA
> Telephone: 214-669-8077
> Fax: 214-669-0684

Appendix

The Billy Graham Evangelistic Association helps give hope to those who are without Christ by presenting the gospel through every means available.

> *Chief Executive Officer: Billy Graham*
> 1300 Harmon Place
> Minneapolis, Minnesota 55403-1988
> USA
> Telephone: 612-338-0500

East Gates Ministries, International helps give hope to the church in mainland China through identifying unmet needs and opportunities as they relate to the fulfilling of the Great Commission as well as by developing indigenous ministries that meet those needs.

> *President: Ned Graham*
> P.O. Box 2010
> Sumner, Washington 98390-0440
> USA
> Telephone: 206-863-5500
> Fax: 206-863-0754

The Evangelical Church of India helps give hope by planting, encouraging, and equipping churches in India that are Christ-centered and Bible-based.

> *Bishop: M. Ezra Sarganum*
> No. 1, Second Street, Ormes Road, Kilpauk
> Madras, India
> Telephone: 44-641-3178

International Reach, Inc., helps give hope to abandoned Brazilian children by processing and arranging for their adoption into Christian homes.

> *Executive Director: Vini Jaquery*
> Alameda dos Arapanes 982/62
> Sao Paulo, Brazil
> Telephone: 04524,001
> P.O. Box 809
> Lake Forest, Illinois 60045
> USA
> Telephone: 708-234-6389

Kids Alive International, Inc. helps give hope to children and youth in Papua, New Guinea, by providing quality care spiritually, educationally, physically, and morally, enabling them to become fully devoted followers of Christ and effective citizens in their national churches.

> *President: John M. Rock*
> 2507 Cumberland Drive
> Valparaiso, Indiana 46383
> USA
> Telephone: 219-464-9035
> Fax: 219-462-5611

Mafraq Sanatorium Association helps give hope to those within the Jordanian Kingdom by supporting Christian missionary projects of all kinds, specifically hospitals and other facilities for medical care and treatment, and schools for medical education.

> *Director: Aileen Coleman*
> P.O. Box 2001
> Boone, North Carolina 28607
> USA
> Telephone: 704-262-1980
> (Inquiries are handled by Samaritan's Purse described later.)

Appendix

Mission Aviation Fellowship helps give hope as a sending agency engaged in aviation and technical services for other agencies in support of community development, relief aid, and other ministries.

> *Chief executive officer: Maxwell H. Meyers*
> P.O. Box 3202
> Redlands, California 92373-0998
> USA
> Telephone: 909-794-1151
> Fax: 909-794-3016

Samaritan's Purse helps give hope to the poor and afflicted around the world by engaging in relief aid, agricultural programs, evangelism, funds transmission, support of national workers, and by supplying equipment.

> *President: Franklin Graham*
> P.O. Box 3000
> Boone, North Carolina 28607-3000
> USA
> Telephone: 704-262-1980
> Fax: 704-262-1796

The Stephen Olford Center for Biblical Preaching helps give hope to the church by equipping and encouraging pastors and laymen in expository preaching and exemplary living, to the end that the church will be revived and the world will be reached with the saving Word of Christ.

> *Founder and Senior Lecturer: Stephen Olford*
> P.O. Box 757800
> Memphis, Tennessee 38175-7800
> USA
> Telephone: 901-757-7977
> Fax: 901-757-1372

World Medical Missions helps give hope to the sick and wounded by mobilizing Christian physicians for placement in mission hospitals around the world and by providing an information service, medical supplies and equipment, and mission orientation for medical personnel.

> *Chairman of the board: Franklin Graham*
> P.O. Box 3000
> Boone, North Carolina 28607-3000
> USA
> Telephone: 704-262-1980
> Fax: 704-262-0175

Wycliffe Bible Translators, Inc., helps give hope to the world by engaging in Bible translation, linguistics, literacy, and missionary training in conjunction with its sister organizations, Wycliffe Bible Translators International, Summer Institute of Linguistics, Jungle Aviation and Radio Service (JAARS), Inc., and Wycliffe Associates.

> *Director: Hyatt Moore*
> P.O. Box 2727
> Huntington Beach, California 92647
> USA
> Telephone: 714-969-4600
> Fax: 714-969-4661

Notes

Introduction

    1.   Rev. 1:9.
    2.   Matt. 24:21.
    3.   Jer. 29:11.
    4.   Isa. 35:3–4.
    5.   John 19:5 KJV.

Chapter 1   Hope When You Are Depressed by the Smallness of Your Life

    1.   See Gen. 3:15.
    2.   See Gen. 12:3.
    3.   See Deut. 18:17–18.
    4.   See Isa. 9:6.
    5.   See Isa. 53:5.
    6.   See Micah 5:2.
    7.   See Zech. 14:9.
    8.   See 2 Pet. 1:20–21.
    9.   See Rom. 8:15.
   10.   See John 14:16, KJV.
   11.   See Matt. 1:21 and Rev. 19:16.
   12.   John 14:3.
   13.   See Col. 2:3.
   14.   Phil. 2:7.
   15.   See Heb. 13:8.
   16.   See Gen. 3:8.
   17.   See Gen. 5:24.
   18.   See Isa. 41:8.
   19.   See Ps. 23:1.
   20.   See Luke 8:2.
   21.   See Acts 9:1–19.
   22.   See Eph. 1:19.

Chapter 2 **Hope for When You Are Depressed by the Greatness of Your Problems**

1. Acts 4:20.
2. See Acts 5:40–41.
3. See John 14:6.
4. See John 14:14.
5. John 1:9.
6. 1 John 2:9.
7. See Matt. 5:15–16.
8. See John 4:24.
9. When my mother heard criticism of my father for what some considered a compromise of evangelistic methods, her comment was, "You don't have to like worms to go fishing!" Obviously, she too was willing to "turn around."
10. See Mal. 3:2–3.
11. See Exodus 28.
12. Heb. 4:14–15 KJV.
13. Heb. 7:25.
14. Dan. 7:9.
15. Isa. 9:6.
16. See Romans 8.
17. Isa. 6:3.
18. See Zech. 2:8.
19. Gen. 12:3a.
20. Deut. 32:35a and Heb. 10:30a.
21. See Matt. 8:26–27, John 11:43, John 20:16, John 1:3, and Heb. 1:3.
22. See John 10:28.
23. See Josh. 5:14, Rev. 19:15, Heb. 4:12, and Eph. 6:17.

Chapter 3 **Hope When You Are Deluded by Your Own Importance**

1. See Matt. 5:16.
2. Matt. 22:36–37.
3. The tree of life represents eternal, abundant life, which includes fullness of love, joy, and peace. See Gen. 2:9, 3:22, 24.
4. Henry H. Halley, *Halley's Bible Handbook,* 24th ed. (Grand Rapids, Mich.: Zondervan, 1965), 702.
5. Ibid., 704.
6. Henry Morris, *The Revelation Record* (San Diego: Creation Life Publishers, 1976), 57.
7. Matt. 24:4.
8. Gen. 3:1 KJV.

9. See Exod. 16:15.
10. See Heb. 9:4.
11. See John 6:51.
12. See John 6:63.
13. See Exod. 28:15–21.
14. David Alexander and Pat Alexander, eds., *Eerdmans' Handbook to the Bible* (Grand Rapids, Mich.: Eerdmans, 1992), 647.
15. Halley, 706.
16. See Rev. 20:11–15.
17. See Genesis 13 and 14.
18. See 2 Cor. 3:18.
19. See Isa. 61:10 and Rev. 7:13–14.
20. See Rev. 19:8.
21. Alexander and Alexander, 648.
22. Halley, 707.
23. 1 Cor. 2:8, Song of Sol. 2:1, and Rev. 22:16 NIV, and Song of Sol. 5:10 KJV, Rev. 5:6.
24. John 15:5.
25. Rom. 7:18.
26. See Isa. 64:6.
27. See Prov. 6:16–17 KJV.
28. Halley, 708.
29. 2 Cor. 3:18 KJV.
30. See 1 John 3:2.

Chapter 4 Hope When You Are Deluded by Your Own Insignificance

1. Halley, 702.
2. See John 16:33.
3. See Psalm 22.
4. John 1:11.
5. See Heb. 13:13.
6. See Matt. 27:35–44.
7. See 2 Cor. 5:21.
8. See Isa. 53:6.
9. Matt. 27:46.
10. The name and some of the details in this story have been changed to protect identities. "Professor Hill" still lives in a country hostile to Christ, where he remains under scrutiny.
11. Esther 4:16, emphasis mine.
12. Dan. 3:15.
13. Dan. 3:16–18, emphasis mine.
14. 2 Tim. 1:7–8a.

15. Halley, 763.
16. Ibid., 703.
17. See Acts 16:13–15.
18. See John 3:14–15.
19. See Matt. 5:27–30.
20. Alexander and Alexander, 648.
21. 2 Sam. 5:7, 9.
22. Rev. 21:2.
23. See John 9:4.
24. Halley, 708.

Chapter 5   Hope When You Are Discouraged by the Majority of the Ungodly

1. See 1 Kings 18.
2. Although two separate women, the Jezebel of Revelation 2 is obviously named after King Ahab's queen. While both were very religious, both were extremely wicked and did great harm to God's people.
3. See 1 Kings 19:4.
4. Ps. 37:1.
5. Jesus Himself gives details concerning the "catching up of believers" in Matt. 24:40–41, Luke 17:34–35, and John 14:1–3. Bible scholars are in disagreement as to whether this historical event takes place at the beginning, midpoint, or end of the Great Tribulation. However, you and I should not be distracted from the main point: We are to be ready to meet Jesus Christ face to face whenever it does occur.
6. 1 Thess. 4:13.
7. See 2 Cor. 5:4–8.
8. See Phil. 3:21.
9. 1 Cor. 15:51–52.
10. Describing the practical impact of the Rapture on daily life, Jesus said, "Two men will be in the field; one will be taken and the other left. Two women will be grinding with a hand mill; one will be taken and the other left" (Matt. 24:40–41). The havoc wreaked on earth by the Rapture of all true believers can only be imagined. When that moment comes, some planes flying in the air will lose their pilots, some cars will lose their drivers, many homes and businesses will be vacated, doctors in the midst of surgery will lose their patients, key government leaders will disappear, and various family members, friends, clients, business associates, soldiers, and students will vanish!

Notes

11. John 14:3, emphasis mine.
12. Acts 1:11, emphasis mine.
13. 1 Cor. 15:52.
14. Luke 12:40.
15. Heb. 10:37.
16. See Ps. 47:8.
17. See Isa. 6:1 and 9:7, and John 12:41.
18. See Ezek. 1:26–28.
19. See Rev. 3:21.
20. See Rev. 5:6, 13.
21. See Exod. 28:15–21.
22. See Genesis 6–9.
23. See 2 Pet. 2:5.
24. The Bible says the earth's crust ruptured and the fountains of the deep erupted like a gigantic, worldwide geyser (see Gen. 7:11). There may have been something like a vapor canopy surrounding planet earth, that kept the temperature pleasantly even (remember, Adam and Eve wore no clothes), and acted like a giant terrarium that allowed no storms or mass air movements. If so, perhaps the "vapor canopy" burst when the floodgates of heaven were opened, and billions of tons of water fell on the earth (Gen. 7:11–12). See Henry M. Morris, *The Genesis Record* (San Diego: Creation Life, 1976), 194–7.
25. Gen. 9:13.
26. See Matt. 26:28.
27. See Exod. 40:15.
28. See Deut. 18:1.
29. Matt. 14:28.
30. See Gal. 5:24.
31. Matt. 21:1–13.
32. See Gen. 3:24.
33. See Isa. 6:2–4.
34. See Isa. 6:6–7.
35. See Ezekiel 1.
36. See Isa. 14:12–15.
37. See Eph. 2:2.
38. Rom. 8:29.
39. See 2 Cor. 3:18.
40. See Isa. 6:4.
41. Ps. 22:3 KJV.
42. 1 Cor. 9:25.
43. 2 Tim. 4:8, KJV.
44. James 1:12.

45. 1 Pet. 5:4.
46. Rev. 3:11.
47. See 1 Cor. 3:10–16.
48. See 2 Pet. 1:11.

Chapter 6   Hope When You Are Discouraged by the Minority of the Godly

1. See Genesis 12 and Heb. 11:8–13.
2. See Heb. 11:24–27 and Deut. 34:1–4.
3. See Jer. 37:2, 44:16.
4. See Daniel 6.
5. See Isaiah 6 and Heb. 11:37. Jewish history indicates Isaiah was one of the prophets described in Heb. 11:37 as being sawn in two.
6. See Matt. 14:1–12.
7. See Luke 1:38 and John 19:25.
8. See Acts 10. Church history records that Peter was crucified upside down.
9. See Rev. 1:9.
10. See Gen. 5:24.
11. See Isa. 41:8.
12. See Gen. 17:17 and 21:1–2.
13. See Num. 12:3.
14. See Judges 13–16.
15. See 1 Sam. 13:14.
16. See 2 Chron. 1:7–12.
17. See 2 Kings 2:11.
18. See Matt. 16:14.
19. Both Jewish and Christian scholars consider Isaiah to be the greatest of the Old Testament prophets.
20. See Matt. 11:11.
21. See Luke 2:4–7.
22. See Acts 2 and 10.
23. See Gen. 3:16–19.
24. As we discussed in chapter 5, there is some debate as to whether these elders were angels or representatives of redeemed men and women. The more obvious fact is that they were kings who served the King of kings!
25. See Lev. 4:27, 32–35.
26. John 1:29.
27. See Heb. 10:3–5.
28. See Heb. 10:5–10.
29. See Eph. 1:7.

Notes

30. See Ps. 137:1–4.
31. See Larry Crabb, *Finding God* (Grand Rapids: Zondervan, 1993), 59.
32. See Isa. 48:11.
33. Phil. 2:10–11.
34. See John 18:3–6.
35. See Isa. 41:4b.

Chapter 7   Hope When You Are Distressed by Evil

1. See Jer. 30:7.
2. See Dan. 9:24, 27.
3. See Rev. 7:14.
4. Jer. 12:1.
5. 2 Pet. 3:9.
6. Rom. 2:4.
7. See 2 Pet. 2:5.
8. Matt. 24:38–39.
9. 2 Pet. 3:4.
10. Some New Testament scholars see the seals, bowls, and trumpets as a three-time repeat of the same judgments. Even if this is so, the judgment still takes place progressively.
11. See Rom. 1:24.
12. See Rom. 1:26–27.
13. See Rom. 1:28.
14. See Acts 1:14 and 2:3.
15. See Acts 2:3.
16. Matt. 24:7–8.
17. See Gen. 3:17–18.
18. Rom. 8:19–22.
19. Hab. 3:2.
20. See Deut. 7:7.
21. See John 5:16–23.
22. See Zech. 12:10–13:1.
23. See 1 Kings 17:1.
24. See 1 Kings 18:42–46.
25. See 2 Kings 2:11.
26. See Mal. 4:5–6.
27. One of the witnesses is thought by some to be Enoch, a great preacher of righteousness in the Old Testament (see Jude 1:14), who likewise never died (see Gen. 5:24).
28. See Exodus 7.
29. See Deut. 34:6 and Jude 1:19.
30. See Matt. 17:3.

31. See Acts 16:25–30.
32. Rom. 10:9.
33. 2 Pet. 3:9.
34. 1 Pet. 2:21–23.

Chapter 8   Hope When You Are Distressed by Evil Alliances

1. Rev. 14:10.
2. Rom. 13:1.
3. See Jer. 25:9 and 27:6.
4. Many Christians today are seeking to "save" our nation through the political process. We need to be careful that we do not find ourselves fighting against God. If we want to turn our nation away from sin, to God, we need to earnestly pray to the One Who is in control, Who establishes all those in authority. (See 2 Chron. 7:13–14.)
5. 2 Thess. 2:3.
6. Dan. 11:36a.
7. Dan. 11:38.
8. Compare 2 Thess. 2:9 with Heb. 2:4.
9. See Dan. 11:37.
10. See Dan. 7:25.
11. See 2 Thess. 2:4 and Dan. 11:36.
12. See Rev. 13:3 and 17:8.
13. Dan. 11:36b.
14. Morris, *The Revelation Record,* 234.
15. See Dan. 7:2–6.
16. See Rev. 12:9.
17. See Dan. 12:10.
18. See Amos 8:11.
19. Rom. 1:25.
20. 2 Thess. 2:10–12.
21. See Gen. 3:1.
22. See Exod. 7:10–12.
23. See Acts 16:16.
24. See Job 28:28 AMP.
25. The events of this battle are described more fully in Zechariah 14. It is also during this battle that there is so much carnage the blood rises to the height of a horse's bridle for a distance of 180 miles, according to Rev. 14:20.
26. Luke 18:7–8, KJV.
27. Rom. 12:19.
28. See Rev. 13:16–17.
29. Gen. 9:1, 7.
30. Gen. 11:4.

Notes

31. Berit Kjos, *Under the Spell of Mother Earth* (Wheaton, Ill.: Victor Books, 1992).
32. See Eph. 1:4.
33. See Eph. 5:25–27.
34. Phil. 1:6.
35. 1 John 3:2.
36. 1 John 3:3.
37. Isa. 63:2–3.
38. See Rev. 5:10. It is obvious that, although we do not know exactly when the Rapture of the church will take place, it will have preceded this event since the Raptured believers are in heaven, returning with Christ as described in Rev. 19:14. (See also 1 Thess. 4:13–18).
39. *Time* magazine, 19 June 1995, 21.

Chapter 9 Hope When You Are Defeated by Life

1. Matt. 25:23.
2. Matt. 6:1, 4. See also Matt. 6:6, 18.
3. Isa. 11:6.
4. See 1 John 3:2.
5. See 1 Pet. 1:15–16.
6. See Col. 3:12–14.
7. See Phil. 1:6.
8. The first resurrection is the resurrection of believers. Jesus Christ Himself was the first fruit of this resurrection. It includes believers raised from the dead in Jerusalem at the time of the resurrection of Christ, the believers raised at the Rapture, as well as believers raised from the dead at the end of the Great Tribulation.
9. John 3:7.
10. John Walvoord, *The Revelation of Jesus Christ* (Chicago: Moody Press, 1966), 301–2.
11. See Isa. 29:13.
12. Jer. 17:9 KJV.
13. Heb. 9:27.
14. John 5:22.
15. See Ps. 69:28.
16. See 2 Cor. 5:19.
17. See John 3:18.
18. See Matt. 13:50.
19. See Rev. 14:11 and 20:10.
20. Rev. 21:4.
21. See Rev. 20:1.
22. Rev. 20:10, 14, 15.

23. See Rev. 21:14.
24. See Jude 13.
25. Rev. 22:5.
26. Matt. 5:22.
27. See Rev. 14:10; 19:20; and 20:10, 14, and 15.
28. See Rev. 22:1–2.
29. See Matt. 7:23.
30. Rev. 22:4.
31. John 3:16–17.
32. On various occasions, people have told me they have often prayed a prayer similar to this one but still are not assured they have truly been saved or born again. I answer by pointing out to them the fact they have prayed this prayer repeatedly suggests they have not prayed it even once by faith, therefore they have NOT been saved (see Eph. 2:8). Because faith takes God at His word, accepts what he says, and says "thank you."

    If you have just prayed this prayer, thank God, through faith in His word, that you are forgiven of your sin. (1 John 1:9), that you have received eternal life (John 3:16), that Jesus Christ now lives within you (Rev. 3:20) in the Person of the Holy Spirit (Luke 11:13, Eph. 1:13), and that God therefore acknowledges you as His own child (John 1:12, Rom. 10:9).
33. *Time* magazine, 17 July 1995, 33.
34. See Matt. 12:26–27.
35. Ps. 103:12.

Chapter 10   Hope When You Are Defeated by Death

1. John 14:2–3.
2. 1 Cor. 2:9.
3. Gen. 2:8–9.
4. John 14:2.
5. Matt. 7:22–23.
6. See John 14:6.
7. See Col. 3:5.
8. 2 Pet. 3:7, 10–11.
9. John 8:12.
10. Matt. 5:14.
11. Although it remains to be seen if these measurements can be taken literally, Dr. Henry Morris, in his book *The Revelation Record* (pp. 450–51), has calculated them mathematically. They describe a cube that is fifteen hundred miles square, which is as large as the area from Canada to Mexico and from the Atlantic Ocean to the Rockies. It could easily

accommodate twenty billion residents, each having his or her own private seventy-five-acre cube "room" or "mansion." This would still leave plenty of room for streets, parks, and public buildings. Heaven is a big place! When Jesus said, "In my Father's house are many rooms," He wanted us to know there would be room enough for anyone and everyone who chooses to be a member of God's family! (See John 14:3.)

12. See 1 Cor. 2:9.
13. While people on earth work and fight and cheat for gold, my mother says you can tell what God thinks of it: He paves the streets of heaven with it!
14. See 1 Pet. 2:4–8.
15. See Matt. 16:18.
16. See Matt. 6:19–20.
17. See Heb. 11:10.
18. See Leviticus 16.
19. Heb. 10:19–20.
20. John 7:38–39.
21. See 2 Cor. 3:17.
22. See Gal. 5:22–23.
23. See Gen. 3:14–19.
24. See Rom. 8:20–21.
25. 1 Cor. 13:12.

Hope That Ignites Our Hearts

1. 1 Sam. 22:2.
2. 1 Tim. 1:1.
3. Charles H. Spurgeon, *Morning and Evening* (London: Passmore and Alabaster, n.d.).
4. See John 9:4.
5. Gal. 6:9.
6. See 1 John 1:7.
7. See 1 John 1:9.
8. See John 4:13–14.
9. See John 6:51, 57–58, 63.
10. See Matt. 1:21; 1 John 1:9, 2:2; and Eph. 1:7.
11. See John 8:12.
12. See Isa. 9:6, Phil. 4:7, and John 14:27.
13. See John 11:25.
14. Gen. 2:17.
15. Gen. 3:1, 3 (italics mine).
16. Jer. 36:2–3.
17. Matt. 5:18.

A Devotional Guide
on
The Book of Revelation

Preface

Is the Book of Revelation confusing to you? Although printed in black and white, translated into English using everyday nouns, verbs, and acceptable sentence structure, do you sometimes read it, thinking it must be written in some form of cryptic code? These worksheets are designed to help you *break the code,* so that rather than being confusing, the Book of Revelation will help you clearly communicate with the Lord Whom the book reveals.

Communication is vitally important in developing a personal relationship with anyone, including God. Could it be that lack of communication, or even miscommunication, could be one reason for your relationship with God seeming to be distant, formal, and impersonal?

Recently I was given this collection of church bulletin misprints:

The rosebud on the altar this morning is to announce the birth of David Alan Belser, the sin of Rev. and Mrs. Julius Belser.

Altar flowers are given to the glory of God in memory of her mother.

The message this evening will be "What Is Hell Like?" Come early and listen to the choir practice.

The outreach committee has enlisted 25 visitors to make calls on people who are not afflicted with any church.

Peacemaking meeting canceled for today due to a conflict.

Ushers will eat latecomers.

Low self-esteem support group, 7 to 8:30 p.m., Eastview Baptist Church (use back door).

Newberg Church tries to assist in servicing a luncheon for families of church members who have died immediately following the funeral.

As humorous as these misprints are, miscommunication is not funny when we are seeking to understand God's Word that we might grow in our personal relationship with Him. Therefore, it is important to take the time and make the effort to read His Word carefully and accurately, that we might hear His voice speaking to us personally and develop our personal relationship with Him.

In the following pages, you will find worksheets designed to help you communicate with God. The worksheets are preceded by an outline for the particular passage they are covering, and correspond with the chapters in the book.

It is my heartfelt prayer that this devotional guide will aid you in developing your communication with God and therefore your personal relationship with Him. And that in the process, you might be thrilled by the vision of His glory!

Instructions

Step 1: To complete the worksheets, begin by reading the designated passage of Scripture. This is on the worksheet in step 1.

Step 2: When you have finished reading the passage, move to step 2, making a verse-by-verse list of the outstanding facts. Don't get caught up in the details, just pinpoint the most obvious facts. Ask yourself who is speaking, what is the subject, where is it taking place, when did it happen, and so on. As you make your list, try not to paraphrase, but use actual words from the passage itself. Take a moment now to read Mark 9:2–8 in the completed example on page 290. When you have read the passage, look over the list of facts so that you understand these instructions more clearly.

Step 3: After looking at the passage and listing the facts, you are ready for step 3. Go back to the list of facts and look for a lesson to learn from each fact. Ask yourself, "What are the people doing that I should be doing? What are they not doing that I should or should not be doing? Is there a command that I should obey? A promise that I should claim? A warning that I should heed? An example that I should follow?" Look over the lessons given in step 3 of the example from Mark 9 on page 291.

Step 4: The most meaningful step is 4, but you cannot do it until steps 1, 2, and 3 have been completed. In order to do step 4, take the lessons you found in step 3, and put them in the form of questions you could ask yourself, your spouse, your child, your friend, your neighbor, or your co-worker. As you write out the questions, listen for God to communicate to you personally through His Word.

The Book of Revelation may be difficult for you in certain passages. (For this reason, only portions of chapters 6 through 19 have been included as a basis for the worksheets, although they are covered in the book.) Don't get hung up on symbolism. Look for the general principles and lessons which can be learned, even when the symbolism is not fully understood. An example is given at the beginning of each column of the worksheets to help you get started.

Remember, don't rush. It may take you several days of prayerful meditation on a given passage in order to discover meaningful lessons and hear God speaking to you. The object of these devotional studies is not to get through the worksheets, but to develop your personal relationship with God as you learn to communicate with Him.

Step 5: Read the Book of Revelation prayerfully, objectively, thoughtfully, and attentively as you listen for God to speak. He may not speak to you through every verse, but He will speak. When He does, record the verse number, what it is He seems to be saying to you, and your response to Him in step 5. You might like to date it as a means not only of keeping a spiritual journal, but also of holding yourself accountable to following through in obedience.

The following example from Mark 9 has been completed in order to illustrate the previous instructions. Track each verse carefully through all five steps so you can see how the facts are developed into lessons, which then unfold into personal questions. God bless you as you seek to learn this simple yet effective method of communicating with Him.

1

Look in His Word:
Feel free to underline,
circle or otherwise mark
text if it will aid your
study.

2

List the Facts: Make
a verse-by-verse list of
the most outstanding,
obvious facts. What does
the passage say? Be literal
as you answer.

*Example of Mark 9:2–8 to
show step by step how to study
Revelation in the following
daily devotionals.*

Mark 9:2 After six days Jesus
took Peter, James and John with
him and led them up a high
mountain, where they were all
alone. There he was transfigured
before them. **3** His clothes
became dazzling white, whiter
than anyone in the world could
bleach them. **4** And there
appeared before them Elijah and
Moses, who were talking with
Jesus. **5** Peter said to Jesus, "Rabbi,
it is good for us to be here. Let us
put up three shelters—one for
you, one for Moses and one for
Elijah." **6** (He did not know what
to say, they were so frightened.) **7**
Then a cloud appeared and
enveloped them, and a voice came
from the cloud: "This is my Son,
whom I love. Listen to him!" **8**
Suddenly, when they looked
around, they no longer saw anyone with them except Jesus.

v.2a Jesus took three disciples
alone up a mountain.

vv.2b–3 He was transfigured
before them with clothes dazzling
white.

v.4 Moses and Elijah appeared
with Jesus.

v.5 Peter said three shelters
should be put up.

v.6 He didn't know what to say.

v.7 A voice spoke from the cloud
saying to listen to Jesus.

v.8 Suddenly they saw no one
except Jesus.

Sample Chapter

3 **Learn from the Lessons:** What lessons can be learned from these facts? What does the passage mean? Be spiritual as you answer.

v.2a Jesus wants to be alone with us.

vv.2b–3 There are times we have to be alone with Jesus in order to have a vision of His glory.

v.4 The vision of His glory will be the focus of believers in eternity.

v.5 Instead of worshiping Christ, some who call themselves Christians want to build earthly monuments to His Name.

v.6 Sometimes our emotions prompt us to speak when we should be silent.

v.7 We are commanded by God to listen to what Jesus says.

v.8 When everything else fades away, including our visions and dreams of glory, our focus should still be on Jesus.

4 **Listen to His Voice:** What does this passage mean to you? Rewrite the lessons from step 3 in the form of questions. Be personal as you answer.

v.2a When do I make time to be alone with Jesus?

vv.2b–3 What fresh vision of Jesus am I lacking because I don't spend time alone with Him each day?

v.4 How drastically will I have to adjust my focus from what it is today to what it will be one day in eternity?

v.5 What earthly monument—a ministry, a church, a denomination, a reputation—am I seeking to build instead of genuine worship of Christ?

v.6 When have I spoken out when I should have been silent in worship?

v.7 Having glimpsed the vision of His glory, how obedient am I to God's command to *listen* to the voice of His beloved Son?

5 **Live in Response:** Pinpoint what God is saying to you from this passage. How will you respond? Write down today's date and what you will do now about what He has said.

I will begin today to make time each day to be alone with Jesus, read my Bible, and listen to His voice.

Suggestions for Study

These worksheets are designed to be used for group public discussion (Sunday School classes, women's or men's church groups, home or neighborhood Bible classes, one-on-one discipleship) or as an individual's private devotions. Believing that God speaks to the individual through His Word, we have designed this Devotional Guide to lead the Bible student through a series of questions concerning the Scripture passage. These exercises enable the readers to not only discover for themselves the eternal truths revealed by God in the Bible, but also to hear God speaking personally through His Word.

Public Discussion

It is suggested that the Preface and Instructions to the Devotional Guide be used as an initial lesson, in order to familiarize the Bible student with the format to be used. The worksheets are subsequently divided into eleven chapters, which, when used with the Preface and Instructions, make up either a three-month-long weekly study, or a one-year-long monthly study.

The preparation for public discussion. In a study that involves more than one person, it is recommended that participants have their own worksheets. The participants should be assigned a specific segment of the material for study and should write out their own answers on the worksheets provided. Participants should complete all the worksheets for the assigned chapter. At this point in the study, it would also be meaningful for participants to read the corresponding chapter in *The Vision of His Glory.*

The participation in public discussion. Once a week or once a month, depending on how often the class meets, the participants should gather for the opportunity to share their insights from the worksheets, under the leadership of a "convener" or "moderator" who would lead the entire group through the public discussion. If the group is large (twelve or more), the class may be divided into

Suggestions for Study

smaller groups for a discussion of the questions with moderators being chosen to lead each small group.

The summation of public discussion. A summary lecture may be given by the "convener" at the end of the group study, emphasizing specific applications from the text of *The Vision of His Glory* to the demographics of the particular group (i.e., age, sex, and interests).

Private Devotions

The Scripture passage for each worksheet corresponds with the Scripture passage in the divisions of the book chapters. For example, the first worksheet on pages 294 and 295 in chapter one covers Revelation 1:1 through Revelation 1:3. In *The Vision of His Glory,* the section entitled Finding Hope by Reflecting on What God Says . . . Through Prophecy, on pages 2 through 9, develops thoughts involving that same passage of Scripture.

Since the number of worksheets varies for each chapter, it is suggested for private devotions that the individual read the introduction to the specific chapter in the book to be studied, then complete one worksheet each day, followed by a reading of the corresponding commentary in the book. Since there are thirty-four worksheets, using this format on a daily basis will take the reader approximately five weeks to complete the entire book.

Other general suggestions for effective daily Bible study are:
- Set aside a regular place and time for private devotions.
- Pray before beginning the day's assignment, asking God to speak to you through His Word.
- Write out your answers for each step of the worksheets in sequence—do not skip a step.
- Make the time to be still and listen, reflecting thoughtfully on your response in step 5.

Spiritual discipline is an essential part of our ability to grow in our personal relationships with God through knowledge and understanding of His Word. I pray that these worksheets will provide an easy, meaningful format for this growth to occur.

1 **Look in His Word:**
Feel free to underline, circle or otherwise mark text if it will aid your study.

2 **List the Facts:** Make a verse-by-verse list of the most outstanding, obvious facts. What does the passage say? Be literal as you answer.

Finding Hope Through Reflecting On What God Says . . . Through Prophecy (1:1–3)

• *received from God v.1*
• *recorded by John v.2*
• *read by you v.3*

v.1 God gave the revelation of Jesus Christ, making it known to John, to show His servants what would take place.

Revelation 1:1 The revelation of Jesus Christ, which God gave him to show his servants what must soon take place. He made it known by sending his angel to his servant John, **2** who testifies to everything he saw—that is, the word of God and the testimony of Jesus Christ. **3** Blessed is the one who reads the words of this prophecy, and blessed are those who hear it and take to heart what is written in it, because the time is near.

3 Learn from the Lessons: What lessons can be learned from these facts? What does the passage mean? Be spiritual as you answer.

v.1 God reveals Jesus to His servants through His Word.

4 Listen to His Voice: What does this passage mean to you? Rewrite the lessons from step 3 in the form of questions. Be personal as you answer.

v.1 Where am I looking for a fresh vision of Jesus?

5 Live in Response: Pinpoint what God is saying to you from this passage. How will you respond? Write down today's date and what you will do now about what He has said.

Look in His Word: Feel free to underline, circle or otherwise mark text if it will aid your study.

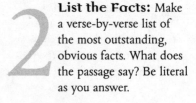

List the Facts: Make a verse-by-verse list of the most outstanding, obvious facts. What does the passage say? Be literal as you answer.

Finding Hope By Refocusing On Who Jesus Is . . . Through Praise (1:4–8)

- *for His deity vv.4–5a*
- *for His humanity vv.5b–7*
- *for His eternity v.8.*

vv.4–5a John greets seven churches with grace and peace from the Eternal, the seven-fold Spirit, and Jesus Christ.

Revelation 1:4 John, to the seven churches in the province of Asia: Grace and peace to you from him who is, and who was, and who is to come, and from the seven spirits before his throne, **5** and from Jesus Christ, who is the faithful witness, the firstborn from the dead, and the ruler of the kings of the earth. To him who loves us and has freed us from our sins by his blood, **6** and has made us to be a kingdom and priests to serve his God and Father—to him be glory and power for ever and ever! Amen. **7** Look, he is coming with the clouds, and every eye will see him, even those who pierced him; and all the peoples of the earth will mourn because of him. So shall it be! Amen. **8** "I am the Alpha and the Omega," says the Lord God, "who is, and who was, and who is to come, the Almighty."

3 Learn from the Lessons: What lessons can be learned from these facts? What does the passage mean? Be spiritual as you answer.

vv.4–5a Grace and peace come from the triune God.

4 Listen to His Voice: What does this passage mean to you? Rewrite the lessons from step 3 in the form of questions. Be personal as you answer.

vv.4–5a From where, what, or whom am I seeking peace?

5 Live in Response: Pinpoint what God is saying to you from this passage. How will you respond? Write down today's date and what you will do now about what He has said.

1

Look in His Word: Feel free to underline, circle or otherwise mark text if it will aid your study.

2

List the Facts: Make a verse-by-verse list of the most outstanding, obvious facts. What does the passage say? Be literal as you answer.

Finding Hope Through the Patience of Christ (1:9–12)

• *during suffering v.9*
• *in solitude v.9*
• *through submission vv.10–12*

v.9 John was suffering patiently on the island of Patmos because of God's Word and the testimony of Jesus.

Revelation 1:9 I, John, your brother and companion in the suffering and kingdom and patient endurance that are ours in Jesus, was on the island of Patmos because of the word of God and the testimony of Jesus. **10** On the Lord's Day I was in the Spirit, and I heard behind me a loud voice like a trumpet, **11** which said: "Write on a scroll what you see and send it to the seven churches: to Ephesus, Smyrna, Pergamum, Thyatira, Sardis, Philadelphia and Laodicea." **12** I turned around to see the voice that was speaking to me. And when I turned I saw seven golden lampstands.

by the Greatness of Your Problems

3 **Learn from the Lessons:** What lessons can be learned from these facts? What does the passage mean? Be spiritual as you answer.

4 **Listen to His Voice:** What does this passage mean to you? Rewrite the lessons from step 3 in the form of questions. Be personal as you answer.

v.9 It is possible to suffer for doing the right thing, yet endure it with patience.

v.9 What is my attitude when suffering unjustly?

5 **Live in Response:** Pinpoint what God is saying to you from this passage. How will you respond? Write down today's date and what you will do now about what He has said.

1 **Look in His Word:**
Feel free to underline, circle or otherwise mark text if it will aid your study.

2 **List the Facts:** Make a verse-by-verse list of the most outstanding, obvious facts. What does the passage say? Be literal as you answer.

Finding Hope Through Preoccupation with Christ (1:13–16)

- *as the Son of Man v.13a*
- *as the High Priest v.13b*
- *as the King of Kings v.13c*
- *as the Everlasting Father v.14a*
- *as the Avenger v.14b*
- *as the Final Judge v.15a*
- *as the Living Word v.15b*
- *as the Lord of Lords v.16a*
- *as the Commander of the Lord's Army v.16b*
- *as the Light of the World v.16c*

Revelation 1:13 and among the lampstands was someone "like a son of man," dressed in a robe reaching down to his feet and with a golden sash around his chest. **14** His head and hair were white like wool, as white as snow, and his eyes were like blazing fire. **15** His feet were like bronze glowing in a furnace, and his voice was like the sound of rushing waters. **16** In his right hand he held seven stars, and out of his mouth came a sharp double-edged sword. His face was like the sun shining in all its brilliance.

v.13 Among the lampstands John saw someone "like a son of man" in a robe and golden sash.

by the Greatness of Your Problems

3 **Learn from the Lessons:** What lessons can be learned from these facts? What does the passage mean? Be spiritual as you answer.

4 **Listen to His Voice:** What does this passage mean to you? Rewrite the lessons from step 3 in the form of questions. Be personal as you answer.

v.13 Jesus Christ should be the focus of our worship.

v.13 What is blurring my focus as I worship?

5 **Live in Response:** Pinpoint what God is saying to you from this passage. How will you respond? Write down today's date and what you will do now about what He has said.

1 **Look in His Word:** Feel free to underline, circle or otherwise mark text if it will aid your study.

2 **List the Facts:** Make a verse-by-verse list of the most outstanding, obvious facts. What does the passage say? Be literal as you answer.

Finding Hope Through Prostration Before Christ (1:17–20)

- *in silence v.17*
- *in stillness v.17*
- *in surrender vv.17–18*
- *for service vv.19–20*

v.17 When John saw Jesus, he fell at His feet, felt His hand, and heard His voice telling him not to be afraid.

Revelation 1:17 When I saw him, I fell at his feet as though dead. Then he placed his right hand on me and said: "Do not be afraid. I am the First and the Last. **18** I am the Living One; I was dead, and behold I am alive for ever and ever! And I hold the keys of death and Hades. **19** "Write, therefore, what you have seen, what is now and what will take place later. **20** The mystery of the seven stars that you saw in my right hand and of the seven golden lampstands is this: The seven stars are the angels of the seven churches, and the seven lampstands are the seven churches.

by the Greatness of Your Problems

3 **Learn from the Lessons:** What lessons can be learned from these facts? What does the passage mean? Be spiritual as you answer.

4 **Listen to His Voice:** What does this passage mean to you? Rewrite the lessons from step 3 in the form of questions. Be personal as you answer.

v.17 A genuine vision of Jesus Christ results in awe-inspired worship and surrender while His Word brings reassuring peace.

v.17 What impact is the vision of Christ having on my life?

5 **Live in Response:** Pinpoint what God is saying to you from this passage. How will you respond? Write down today's date and what you will do now about what He has said.

A Devotional Guide / 303

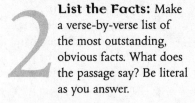

Look in His Word:
Feel free to underline, circle or otherwise mark text if it will aid your study.

List the Facts: Make a verse-by-verse list of the most outstanding, obvious facts. What does the passage say? Be literal as you answer.

Deluded by the Importance of Service: Finding Hope through . . . (2:1–7)

• *looking at Jesus v.1*
• *learning from Jesus vv.2–6*
• *listening to Jesus v.7*

Revelation 2:1 "To the angel of the church in Ephesus write: These are the words of him who holds the seven stars in his right hand and walks among the seven golden lampstands: **2** I know your deeds, your hard work and your perseverance. I know that you cannot tolerate wicked men, that you have tested those who claim to be apostles but are not, and have found them false. **3** You have persevered and have endured hardships for my name, and have not grown weary. **4** Yet I hold this against you: You have forsaken your first love. **5** Remember the height from which you have fallen! Repent and do the things you did at first. If you do not repent, I will come to you and remove your lampstand from its place. **6** But you have this in your favor: You hate the practices of the Nicolaitans, which I also hate. **7** He who has an ear, let him hear what the Spirit says to the churches. To him who overcomes, I will give the right to eat from the tree of life, which is in the paradise of God.

v.1 The One Who holds the stars and walks amongst the lampstands writes a word to the Ephesian church.

3 **Learn from the Lessons:** What lessons can be learned from these facts? What does the passage mean? Be spiritual as you answer.

4 **Listen to His Voice:** What does this passage mean to you? Rewrite the lessons from step 3 in the form of questions. Be personal as you answer.

v.1 Through His written Word, Jesus reveals His presence in our midst.

v.1 If I lack an awareness of His presence in my life, could it be because I have neglected my Bible reading?

5 **Live in Response:** Pinpoint what God is saying to you from this passage. How will you respond? Write down today's date and what you will do now about what He has said.

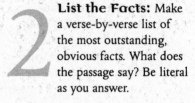

1 **Look in His Word:** Feel free to underline, circle or otherwise mark text if it will aid your study.

2 **List the Facts:** Make a verse-by-verse list of the most outstanding, obvious facts. What does the passage say? Be literal as you answer.

Deluded by the Importance of Society: Finding Hope through . . . (2:12–17)

- *looking at Jesus v.12*
- *learning from Jesus vv.13–16*
- *listening to Jesus v.17*

him hear what the Spirit says to the churches. To him who overcomes, I will give some of the hidden manna. I will also give him a white stone with a new name written on it, known only to him who receives it.

Revelation 2:12 "To the angel of the church in Pergamum write: These are the words of him who has the sharp, double-edged sword. **13** I know where you live—where Satan has his throne. Yet you remain true to my name. You did not renounce your faith in me, even in the days of Antipas, my faithful witness, who was put to death in your city—where Satan lives. **14** Nevertheless, I have a few things against you: You have people there who hold to the teaching of Balaam, who taught Balak to entice the Israelites to sin by eating food sacrificed to idols and by committing sexual immorality. **15** Likewise you also have those who hold to the teaching of the Nicolaitans. **16** Repent therefore! Otherwise, I will soon come to you and will fight against them with the sword of my mouth. **17** He who has an ear, let

v.12 The One Who has the sword has a word for the church at Pergamum.

by Your Own Importance

3 **Learn from the Lessons:** What lessons can be learned from these facts? What does the passage mean? Be spiritual as you answer.

4 **Listen to His Voice:** What does this passage mean to you? Rewrite the lessons from step 3 in the form of questions. Be personal as you answer.

v.12 Jesus reminds the church that the Bible, which is His Word, is also an offensive spiritual weapon.

v.12 As I seek to have victory over Satan, what weapons am I using?

5 **Live in Response:** Pinpoint what God is saying to you from this passage. How will you respond? Write down today's date and what you will do now about what He has said.

1 **Look in His Word:**
Feel free to underline, circle or otherwise mark text if it will aid your study.

2 **List the Facts:** Make a verse-by-verse list of the most outstanding, obvious facts. What does the passage say? Be literal as you answer.

Deluded by the Importance of Status: Finding Hope through . . . (3:1–6)

• *looking at Jesus v. 1*
• *learning from Jesus vv. 1–4*
• *listening to Jesus vv. 5–6*

Revelation 3:1 "To the angel of the church in Sardis write: These are the words of him who holds the seven spirits of God and the seven stars. I know your deeds; you have a reputation of being alive, but you are dead. **2** Wake up! Strengthen what remains and is about to die, for I have not found your deeds complete in the sight of my God. **3** Remember, therefore, what you have received and heard; obey it, and repent. But if you do not wake up, I will come like a thief, and you will not know at what time I will come to you. **4** Yet you have a few people in Sardis who have not soiled their clothes. They will walk with me, dressed in white, for they are worthy. **5** He who overcomes will, like them, be dressed in white. I will never blot out his name from the book of life, but will acknowledge his name before my Father and his angels. **6** He who has an ear, let him hear what the Spirit says to the churches.

v. 1 The One Who holds the Spirit of God and the stars knows the deeds and reputation of the church at Sardis.

by Your Own Importance

3 **Learn from the Lessons:** What lessons can be learned from these facts? What does the passage mean? Be spiritual as you answer.

4 **Listen to His Voice:** What does this passage mean to you? Rewrite the lessons from step 3 in the form of questions. Be personal as you answer.

v.1 God is not impressed by our reputation.

v.1 How closely does my reputation before others resemble what God knows to be accurate?

5 **Live in Response:** Pinpoint what God is saying to you from this passage. How will you respond? Write down today's date and what you will do now about what He has said.

Look in His Word: Feel free to underline, circle or otherwise mark text if it will aid your study.

List the Facts: Make a verse-by-verse list of the most outstanding, obvious facts. What does the passage say? Be literal as you answer.

Deluded by the Importance of Self: Finding Hope through . . . (3:14–22)

- *looking at Jesus v.14*
- *learning from Jesus vv.15–20*
- *listening to Jesus vv.21–22*

Revelation 3:14 "To the angel of the church in Laodicea write: These are the words of the Amen, the faithful and true witness, the ruler of God's creation. **15** I know your deeds, that you are neither cold nor hot. I wish you were either one or the other! **16** So, because you are lukewarm—neither hot nor cold—I am about to spit you out of my mouth. **17** You say, 'I am rich; I have acquired wealth and do not need a thing.' But you do not realize that you are wretched, pitiful, poor, blind and naked. **18** I counsel you to buy from me gold refined in the fire, so you can become rich; and white clothes to wear, so you can cover your shameful nakedness; and salve to put on your eyes, so you can see. **19** Those whom I love I rebuke and discipline. So be earnest, and repent. **20** Here I am! I stand at the door and knock. If anyone hears my voice and opens the door, I will come in and eat with him, and he with me. **21** To him who overcomes, I will give the right to sit with me on my throne, just as I overcame and sat down with my Father on his throne. **22** He who has an ear, let him hear what the Spirit says to the churches."

v.14 The One Who is the Amen, the witness, the ruler of creation, has a word for the church at Laodicea.

3 **Learn from the Lessons:** What lessons can be learned from these facts? What does the passage mean? Be spiritual as you answer.

4 **Listen to His Voice:** What does this passage mean to you? Rewrite the lessons from step 3 in the form of questions. Be personal as you answer.

v.14 Jesus is the Amen—He will have the last word.

v.14 Do I acknowledge the final authority of God's Word?

5 **Live in Response:** Pinpoint what God is saying to you from this passage. How will you respond? Write down today's date and what you will do now about what He has said.

1 **Look in His Word:**
Feel free to underline,
circle or otherwise mark
text if it will aid your
study.

2 **List the Facts:** Make
a verse-by-verse list of
the most outstanding,
obvious facts. What does
the passage say? Be literal
as you answer.

*The Insignificance of Your
Testimony: Finding Hope
through . . . (2:8–11)*

• *looking at Jesus v.8*
• *learning from Jesus vv.9–10*
• *listening to Jesus vv.10–11*

v.8 The One Who is First and
Last, Who died and rose, has a
word for the church at Smyrna.

Revelation 2:8 "To the angel of
the church in Smyrna write: These
are the words of him who is the
First and the Last, who died and
came to life again. **9** I know your
afflictions and your poverty—yet
you are rich! I know the slander
of those who say they are Jews
and are not, but are a synagogue
of Satan. **10** Do not be afraid of
what you are about to suffer. I tell
you, the devil will put some of
you in prison to test you, and you
will suffer persecution for ten
days. Be faithful, even to the point
of death, and I will give you the
crown of life. **11** He who has an
ear, let him hear what the Spirit
says to the churches. He who
overcomes will not be hurt at all
by the second death.

by Your Own Insignificance

3 **Learn from the
Lessons:** What lessons
can be learned from these
facts? What does the pas-
sage mean? Be spiritual as
you answer.

4 **Listen to His Voice:**
What does this passage
mean to you? Rewrite the
lessons from step 3 in the
form of questions. Be
personal as you answer.

v.8 The Eternal, Risen, Living
Lord speaks through His written
Word to the church today.

v.8 If His Word is not faithfully
proclaimed, how can Christ
speak?

5 **Live in Response:** Pinpoint what God is saying to you from
this passage. How will you respond? Write down today's date and
what you will do now about what He has said.

1 Look in His Word:
Feel free to underline, circle or otherwise mark text if it will aid your study.

2 List the Facts: Make
a verse-by-verse list of the most outstanding, obvious facts. What does the passage say? Be literal as you answer.

The Insignificance of Your Purity: Finding Hope through . . . (2:18–29)

- *looking at Jesus v.18*
- *learning from Jesus vv.19–25*
- *listening to Jesus vv.26–29*

Revelation 2:18 "To the angel of the church in Thyatira write: These are the words of the Son of God, whose eyes are like blazing fire and whose feet are like burnished bronze. **19** I know your deeds, your love and faith, your service and perseverance, and that you are now doing more than you did at first. **20** Nevertheless, I have this against you: You tolerate that woman Jezebel, who calls herself a prophetess. By her teaching she misleads my servants into sexual immorality and the eating of food sacrificed to idols. **21** I have given her time to repent of her immorality, but she is unwilling. **22** So I will cast her on a bed of suffering, and I will make those who commit adultery with her suffer intensely, unless they repent of her ways. **23** I will strike her children dead. Then all the churches will know that I am he who searches hearts and minds, and I will repay each of you according to your deeds. **24** Now I say to the rest of you in Thyatira, to you who do not hold to her teaching and have not

learned Satan's so-called deep secrets (I will not impose any other burden on you): **25** Only hold on to what you have until I come. **26** To him who overcomes and does my will to the end, I will give authority over the nations— **27** 'He will rule them with an iron scepter; he will dash them to pieces like pottery'—just as I have received authority from my Father. **28** I will also give him the morning star. **29** He who has an ear, let him hear what the Spirit says to the churches.

v.18 The Son of God, with eyes like fire and feet like bronze, has a word for the church at Thyatira.

3 **Learn from the Lessons:** What lessons can be learned from these facts? What does the passage mean? Be spiritual as you answer.

4 **Listen to His Voice:** What does this passage mean to you? Rewrite the lessons from step 3 in the form of questions. Be personal as you answer.

v.18 It is possible for God's wrath and impending judgment to be directed at those who call themselves by His Name.

v.18 What am I doing—or could I do—to provoke the wrath and judgment of God?

5 **Live in Response:** Pinpoint what God is saying to you from this passage. How will you respond? Write down today's date and what you will do now about what He has said.

Chapter 4: Hope When You are Deluded . . .

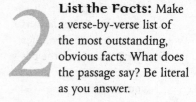

1 **Look in His Word:** Feel free to underline, circle or otherwise mark text if it will aid your study.

2 **List the Facts:** Make a verse-by-verse list of the most outstanding, obvious facts. What does the passage say? Be literal as you answer.

The Insignificance of Your Ability: Finding Hope through . . . (3:7–13)

- *looking at Jesus v.7*
- *learning from Jesus vv.8–11*
- *listening to Jesus vv.12–13*

Revelation 3:7 "To the angel of the church in Philadelphia write: These are the words of him who is holy and true, who holds the key of David. What he opens no one can shut, and what he shuts no one can open. **8** I know your deeds. See, I have placed before you an open door that no one can shut. I know that you have little strength, yet you have kept my word and have not denied my name. **9** I will make those who are of the synagogue of Satan, who claim to be Jews though they are not, but are liars—I will make them come and fall down at your feet and acknowledge that I have loved you. **10** Since you have kept my command to endure patiently, I will also keep you from the hour of trial that is going to come upon the whole world to test those who live on the earth. **11** I am coming soon. Hold on to what

you have, so that no one will take your crown. **12** Him who overcomes I will make a pillar in the temple of my God. Never again will he leave it. I will write on him the name of my God and the name of the city of my God, the new Jerusalem, which is coming down out of heaven from my God; and I will also write on him my new name. **13** He who has an ear, let him hear what the Spirit says to the churches.

v.7 The One Who holds the key of David opens and shuts the door.

by Your Own Insignificance

3 **Learn from the Lessons:** What lessons can be learned from these facts? What does the passage mean? Be spiritual as you answer.

v.7 Jesus Christ is the One Who determines which doors of opportunity are opened and shut for me.

4 **Listen to His Voice:** What does this passage mean to you? Rewrite the lessons from step 3 in the form of questions. Be personal as you answer.

v.7 To whom or to what am I looking to give me an opportunity?

5 **Live in Response:** Pinpoint what God is saying to you from this passage. How will you respond? Write down today's date and what you will do now about what He has said.

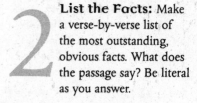

1 **Look in His Word:** Feel free to underline, circle or otherwise mark text if it will aid your study.

2 **List the Facts:** Make a verse-by-verse list of the most outstanding, obvious facts. What does the passage say? Be literal as you answer.

Finding Hope in Expecting the Lord to Enter to Claim His People (4:1; 1 Thessalonians 4:13–18)

1 Thessalonians 4:13 Brothers, we do not want you to be ignorant about those who fall asleep, or to grieve like the rest of men, who have no hope. **14** We believe that Jesus died and rose again and so we believe that God will bring with Jesus those who have fallen asleep in him. **15** According to the Lord's own word, we tell you that we who are still alive, who are left till the coming of the Lord, will certainly not precede those who have fallen asleep. **16** For the Lord himself will come down from heaven, with a loud command, with the voice of the archangel and with the trumpet call of God, and the dead in Christ will rise first. **17** After that, we who are still alive and are left will be caught up together with them in the clouds to meet the Lord in the air. And so we will be with the Lord forever. **18** Therefore encourage each other with these words.

v.13 We are not to be ignorant about those who fall asleep or grieve like others without hope.

3 **Learn from the Lessons:** What lessons can be learned from these facts? What does the passage mean? Be spiritual as you answer.

4 **Listen to His Voice:** What does this passage mean to you? Rewrite the lessons from step 3 in the form of questions. Be personal as you answer.

v.13 Ignorance is the only reason for hopelessness at the funeral of a believer.

v.13 Is ignorance of God's Word the real reason for my hopelessness and grief?

5 **Live in Response:** Pinpoint what God is saying to you from this passage. How will you respond? Write down today's date and what you will do now about what He has said.

1 **Look in His Word:** Feel free to underline, circle or otherwise mark text if it will aid your study.

2 **List the Facts:** Make a verse-by-verse list of the most outstanding, obvious facts. What does the passage say? Be literal as you answer.

Finding Hope in Knowing the Lord is Enthroned at the Center of the Universe (4:1–3a)

• *in sovereignty vv.1–2*
• *in beauty v.3a*

v.1 John saw heaven opened and heard a voice telling him to come and be shown what would take place.

Revelation 4:1 After this I looked, and there before me was a door standing open in heaven. And the voice I had first heard speaking to me like a trumpet said, "Come up here, and I will show you what must take place after this." **2** At once I was in the Spirit, and there before me was a throne in heaven with someone sitting on it. **3** And the one who sat there had the appearance of jasper and carnelian.

3 **Learn from the Lessons:** What lessons can be learned from these facts? What does the passage mean? Be spiritual as you answer.

4 **Listen to His Voice:** What does this passage mean to you? Rewrite the lessons from step 3 in the form of questions. Be personal as you answer.

v.1 Through His Word, God reveals His presence, inviting us to know His plan and purpose.

v.1 Do my circumstances seem confusing or frightening because I have neglected my Bible reading, therefore lack an awareness of His presence and purpose in my life?

5 **Live in Response:** Pinpoint what God is saying to you from this passage. How will you respond? Write down today's date and what you will do now about what He has said.

Look in His Word: Feel free to underline, circle or otherwise mark text if it will aid your study.

List the Facts: Make a verse-by-verse list of the most outstanding, obvious facts. What does the passage say? Be literal as you answer.

Finding Hope by Seeing the Lord Encircled by the Court of Heaven (4:3b–8)

- *security v.3b*
- *sincerity v.4*
- *activity v.5a*
- *purity v.5b*
- *authority v.6a*
- *piety vv.6b–8*

Revelation 4:3b A rainbow, resembling an emerald, encircled the throne. **4** Surrounding the throne were twenty-four other thrones, and seated on them were twenty-four elders. They were dressed in white and had crowns of gold on their heads. **5** From the throne came flashes of lightning, rumblings and peals of thunder. Before the throne, seven lamps were blazing. These are the seven spirits of God. **6** Also before the throne there was what looked like a sea of glass, clear as crystal. In the center, around the throne, were four living creatures, and they were covered with eyes, in front and in back. **7** The first living creature was like a lion, the second was like an ox, the third had a face like a man, the fourth was like a flying eagle. **8** Each of the four living creatures had six wings and was covered with eyes all around, even under his wings. Day and night they never stop saying: "Holy, holy, holy is the Lord God Almighty, who was, and is, and is to come."

v.3b An emerald rainbow encircles the throne.

3 **Learn from the Lessons:** What lessons can be learned from these facts? What does the passage mean? Be spiritual as you answer.

4 **Listen to His Voice:** What does this passage mean to you? Rewrite the lessons from step 3 in the form of questions. Be personal as you answer.

v.3b God's covenant of faithfulness is evident to us when He is in absolute authority.

v.3b If I am doubting God's mercy, or fearful of losing my eternal security, then Who is sitting on the throne of my life?

5 **Live in Response:** Pinpoint what God is saying to you from this passage. How will you respond? Write down today's date and what you will do now about what He has said.

1 **Look in His Word:**
Feel free to underline,
circle or otherwise mark
text if it will aid your
study.

2 **List the Facts:** Make
a verse-by-verse list of
the most outstanding,
obvious facts. What does
the passage say? Be literal
as you answer.

*Finding Hope in Hearing the
Lord Enveloped in a Crescendo
of Praise; Praising the Lord in
. . . (4:8–11)*

• *continuous worship v.8*
• *contagious worship vv.9–10*
• *costly worship vv.10b–11*

v.8 The four living creatures never
stop saying, "Holy is the Lord."

Revelation 4:8 Each of the four
living creatures had six wings and
was covered with eyes all around,
even under his wings. Day and
night they never stop saying:
"Holy, holy, holy is the Lord God
Almighty, who was, and is, and is
to come." **9** Whenever the living
creatures give glory, honor and
thanks to him who sits on the
throne and who lives for ever and
ever, **10** the twenty-four elders
fall down before him who sits on
the throne, and worship him who
lives for ever and ever. They lay
their crowns before the throne
and say: **11** "You are worthy, our
Lord and God, to receive glory
and honor and power, for you created all things, and by your will
they were created and have their
being."

by the Majority of the Ungodly

3 **Learn from the Lessons:** What lessons can be learned from these facts? What does the passage mean? Be spiritual as you answer.

4 **Listen to His Voice:** What does this passage mean to you? Rewrite the lessons from step 3 in the form of questions. Be personal as you answer.

v.8 Our worship of the Lord should never cease.

v.8 What has interrupted my worship of Christ?

5 **Live in Response:** Pinpoint what God is saying to you from this passage. How will you respond? Write down today's date and what you will do now about what He has said.

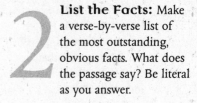

Look in His Word:
Feel free to underline, circle or otherwise mark text if it will aid your study.

List the Facts: Make a verse-by-verse list of the most outstanding, obvious facts. What does the passage say? Be literal as you answer.

Finding Hope in the Unequaled Position of Jesus Christ (5:1–5)

v. 1 The One Who sits on the throne holds in His hand a scroll with writing and seals.

Revelation 5:1 Then I saw in the right hand of him who sat on the throne a scroll with writing on both sides and sealed with seven seals. **2** And I saw a mighty angel proclaiming in a loud voice, "Who is worthy to break the seals and open the scroll?" **3** But no one in heaven or on earth or under the earth could open the scroll or even look inside it. **4** I wept and wept because no one was found who was worthy to open the scroll or look inside. **5** Then one of the elders said to me, "Do not weep! See, the Lion of the tribe of Judah, the Root of David, has triumphed. He is able to open the scroll and its seven seals."

by the Minority of the Godly

3 **Learn from the Lessons:** What lessons can be learned from these facts? What does the passage mean? Be spiritual as you answer.

4 **Listen to His Voice:** What does this passage mean to you? Rewrite the lessons from step 3 in the form of questions. Be personal as you answer.

v. 1 There is Someone sitting on the throne at the center of the Universe.

v. 1 What difference does the knowledge of an actual physical Person ruling the Universe make in my daily life?

5 **Live in Response:** Pinpoint what God is saying to you from this passage. How will you respond? Write down today's date and what you will do now about what He has said.

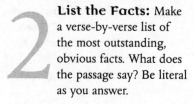

Look in His Word:
Feel free to underline, circle or otherwise mark text if it will aid your study.

List the Facts: Make a verse-by-verse list of the most outstanding, obvious facts. What does the passage say? Be literal as you answer.

Finding Hope in the Undisputed Power of Jesus Christ (5:6–8)

v.6 A Lamb that had been slain, with seven horns and eyes, stood in the throne, surrounded by the creatures and elders.

Revelation 5:6 Then I saw a Lamb, looking as if it had been slain, standing in the center of the throne, encircled by the four living creatures and the elders. He had seven horns and seven eyes, which are the seven spirits of God sent out into all the earth. **7** He came and took the scroll from the right hand of him who sat on the throne. **8** And when he had taken it, the four living creatures and the twenty-four elders fell down before the Lamb. Each one had a harp and they were holding golden bowls full of incense, which are the prayers of the saints.

by the Minority of the Godly

3 **Learn from the Lessons:** What lessons can be learned from these facts? What does the passage mean? Be spiritual as you answer.

4 **Listen to His Voice:** What does this passage mean to you? Rewrite the lessons from step 3 in the form of questions. Be personal as you answer.

v.6 At the end of human history, the risen, crucified Lamb of God still stands supreme, in full authority over the Universe.

v.6 If the Lamb of God is still supreme at the end of human history, why is He not supreme with full authority in my life today?

5 **Live in Response:** Pinpoint what God is saying to you from this passage. How will you respond? Write down today's date and what you will do now about what He has said.

Look in His Word:
Feel free to underline, circle or otherwise mark text if it will aid your study.

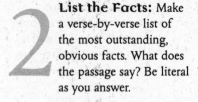

List the Facts: Make a verse-by-verse list of the most outstanding, obvious facts. What does the passage say? Be literal as you answer.

Finding Hope in the Universal Praise of Jesus Christ (5:9–14)

Revelation 5:9 And they sang a new song: "You are worthy to take the scroll and to open its seals, because you were slain, and with your blood you purchased men for God from every tribe and language and people and nation. **10** You have made them to be a kingdom and priests to serve our God, and they will reign on the earth." **11** Then I looked and heard the voice of many angels, numbering thousands upon thousands, and ten thousand times ten thousand. They encircled the throne and the living creatures and the elders. **12** In a loud voice they sang: "Worthy is the Lamb, who was slain, to receive power and wealth and wisdom and strength and honor and glory and praise!" **13** Then I heard every creature in heaven and on earth and under the earth and on the sea, and all that is in them, singing: "To him who sits on the throne and to the Lamb be praise and honor and glory and power, for ever and ever!" **14** The four living creatures said, "Amen," and the elders fell down and worshiped.

v.9 They sang a new song about the worthiness of Christ to take the scroll, because He was slain and purchased men with His blood.

by the Minority of the Godly

3 **Learn from the Lessons:** What lessons can be learned from these facts? What does the passage mean? Be spiritual as you answer.

4 **Listen to His Voice:** What does this passage mean to you? Rewrite the lessons from step 3 in the form of questions. Be personal as you answer.

v.9 For all eternity, the Cross of Christ will be reason for rejoicing.

v.9 In light of the Cross, what reason do I have for losing my joy?

5 **Live in Response:** Pinpoint what God is saying to you from this passage. How will you respond? Write down today's date and what you will do now about what He has said.

1 **Look in His Word:** Feel free to underline, circle or otherwise mark text if it will aid your study.

2 **List the Facts:** Make a verse-by-verse list of the most outstanding, obvious facts. What does the passage say? Be literal as you answer.

Finding Hope in Knowing God is Just (6–9)

- *He judges with patience 6:9–11*
- *He judges with progression 6:1–17*
- *He judges with a pause 7:1–8:5*
- *He judges with precision 8:6–9:21*

This lesson will focus on Revelation 7:9 After this I looked and there before me was a great multitude that no one could count, from every nation, tribe, people and language, standing before the throne and in front of the Lamb. They were wearing white robes and were holding palm branches in their hands. **10** And they cried out in a loud voice: "Salvation belongs to our God, who sits on the throne, and to the Lamb." **11** All the angels were standing around the throne and around the elders and the four living creatures. They fell down on their faces before the throne and worshiped God, **12** saying: "Amen! Praise and glory and wisdom and thanks and honor and power and strength be to our God for ever and ever. Amen!" **13** Then one of the elders asked me, "These in white robes—who are they, and where did they come from?" **14** I answered, "Sir, you know." And he said, "These are they who have come out of the great tribulation; they have washed their robes and made them white in the blood of the Lamb." **15** Therefore, "they are before the throne of God and serve him day and night in his temple; and he who sits on the throne will spread his tent over them. **16** Never again will they hunger; never again will they thirst. The sun will not beat upon them, nor any scorching heat. **17** For the Lamb at the center of the throne will be their shepherd; he will lead them to springs of living water. And God will wipe away every tear from their eyes."

v.9 John saw a great multitude standing before the throne wearing white robes and holding palm branches.

3 **Learn from the Lessons:** What lessons can be learned from these facts? What does the passage mean? Be spiritual as you answer.

v.9 There will be a great number of people in heaven who have been faithful to Christ on earth.

4 **Listen to His Voice:** What does this passage mean to you? Rewrite the lessons from step 3 in the form of questions. Be personal as you answer.

v.9 Why do I think I am the only one in the midst of stress and suffering living faithfully for Christ?

5 **Live in Response:** Pinpoint what God is saying to you from this passage. How will you respond? Write down today's date and what you will do now about what He has said.

1 **Look in His Word:** Feel free to underline, circle or otherwise mark text if it will aid your study.

2 **List the Facts:** Make a verse-by-verse list of the most outstanding, obvious facts. What does the passage say? Be literal as you answer.

Finding Hope in Knowing God is Merciful (7–14)

- *provision of 144,000 preachers 7:1–8*
- *provision of two prophets 11:3*
- *provision of transformed people 12:11*
- *provision of angelic proclamation 14:6–7*

This lesson will focus on Revelation 11:15 The seventh angel sounded his trumpet, and there were loud voices in heaven, which said: "The kingdom of the world has become the kingdom of our Lord and of his Christ, and he will reign for ever and ever." **16** And the twenty-four elders, who were seated on their thrones before God, fell on their faces and worshiped God, **17** saying: "We give thanks to you, Lord God Almighty, the One who is and who was, because you have taken your great power and have begun to reign. **18** The nations were angry; and your wrath has come. The time has come for judging the dead, and for rewarding your servants the prophets and your saints and those who reverence your name, both small and great—and for destroying those who destroy the earth." **19** Then God's temple in heaven was opened, and within his temple was seen the ark of his covenant. And there came flashes of lightning, rumblings, peals of thunder, an earthquake and a great hailstorm.

v.15 A trumpet and loud voices in heaven said: "The world has become the kingdom of Christ and He will reign forever."

by Evil Actions

3 **Learn from the Lessons:** What lessons can be learned from these facts? What does the passage mean? Be spiritual as you answer.

4 **Listen to His Voice:** What does this passage mean to you? Rewrite the lessons from step 3 in the form of questions. Be personal as you answer.

v.15 One day the world that was made by Christ at Creation and bought by Him at Calvary, will be reigned by Him.

v.15 How can I be hopeless when I consider what the world is really coming to?

5 **Live in Response:** Pinpoint what God is saying to you from this passage. How will you respond? Write down today's date and what you will do now about what He has said.

1 **Look in His Word:** Feel free to underline, circle or otherwise mark text if it will aid your study.

2 **List the Facts:** Make a verse-by-verse list of the most outstanding, obvious facts. What does the passage say? Be literal as you answer.

Finding Hope in Knowing God is Merciful (7–14)

- *provision of 144,000 preachers 7:1–8*
- *provision of two prophets 11:3*
- *provision of transformed people 12:11*
- *provision of angelic proclamation 14:6–7*

This lesson will focus on Revelation 12:10 Then I heard a loud voice in heaven say: "Now have come the salvation and the power and the kingdom of our God, and the authority of his Christ. For the accuser of our brothers, who accuses them before our God day and night, has been hurled down. **11** They overcame him by the blood of the Lamb and by the word of their testimony; they did not love their lives so much as to shrink from death. **12** Therefore rejoice, you heavens and you who dwell in them! But woe to the earth and the sea, because the devil has gone down to you! He is filled with fury, because he knows that his time is short."

v.10 Salvation, the power of God, and the authority of Christ, have come, for the accuser has been hurled down.

by Evil Actions

3 **Learn from the Lessons:** What lessons can be learned from these facts? What does the passage mean? Be spiritual as you answer.

4 **Listen to His Voice:** What does this passage mean to you? Rewrite the lessons from step 3 in the form of questions. Be personal as you answer.

v.10 Rather than thwart the power of God and authority of Christ, Satan's activity actually gives opportunity for us to experience it.

v.10 When Satan attacks, how expectant am I of experiencing the power of God in a new way?

5 **Live in Response:** Pinpoint what God is saying to you from this passage. How will you respond? Write down today's date and what you will do now about what He has said.

1 **Look in His Word:** Feel free to underline, circle or otherwise mark text if it will aid your study.

2 **List the Facts:** Make a verse-by-verse list of the most outstanding, obvious facts. What does the passage say? Be literal as you answer.

Finding Hope in Knowing Jesus Christ Will Assert His Power (13:1–16:21)

- *through political leaders 13:1–2, 4–5, 7–8, 16–18*
- *through preachers/prophets (religious leaders) 13:11–13*
- *through plagues 14:1–16:21*

This lesson will focus on Revelation 15:1 I saw in heaven another great and marvellous sign: seven angels with the seven last plagues—last, because with them God's wrath is completed. **2** And I saw what looked like a sea of glass mixed with fire and, standing beside the sea, those who had been victorious over the beast and his image and over the number of his name. They held harps given them by God **3** and sang the song of Moses the servant of God and the song of the Lamb: "Great and marvellous are your deeds, Lord God Almighty. Just and true are your ways, King of the ages. **4** Who will not fear you, O Lord, and bring glory to your name? For you alone are holy. All nations will come and worship before you, for your righteous acts have been revealed." **5** After this I

looked and in heaven the temple, that is, the tabernacle of the Testimony, was opened.

v.1 John saw seven angels with seven last plagues because God's wrath was complete.

by Evil Alliances

3 **Learn from the Lessons:** What lessons can be learned from these facts? What does the passage mean? Be spiritual as you answer.

v.1 God's wrath is thorough, complete, and final.

4 **Listen to His Voice:** What does this passage mean to you? Rewrite the lessons from step 3 in the form of questions. Be personal as you answer.

v.1 Whom do I know who believes he or she can sin and get by with it?

5 **Live in Response:** Pinpoint what God is saying to you from this passage. How will you respond? Write down today's date and what you will do now about what He has said.

1 **Look in His Word:**
Feel free to underline, circle or otherwise mark text if it will aid your study.

2 **List the Facts:** Make a verse-by-verse list of the most outstanding, obvious facts. What does the passage say? Be literal as you answer.

Finding Hope in Knowing Jesus Christ Will Appear in Person (19:1–10)—The Saints Rejoice . . .

• *over the destruction of the wicked vv. 1–5*
• *at the celebration of the wedding vv. 6–10*

Revelation 19:1 After this I heard what sounded like the roar of a great multitude in heaven shouting: "Hallelujah! Salvation and glory and power belong to our God, **2** for true and just are his judgments. He has condemned the great prostitute who corrupted the earth by her adulteries. He has avenged on her the blood of his servants." **3** And again they shouted: "Hallelujah! The smoke from her goes up for ever and ever." **4** The twenty-four elders and the four living creatures fell down and worshiped God, who was seated on the throne. And they cried: "Amen, Hallelujah!" **5** Then a voice came from the throne, saying: "Praise our God, all you his servants, you who fear him, both small and great!" **6** Then I heard what sounded like a great multitude, like the roar of rushing waters and like loud peals of thunder, shouting: "Hallelujah! For our Lord God Almighty reigns. **7** Let us rejoice and be glad and give him glory! For the wedding of the Lamb has come, and his bride has made herself ready. **8** Fine linen, bright and clean, was given her to wear." (Fine linen stands for the

righteous acts of the saints.) **9** Then the angel said to me, "Write: 'Blessed are those who are invited to the wedding supper of the Lamb!'" And he added, "These are the true words of God." **10** At this I fell at his feet to worship him. But he said to me, "Do not do it! I am a fellow-servant with you and with your brothers who hold to the testimony of Jesus. Worship God! For the testimony of Jesus is the spirit of prophecy."

vv. 1–2a John heard a great multitude in heaven shouting: "Hallelujah! Salvation, glory, and power belong to God."

3 **Learn from the Lessons:** What lessons can be learned from these facts? What does the passage mean? Be spiritual as you answer.

4 **Listen to His Voice:** What does this passage mean to you? Rewrite the lessons from step 3 in the form of questions. Be personal as you answer.

vv. 1–2a All heaven rejoices in the salvation of the righteous.

vv. 1–2a When have I caused heaven to rejoice because I was instrumental in someone's salvation?

5 **Live in Response:** Pinpoint what God is saying to you from this passage. How will you respond? Write down today's date and what you will do now about what He has said.

1 Look in His Word: Feel free to underline, circle or otherwise mark text if it will aid your study.

2 List the Facts: Make a verse-by-verse list of the most outstanding, obvious facts. What does the passage say? Be literal as you answer.

Finding Hope in Knowing Jesus Christ Will Appear in Person (19:11–16)—The Saints Rejoice . . .

• *as the Son returns v.11–16*

v.11 John saw heaven open and a rider called Faithful and True on a white horse, making war with justice.

Revelation 19:11 I saw heaven standing open and there before me was a white horse, whose rider is called Faithful and True. With justice he judges and makes war. **12** His eyes are like blazing fire, and on his head are many crowns. He has a name written on him that no one knows but he himself. **13** He is dressed in a robe dipped in blood, and his name is the Word of God. **14** The armies of heaven were following him, riding on white horses and dressed in fine linen, white and clean. **15** Out of his mouth comes a sharp sword with which to strike down the nations. "He will rule them with an iron scepter." He treads the winepress of the fury of the wrath of God Almighty. **16** On his robe and on his thigh he has this name written: KING OF KINGS AND LORD OF LORDS.

by Evil Alliances

3 **Learn from the Lessons:** What lessons can be learned from these facts? What does the passage mean? Be spiritual as you answer.

4 **Listen to His Voice:** What does this passage mean to you? Rewrite the lessons from step 3 in the form of questions. Be personal as you answer.

v.11 One day heaven will open, and Jesus will appear to judge the earth.

v.11 Five minutes before heaven opens and Jesus returns to judge the world, what will I wish I had done differently?

5 **Live in Response:** Pinpoint what God is saying to you from this passage. How will you respond? Write down today's date and what you will do now about what He has said.

1

Look in His Word:
Feel free to underline,
circle or otherwise mark
text if it will aid your
study.

2

List the Facts: Make
a verse-by-verse list of
the most outstanding,
obvious facts. What does
the passage say? Be literal
as you answer.

Finding Hope in Knowing We
Will Experience the Glory of
Christ (20:1–6)—Experiencing
His glory through . . .

• *service v.4*
• *serenity-Isaiah 11*
• *satisfaction v.6*
• *sanctification v.6*
• *security v.6*

Revelation 20:1 And I saw an angel
coming down out of heaven, having
the key to the Abyss and holding in
his hand a great chain. **2** He seized
the dragon, that ancient serpent, who
is the devil, or Satan, and bound him
for a thousand years. **3** He threw him
into the Abyss, and locked and sealed
it over him, to keep him from deceiving the nations any more until the
thousand years were ended. After
that, he must be set free for a short
time. **4** I saw thrones on which were
seated those who had been given
authority to judge. And I saw the
souls of those who had been
beheaded because of their testimony
for Jesus and because of the word of
God. They had not worshiped the
beast or his image and had not
received his mark on their foreheads
or their hands. They came to life and
reigned with Christ for a thousand
years. **5** (The rest of the dead did not
come to life until the thousand years

were ended.) This is the first resurrection. **6** Blessed and holy are those
who have part in the first resurrection. The second death has no power
over them, but they will be priests of
God and of Christ and will reign
with him for a thousand years.

v.1 John saw an angel coming
from heaven, having the key to
the Abyss and holding a chain.

by Life

3 **Learn from the Lessons:** What lessons can be learned from these facts? What does the passage mean? Be spiritual as you answer.

4 **Listen to His Voice:** What does this passage mean to you? Rewrite the lessons from step 3 in the form of questions. Be personal as you answer.

v.1 Access to the Abyss, or hell, is controlled by heaven, not Satan or anyone else.

v.1 What difference would it make in my witness if I truly believed there was a hell?

5 **Live in Response:** Pinpoint what God is saying to you from this passage. How will you respond? Write down today's date and what you will do now about what He has said.

1 **Look in His Word:** Feel free to underline, circle or otherwise mark text if it will aid your study.

2 **List the Facts:** Make a verse-by-verse list of the most outstanding, obvious facts. What does the passage say? Be literal as you answer.

Finding Hope in Knowing We Will Exult in the Victory of Christ (20:7–10)—Victory over the . . .

• *deception vv.7–8*
• *deceived v.9*
• *deceiver v.10*

v.7 After 1,000 years, Satan will be released.

Revelation 20:7 When the thousand years are over, Satan will be released from his prison **8** and will go out to deceive the nations in the four corners of the earth— Gog and Magog—to gather them for battle. In number they are like the sand on the seashore. **9** They marched across the breadth of the earth and surrounded the camp of God's people, the city he loves. But fire came down from heaven and devoured them. **10** And the devil, who deceived them, was thrown into the lake of burning sulfur, where the beast and the false prophet had been thrown. They will be tormented day and night for ever and ever.

3 **Learn from the Lessons:** What lessons can be learned from these facts? What does the passage mean? Be spiritual as you answer.

v.7 Satan's freedom to act, attack, and tempt is under God's authority.

4 **Listen to His Voice:** What does this passage mean to you? Rewrite the lessons from step 3 in the form of questions. Be personal as you answer.

v.7 When Satan seems to have the upper hand, do I cower in fear, or do I look to see what purpose God may have in allowing his attack?

5 **Live in Response:** Pinpoint what God is saying to you from this passage. How will you respond? Write down today's date and what you will do now about what He has said.

1 **Look in His Word:** Feel free to underline, circle or otherwise mark text if it will aid your study.

2 **List the Facts:** Make a verse-by-verse list of the most outstanding, obvious facts. What does the passage say? Be literal as you answer.

Finding Hope in Knowing We Will Escape the Penalty of Christ (20:11–15)—Escape the . . .

• *place of judgment v.11*
• *presence of the judge v.11*
• *people who will be judged vv.12–14*
• *proof of justice v.15*

Revelation 20:11 Then I saw a great white throne and him who was seated on it. Earth and sky fled from his presence, and there was no place for them. **12** And I saw the dead, great and small, standing before the throne, and books were opened. Another book was opened, which is the book of life. The dead were judged according to what they had done as recorded in the books. **13** The sea gave up the dead that were in it, and death and Hades gave up the dead that were in them, and each person was judged according to what he had done. **14** Then death and Hades were thrown into the lake of fire. The lake of fire is the second death. **15** If anyone's name was not found written in the book of life, he was thrown into the lake of fire.

v.11 John saw a Person sitting on a white throne, from Whom earth and sky fled.

by Life

3 **Learn from the Lessons:** What lessons can be learned from these facts? What does the passage mean? Be spiritual as you answer.

4 **Listen to His Voice:** What does this passage mean to you? Rewrite the lessons from step 3 in the form of questions. Be personal as you answer.

v.11 There will be no hiding place from final judgment.

v.11 Who will face the final judgment unless I share with them how to be saved from it?

5 **Live in Response:** Pinpoint what God is saying to you from this passage. How will you respond? Write down today's date and what you will do now about what He has said.

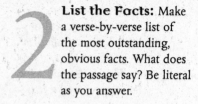

Look in His Word: Feel free to underline, circle or otherwise mark text if it will aid your study.

List the Facts: Make a verse-by-verse list of the most outstanding, obvious facts. What does the passage say? Be literal as you answer.

Our Hope of a Beautiful Place (21:1–8)—That is a . . .

• *prepared place vv.1–2, 7–8*
• *perfect place vv.3–6*

Revelation 21:1 Then I saw a new heaven and a new earth, for the first heaven and the first earth had passed away, and there was no longer any sea. **2** I saw the Holy City, the new Jerusalem, coming down out of heaven from God, prepared as a bride beautifully dressed for her husband. **3** And I heard a loud voice from the throne saying, "Now the dwelling of God is with men, and he will live with them. They will be his people, and God himself will be with them and be their God. **4** He will wipe every tear from their eyes. There will be no more death or mourning or crying or pain, for the old order of things has passed away." **5** He who was seated on the throne said, "I am making everything new!" Then he said, "Write this down, for these words are trustworthy and true." **6** He said to me: "It is done. I am the Alpha and the Omega, the Beginning and the End. To him who is thirsty I will give to drink without cost from the spring of the water of life. **7** He who overcomes will inherit all this, and I will be his God and he will be my son. **8** But the cowardly, the unbelieving, the vile, the murderers, the sexually immoral, those who practice magic arts, the idolaters and all liars—their place will be in the fiery lake of burning sulfur. This is the second death."

v.1 John saw a new heaven and earth, for the old had passed away.

3 **Learn from the Lessons:** What lessons can be learned from these facts? What does the passage mean? Be spiritual as you answer.

4 **Listen to His Voice:** What does this passage mean to you? Rewrite the lessons from step 3 in the form of questions. Be personal as you answer.

v.1 One day everything we see around us will no longer exist.

v.1 How much time am I spending on that which is going to perish?

5 **Live in Response:** Pinpoint what God is saying to you from this passage. How will you respond? Write down today's date and what you will do now about what He has said.

Look in His Word: Feel free to underline, circle or otherwise mark text if it will aid your study.

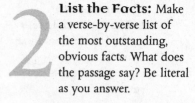

List the Facts: Make a verse-by-verse list of the most outstanding, obvious facts. What does the passage say? Be literal as you answer.

Our Hope of a Beautiful Place (21:9–21)—That is a . . .

• *physical place vv.9–21*

Revelation 21:9 One of the seven angels who had the seven bowls full of the seven last plagues came and said to me, "Come, I will show you the bride, the wife of the Lamb." **10** And he carried me away in the Spirit to a mountain great and high, and showed me the Holy City, Jerusalem, coming down out of heaven from God. **11** It shone with the glory of God, and its brilliance was like that of a very precious jewel, like a jasper, clear as crystal. **12** It had a great, high wall with twelve gates, and with twelve angels at the gates. On the gates were written the names of the twelve tribes of Israel. **13** There were three gates on the east, three on the north, three on the south and three on the west. **14** The wall of the city had twelve foundations, and on them were the names of the twelve apostles of the Lamb. **15** The angel who talked with me had a measuring rod of gold to measure the city, its gates and its walls. **16** The city was laid out like a square, as long as it was wide. He measured the city with the rod and found it to be 12,000 stadia in length, and as wide and high as it is long. **17** He measured its wall and it was 144 cubits thick, by man's measure-ment, which the angel was using. **18** The wall was made of jasper, and the city of pure gold, as pure as glass. **19** The foundations of the city walls were decorated with every kind of precious stone. The first foundation was jasper, the second sapphire, the third chalcedony, the fourth emerald, **20** the fifth sardonyx, the sixth carnelian, the seventh chrysolite, the eighth beryl, the ninth topaz, the tenth chrysoprase, the eleventh jacinth, and the twelfth amethyst. **21** The twelve gates were twelve pearls, each gate made of a single pearl. The great street of the city was of pure gold, like transparent glass.

v.9 One of the angels showed John the Bride of the Lamb.

3 **Learn from the Lessons:** What lessons can be learned from these facts? What does the passage mean? Be spiritual as you answer.

v.9 The Lamb is deeply, permanently, emotionally involved in a love relationship.

4 **Listen to His Voice:** What does this passage mean to you? Rewrite the lessons from step 3 in the form of questions. Be personal as you answer.

v.9 Am I a responsive and passionate bride with eyes only for her husband?

5 **Live in Response:** Pinpoint what God is saying to you from this passage. How will you respond? Write down today's date and what you will do now about what He has said.

1

Look in His Word:
Feel free to underline,
circle or otherwise mark
text if it will aid your
study.

2

List the Facts: Make
a verse-by-verse list of
the most outstanding,
obvious facts. What does
the passage say? Be literal
as you answer.

*Our Hope of a Beautiful Place
(21:22–27)—That is a . . .*

• *populated place vv.22–27*

v.22 The temple was not seen,
because the Lord and the Lamb
are the temple in the city.

Revelation 21:22 I did not see a
temple in the city, because the
Lord God Almighty and the Lamb
are its temple. **23** The city does
not need the sun or the moon to
shine on it, for the glory of God
gives it light, and the Lamb is its
lamp. **24** The nations will walk by
its light, and the kings of the
earth will bring their splendor
into it. **25** On no day will its
gates ever be shut, for there will
be no night there. **26** The glory
and honor of the nations will be
brought into it. **27** Nothing
impure will ever enter it, nor will
anyone who does what is shameful or deceitful, but only those
whose names are written in the
Lamb's book of life.

by Death

3 **Learn from the Lessons:** What lessons can be learned from these facts? What does the passage mean? Be spiritual as you answer.

4 **Listen to His Voice:** What does this passage mean to you? Rewrite the lessons from step 3 in the form of questions. Be personal as you answer.

v.22 I will never lack an awareness of the Presence of Christ in my life when in heaven.

v.22 When lonely or discouraged, do I take comfort in the hope that one day I will be in His Presence forever?

5 **Live in Response:** Pinpoint what God is saying to you from this passage. How will you respond? Write down today's date and what you will do now about what He has said.

Look in His Word: Feel free to underline, circle or otherwise mark text if it will aid your study.

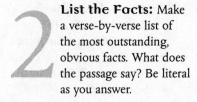

List the Facts: Make a verse-by-verse list of the most outstanding, obvious facts. What does the passage say? Be literal as you answer.

To Be Faithful To His Word (22:6–7)

To Be Faithful to Worship (22:8–9)

v.6 These words are true. The Lord sent His angel to show His servants what must take place.

Revelation 22:6 The angel said to me, "These words are trustworthy and true. The Lord, the God of the spirits of the prophets, sent his angel to show his servants the things that must soon take place." **7** "Behold, I am coming soon! Blessed is he who keeps the words of the prophecy in this book." **8** I, John, am the one who heard and saw these things. And when I had heard and seen them, I fell down to worship at the feet of the angel who had been showing them to me. **9** But he said to me, "Do not do it! I am a fellow servant with you and with your brothers the prophets and of all who keep the words of this book. Worship God!"

Hope That Ignites Our Hearts

3 **Learn from the Lessons:** What lessons can be learned from these facts? What does the passage mean? Be spiritual as you answer.

4 **Listen to His Voice:** What does this passage mean to you? Rewrite the lessons from step 3 in the form of questions. Be personal as you answer.

v.6 God does not lie, and wants His servants to have hope for the future.

v.6 Is my hopelessness concerning the future based on my doubt of the truth of God's Word?

5 **Live in Response:** Pinpoint what God is saying to you from this passage. How will you respond? Write down today's date and what you will do now about what He has said.

Chapter 11: Hope That Ignites Our Hearts

1 **Look in His Word:** Feel free to underline, circle or otherwise mark text if it will aid your study.

2 **List the Facts:** Make a verse-by-verse list of the most outstanding, obvious facts. What does the passage say? Be literal as you answer.

To Be Faithful To His Work (22:10–13)

To Be Faithful To Wash (22:14–15)

v.10 Don't seal this book, because the time is near.

Revelation 22:10 Then he told me, "Do not seal up the words of the prophecy of this book, because the time is near. **11** Let him who does wrong continue to do wrong; let him who is vile continue to be vile; let him who does right continue to do right; and let him who is holy continue to be holy." **12** "Behold, I am coming soon! My reward is with me, and I will give to everyone according to what he has done. **13** I am the Alpha and the Omega, the First and the Last, the Beginning and the End. **14** "Blessed are those who wash their robes, that they may have the right to the tree of life and may go through the gates into the city. **15** Outside are the dogs, those who practice magic arts, the sexually immoral, the murderers, the idolaters and everyone who loves and practices falsehood.

3 **Learn from the Lessons:** What lessons can be learned from these facts? What does the passage mean? Be spiritual as you answer.

4 **Listen to His Voice:** What does this passage mean to you? Rewrite the lessons from step 3 in the form of questions. Be personal as you answer.

v.10 As the end of human history draws near, we will do well to read, study and apply the Book of Revelation.

v.10 How much time have I given to reading, studying and applying the Book of Revelation?

5 **Live in Response:** Pinpoint what God is saying to you from this passage. How will you respond? Write down today's date and what you will do now about what He has said.

1 **Look in His Word:**
Feel free to underline, circle or otherwise mark text if it will aid your study.

2 **List the Facts:** Make a verse-by-verse list of the most outstanding, obvious facts. What does the passage say? Be literal as you answer.

To Be Faithful To Witness (22:16–17)

To Be Faithful To Warn (22:18–19)

To Be Faithful To Watch (22:20–21)

Revelation 22:16 "I, Jesus, have sent my angel to give you this testimony for the churches. I am the Root and the Offspring of David, and the bright Morning Star." **17** The Spirit and the bride say, "Come!" And let him who hears say, "Come!" Whoever is thirsty, let him come; and whoever wishes, let him take the free gift of the water of life. **18** I warn everyone who hears the words of the prophecy of this book: If anyone adds anything to them, God will add to him the plagues described in this book. **19** And if anyone takes words away from this book of prophecy, God will take away from him his share in the tree of life and in the holy city, which are described in this book. **20** He who testifies to these things says, "Yes, I am coming soon." Amen. Come, Lord Jesus. **21** The grace of the Lord Jesus be with God's people. Amen.

v.16 Jesus, the Offspring of David, the Morning Star, sent His angel to give this testimony to the church.

3 **Learn from the Lessons:** What lessons can be learned from these facts? What does the passage mean? Be spiritual as you answer.

v.16 The Book of Revelation was given specifically by Christ to those who call themselves by His Name.

4 **Listen to His Voice:** What does this passage mean to you? Rewrite the lessons from step 3 in the form of questions. Be personal as you answer.

v.16 If I am one of those to whom the Book of Revelation was originally given, how diligently have I read, studied and applied it?

5 **Live in Response:** Pinpoint what God is saying to you from this passage. How will you respond? Write down today's date and what you will do now about what He has said.

Afterword

At the beginning of this Devotional Guide, after the Preface and Instructions, a Completed Example was given using Mark 9, which describes the experience three disciples had as they witnessed the transfiguration of Jesus Christ. I wonder if Jesus had invited all of His disciples to draw aside and spend some time alone with Him, but only three out of the twelve accepted His invitation. However that may be, the three who spent time alone with Him received a fresh vision of His glory (vv.2–3), while those who had not, faced massive confusion and problems which they had no power to solve (vv.14, 17–18).

One of the problems the nine disciples faced was that of a father who brought to them his son, who was completely out of control. You can hear the father's anguished despair and frustration as he tells Jesus of his disappointment with the disciples' inability to help: "Teacher, I brought you my son . . . I asked your disciples to drive out the spirit, but they could not" (vv.17–18).

Later, when His disciples asked Jesus why they had no power to help the father or his son, He answered in a way that gives tremendous insight into our powerlessness to help others: "This kind can come out only by prayer and fasting" (v.29 alternate translation). In other words, our power to help others is directly related to the time we spend in fasting—going without anything and everything in order to make the time to get alone with Jesus in prayer and the reading of His Word. Too often we put our work before our worship and end up with powerless, fruitless service.

As you complete this Devotional Guide, make plans now for the continued reading of God's Word. I pray God will richly bless you as you seek to maintain your vision of His glory, and in so doing, receive the power to make an impact in the lives of others.

About the Author

Anne Graham Lotz, the second child of Billy and Ruth Graham, is an acclaimed Bible teacher. Born in the mountains of North Carolina and married to Dr. Daniel M. Lotz, she is the mother of three adult children. After teaching Bible Study Fellowship each week for twelve years without missing a class, Anne responded to God's call to an itinerant ministry of Bible teaching in 1988. At that time she founded AnGeL Ministries, a non-profit organization which gives out messages of biblical exposition, so that God's Word is relevant and personal to ordinary people. On every continent, and in over twenty foreign countries, Anne has been used to bring revival to the hearts of people as she imparts knowledge of God through His Word.